Top im Abi
Abiwissen kompakt

Englisch

Schroedel

Englisch

Autorin:
Sarah Nowotny stammt aus London und verfügt über langjährige Erfahrung als Englisch-Lehrerin. Außerdem arbeitet sie als freie Autorin und Übersetzerin.

© 2014 Bildungshaus Schulbuchverlage
Westermann Schroedel Diesterweg Schöningh Winklers GmbH, Braunschweig
www.schroedel.de

Das Werk und seine Teile sind urheberrechtlich geschützt. Jede Nutzung in anderen als den gesetzlich zugelassenen Fällen bedarf der vorherigen schriftlichen Einwilligung des Verlages. Hinweis zu § 52a UrhG: Weder das Werk noch seine Teile dürfen ohne eine solche Einwilligung gescannt und in ein Netzwerk eingestellt werden. Dies gilt auch für Intranets von Schulen und sonstigen Bildungseinrichtungen.
Auf verschiedenen Seiten dieses Buches befinden sich Verweise (Links) auf Internet-Adressen. Haftungshinweis: Trotz sorgfältiger inhaltlicher Kontrolle wird die Haftung für die Inhalte der externen Seiten ausgeschlossen. Für den Inhalt dieser externen Seiten sind ausschließlich deren Betreiber verantwortlich. Sollten Sie bei dem angegebenen Inhalt des Anbieters dieser Seite auf kostenpflichtige, illegale oder anstößige Inhalte treffen, so bedauern wir dies ausdrücklich und bitten Sie, uns umgehend per E-Mail davon in Kenntnis zu setzen, damit beim Nachdruck der Verweis gelöscht wird.

Druck 2 / Jahr 2016

Redaktion: imprint, Zusmarshausen
Kontakt: lernhilfen@schroedel.de
Herstellung: Druckreif! Sandra Grünberg, Braunschweig
Umschlaggestaltung und Layout: Janssen Kahlert Design & Kommunikation, Hannover
Satz und Grafik: imprint, Zusmarshausen
Druck und Bindung: westermann druck GmbH, Braunschweig

ISBN 978-3-507-**23113**-9

Vorwort

Prüfungen in einer Fremdsprache vorzubereiten, ist nicht immer leicht, weil es so viele verschiedene Aspekte zu bedenken gibt. Man muss nicht nur Vokabeln und Grammatik lernen, sondern auch wissen, wie diese in verschiedenen Aufgaben einzusetzen sind. Man soll die Sprache verstehen, analysieren und sie schreibend und sprechend anwenden können. Zudem sollte man auch über die wichtigsten landeskundlichen Themen Bescheid wissen.

Dieses Buch soll Ihnen helfen, alle diese prüfungsrelevanten Themen vorzubereiten. Sie finden hier nützliche Vokabeln zu typischen Prüfungsthemen, eine Zusammenfassung der englischen Grammatik sowie eine Übersicht über die zentralen Begriffe aus dem Bereich Landeskunde. Zusätzlich gibt es praktische Hilfe für spezifische Prüfungsaufgaben wie Textanalyse, Textproduktion und Übersetzung mit vielen anschaulichen Beispielen. Das Buch enthält zahlreiche Merkkästen, Abi-Tipps und Checklisten, die Ihnen das Lernen erleichtern sollen. Es wird auf Fallstricke und typische Fehler hingewiesen – und darauf, wie Sie diese vermeiden können.

Es ist nicht notwendig, das Buch von vorne nach hinten durchzuarbeiten. Jedes Kapitel steht für sich und behandelt einen anderen Aspekt der Prüfung. Deshalb ist es auch möglich, nur einzelne Bereiche, wie beispielsweise die Benutzung bestimmter Zeitformen, nachzuschlagen und zu wiederholen.

Passend zum Buch gibt es eine **Abi-App**. 100 interaktive Test-Aufgaben zu allen Kapiteln dieses Buches warten auf Sie! Einfach im jeweiligen App-Store „Top im Abi" eingeben und mit dem Code **e n 5 – 8 g w** die Version für das Fach Englisch herunterladen.

Buch plus App – der clevere Weg zum Abitur.

Wir wünschen Ihnen viel Erfolg für die Prüfung!

Inhalt

Vorwort		3

1 Vocabulary — 6

- 1.1 Topics — 6
- 1.2 Idioms — 37
- 1.3 Recording and learning vocabulary — 46
- 1.4 Getting the most from your dictionary — 49
- 1.5 Coping without a dictionary — 51

2 English grammar – a brief overview — 55

- 2.1 Use of the tenses — 55
- 2.2 The passive — 68
- 2.3 Irregular English verbs — 70
- 2.4 Use of the gerund — 73
- 2.5 Use of participles — 75
- 2.6 Phrasal verbs — 78
- 2.7 "False Friends" — 82
- 2.8 Problem areas of English — 88

3 Understanding Britain and America – important terms — 97

- 3.1 Britain — 97
- 3.2 The British Empire and the Commonwealth — 108
- 3.3 USA — 114
- 3.4 English as a world language — 123

4	**Textanalyse**	128
4.1	Wie man an eine Textanalyse herangeht	128
4.2	Sprachstile	132
4.3	Stilistische und rhetorische Mittel	135
4.4	Die Analyse literarischer Texte	140
4.5	Examples of text analysis	148

5	**Textproduktion**	169
5.1	Wie man eine Zusammenfassung schreibt	169
5.2	Wie man einen Aufsatz schreibt	176

6	**Übersetzung**	195
6.1	Wie man an eine Übersetzung herangeht	195
6.2	Einige typische Übersetzungsprobleme	199
6.3	Schlüsselwörter	208
6.4	Example texts	210

Stichwortverzeichnis ... 220

1 Vocabulary

Ein guter Wortschatz ist wichtig, um sich mündlich wie schriftlich treffend ausdrücken zu können. Im Folgenden finden Sie nützliche Begriffe zu verschiedenen Themen, gefolgt von einem kurzen Text, in dem einige der Wörter im Kontext benutzt werden. Wie aber soll man sich dies alles merken? Hierzu finden Sie viele hilfreiche Tipps, vom Erfassen und Sortieren von Vokabeln bis zu Hinweisen, wie man am besten mit verschiedenen Arten von Wörterbüchern umgeht.

1.1 Topics

Politics

Politics in Britain

People	
Prime Minister	Premierminister(in)
Member of Parliament (MP)	Abgeordnete(r)
Home Secretary	Innenminister(in)
Chancellor of the Exchequer	Finanzminister(in)
Defence Secretary	Verteidigungsminister(in)
Foreign Secretary	Außenminister(in)
Education Secretary	Bildungsminister(in)
the government	Regierung
the cabinet	Kabinett
the Speaker	Präsident des Unterhauses
backbenchers	Abgeordnete, die nicht Mitglieder des Kabinetts sind
the opposition	Oppositionspartei
the shadow cabinet	Schattenkabinett

Government departments	
Government department	Ministerium, Ressort
the Home Office	Innenministerium
the Foreign Office	Außenministerium
the Treasury	Finanzministerium
the Ministry of Defence	Verteidigungsministerium
Department of Health	Gesundheitsministerium
Department for Children, Schools and Families	Bildungs- und Familienministerium

Activities in Parliament	
to debate	debattieren
to vote	abstimmen
to pass laws	Gesetze verabschieden

Politics in the USA

People	
The President	Präsident(in)
The Vice President	Vizepräsident(in)
Senator	Senator(in)
Congressman/woman	Kongressabgeordnete(r)
Secretary of the Interior	Innenminister(in)
Secretary of the Treasury	Finanzminister(in)
Secretary of Defense	Verteidigungsminister(in)
Secretary of State	Außenminister(in)
Attorney General	Justizminister(in)

Government departments	
Department of the Interior	Innenministerium
Department of State	Außenministerium
Department of the Treasury	Finanzministerium
Department of Defense	Verteidigungsministerium
Department of Education	Bildungsministerium
Department of Health and Human Services	das Gesundheitsministerium

Political issues	
legislation	Gesetzgebung
the Budget	öffentlicher Haushaltsplan
tax	Steuer
tax reform	Steuerreform
tax increase	Steuererhöhung
benefits	Sozialleistungen
benefits cuts	Kürzungen bei Sozialleistungen
child benefit	Kindergeld
childcare	Kinderbetreuung
unemployment	Arbeitslosigkeit
education	Bildung
privatization	Privatisierung
defence	Verteidigung
environmental issues	Fragen der Umwelt

Terrorism and war – buzzwords

terrorism	Terrorismus
threat	Bedrohung
chemical warfare	chemische Kriegsführung
biological warfare	biologische Kriegsführung
cyberterrorism	Cyberterrorismus
weapons of mass destruction	Massenvernichtungswaffen
treaty	Abkommen
resolution	Resolution
skyjacker	Flugzeugentführer(in)
sleeper terrorist	Schläfer
homeland security (AE)	Innere Sicherheit
regime change	Regimewechsel
interim government	Übergangsregierung
disarmament	Entwaffnung
friendly fire	Beschuss durch die eigene Seite
embedded journalists	„eingebettete" Journalisten (die eine Armeeeinheit begleiten)

Britain and Europe

insularity	Provinzialität
"island mentality"	„Insel-Mentalität"
(loss of) sovereignty	(Verlust von) Eigenstaatlichkeit
single currency	Einheitswährung
free trade	freier Handel
Eurosceptic	Euroskeptiker(in)
influx of immigrants	Immigrantenzustrom
referendum on membership	Volksentscheid über Mitgliedschaft

Vocabulary in context: The British Prime Minister and the President of the United States have been meeting to discuss the latest terrorist threats. Fears of biological or chemical warfare have led to calls for tighter homeland security. The Chancellor of the Exchequer has promised to increase the defence budget, and legislation is being discussed to help fight terrorism. Meanwhile, the Foreign Secretary and the Secretary of State have been meeting with other world leaders to discuss an international disarmament treaty.

The question of whether Britain should join the European single currency continues to be a controversial one. Supporters of the idea emphasize the importance of free trade between European nations, which is made easier if the Euro is used as currency. Eurosceptics, however, are still extremely concerned about the loss of sovereignty which might result from this move, as well as possible negative economic consequences. Those in favour of closer integration into the European Union criticize the sceptics for their "island mentality", stating that, economically, Britain will not be able to survive independently from the rest of Europe.

In the last few years, Britain has become more Eurosceptic than ever. Polls show that many people fear an influx of immigrants every time another country joins the EU, such as when Bulgaria and Romania became members in 2014. Prime Minister David Cameron promised to have a referendum on membership no later than 2017; given current public opinion, it is possible that the citizens of Britain would vote to leave the EU.

The environment

Environmental issues

air, river and sea pollution	Luft-, Fluss- und Meeresverschmutzung
exhaust fumes	Abgase
CO_2 emissions	CO_2-Emissionen
fossil fuel	fossiler Brennstoff
nuclear waste	Atommüll
oil spill	Ölverschmutzung
oil slick	Ölteppich
global warming	globale Erwärmung
climatic changes	Klimaänderungen
greenhouse effect	Treibhauseffekt
rainforest	Regenwald
shrinking habitats	verschwindende Lebensräume
endangered species	vom Aussterben bedrohte Tierart
overpopulation	Überbevölkerung
water shortage	Wasserknappheit, Wassermangel
waste disposal	Abfallentsorgung
packaging	Verpackung
pesticides	Pestizide

Ways of saving natural resources

recycling	Recycling
biodegradable packaging	biologisch abbaubare Verpackung
unleaded petrol	bleifreies Benzin
alternative energy sources	alternative Energiequellen
solar power	Solarenergie
energy conservation	Energie sparen
car pool	Fahrgemeinschaft
public transport	öffentliche Verkehrsmittel

Vocabulary in context: Nowadays everyone in the western world is aware of the problems facing our environment. Global warming is causing climatic changes which will alter the face of our planet forever, doing irreparable damage to the natural world. The destruction of the rainforest means shrinking habitats for many animals and plants, some of which are now hardly able to survive: the list of endangered species in the world grows longer almost daily. In other places the worst problems are caused by overpopulation: too many people in one place means that there are simply not enough resources to go round. Some of these overpopulated areas are already suffering from water shortages, which in its turn affects agriculture, food supply and sanitation.

In developed countries the most damage to the environment is done by pollution: exhaust fumes from our beloved cars damage the very air that we breathe, and factories pollute the air with CO_2 emissions while manufacturing more consumer goods for us, which reach us wrapped in plenty of non-biodegradable packaging, of course. We might think that it's enough to fill our cars with unleaded petrol, but there is much more that we could do to conserve fossil fuels and other resources. For example, we could use public transport more often or form car pools for the journey to work every day. Alternative energy sources such as solar power may also become more common in the years to come, but at the moment use of these is the exception rather than the rule.

Natural disasters

Disasters

earthquake	Erdbeben
volcanic eruption	Vulkanausbruch
hurricane	Orkan
tornado	Tornado
flood	Überschwemmung
flood damage	Hochwasserschaden
epidemic	Epidemie
famine	Hungersnot
starvation	Verhungern
drought	Dürre
wildfire	Großflächenbrand (etwa von Wald)
avalanche	Lawine

People involved in disasters

casualty	Todesfall, (Unfall-)Opfer
victim	Opfer
survivor	Überlebende(r)
refugee	Flüchtling
homeless person	Obdachlose/r
volunteer	Freiwillige(r)
aid worker	Mitarbeiter(in) einer Hilfsorganisation

Ways of helping

aid	(finanzielle und materielle) Hilfe
emergency aid	Soforthilfe
foreign aid	Entwicklungshilfe
charity	Wohltätigkeits-/Hilfsorganisation
donation	Spende
to give/donate to charity	spenden
to volunteer	Hilfe anbieten

Vocabulary in context: It seems that we can hardly switch on the news nowadays without hearing about the latest natural disaster. Some are so common that they don't even surprise us any more, such as when yet another tornado hits the east coast of the United States. Earthquakes are fairly commonplace in some parts of the world, too, and everyone is familiar with the pictures of the helpless victims standing in despair beside the heap of rubble that was once their home, or helping the army to look for survivors in the ruins. One thing is clear, though: people in the western world are usually very generous when it comes to making donations to charities in order to help these people. The European Union sends more aid to countries suffering from famine or drought than any other group, and supports several foreign aid projects so that the people in those countries can help themselves long-term. But people are not afraid to give practical help, either. For example, when much of eastern Europe was hit by severe floods, thousands of volunteers offered their services, and helped to build sandbanks in an attempt to limit the flood damage.

The media

Newspapers

the press	die Presse
tabloid	Boulevardzeitung
quality papers/broadsheets	seriöse Zeitungen
editor	Redakteur(in), Herausgeber(in)
journalist/reporter	Journalist(in)
headline	Schlagzeile
editorial	Leitartikel
report	Reportage
feature	Sonderbeitrag
interview	Interview
review	Kritik, Rezension
TV listings, TV guide	Fernsehprogramm
colour supplement	Beilagemagazin, Farbbeilage

Radio

radio station	Radiosender
transmission	Übertragung
broadcast	Sendung, Übertragung
music programme	Musiksendung
news and current affairs	Nachrichten und Zeitgeschehen
call-in show, talk-back radio	Sendung mit Zuhörerbeteiligung

Television

channel	Sender
programme (AE: program)	Sendung
cable TV	Kabelfernsehen
satellite TV	Satellitenfernsehen
digital TV	Digitalfernsehen
pay TV	Pay-TV
to subscribe to	abonnieren

to switch/turn on	anschalten
to switch/turn off	ausschalten
to change/switch channels	umschalten
to zap, to channel-hop	zappen
remote control	Fernbedienung
prime time	Hauptsendezeit
ratings	Einschaltquoten
documentary	Dokumentarfilm
soap opera	Seifenoper
sitcom	Fernsehkomödie
chat show	Talkshow
game show	Quizsendung
drama	Fernsehspiel
travel program(me)	Reisesendung
commercials/advertisements	Werbung
newsreader	Nachrichtensprecher(in)
presenter	Moderator(in)
host (e.g. of a game show)	Moderator(in), Showmaster
anchorman/woman (AE)	Moderator(in) einer Nachrichtensendung

Vocabulary in context: I sometimes quite enjoy reading the tabloids: there's always plenty of celebrity gossip, sport, and detailed TV listings. However, to get factual, in-depth information about news and current affairs, you really need to read a report written by a good investigative journalist in one of the quality papers, such as The Guardian. The editorial always provokes interesting discussions, and some of the features about foreign countries are simply fascinating. And the colour supplement helps me keep up to date with the latest trends in the world of art and culture.

After a long day at work, I find there's nothing more relaxing than just flopping down in front of the television. I don't have digital TV at the moment, but I've had satellite TV for a couple of years now, and I have to admit that I love the variety. Of course there are a couple of channels that I watch more than the others – for example the one that broadcasts my favourite soap opera, East Enders – but I've also come across some great programmes on other channels, too, usually purely by chance. When the commercials come on, I tend to pick up the remote control and just start zapping: there's always something good on somewhere. I once even applied to take part in a game show, but didn't get chosen. In a way I was relieved, because, although the prize money is good, I find the host extremely irritating.

Society today

Family life

single-parent family	Familie mit nur einem Elternteil
single parent	Alleinerziehende(r)
divorce	Scheidung
divorce rate	Scheidungsrate
step-father/-mother	Stiefvater/-mutter
half-brother/-sister	Halbbruder/-schwester
cohabitation	Zusammenleben
birth-rate	Geburtenrate
elderly population	ältere Bevölkerung

Issues affecting families

childcare	Kinderpflege
healthcare	Gesundheitsversorgung
schooling	schulische Ausbildung
housing	Wohnungen, Wohnungsbau

Social issues: poverty

poverty line	Armutsgrenze
to live below the poverty line	unter der Armutsgrenze leben
to live on the breadline	am Existenzminimum leben
to be destitute	mittellos sein
minimum wage	Mindestlohn

social security	Sozialhilfe
long-term unemployment	Langzeit-Arbeitslosigkeit
to be in debt	Schulden haben
homelessness	Obdachlosigkeit
a homeless person	Obdachlose(r)

Social issues: crime and punishment

to commit a crime	ein Verbrechen begehen
a criminal	Verbrecher(in)
juvenile delinquency	Jugendkriminalität
juvenile offender/delinquent	jugendliche Straftäter(in)
murder	Mord
a murderer	Mörder(in)
theft	Diebstahl
a thief	Dieb(in)
mugging	Überfall (auf offener Straße)
a mugger	(Straßen)räuber(in)
shoplifting	Ladendiebstahl
a shoplifter	Ladendieb
drug-trafficking	Drogenhandel
a drug dealer	Drogenhändler(in)
court	Gericht
trial	Verhandlung
lenient	milde
judge	Richter(in)
jury	die Geschworenen
to plead guilty/not guilty	sich (nicht) schuldig bekennen
to pass verdict (on someone)	(über jdn.) ein Urteil fällen
to sentence someone	jemanden verurteilen
a fine	eine Geldstrafe
a prison sentence	eine Freiheitsstrafe
a 6-month suspended sentence	6 Monate auf Bewährung

community service	Sozialstunden, gemeinnützige Arbeit
to acquit	freisprechen
to release (from prison)	freilassen

Social structure: immigration

multicultural	multikulturell
cultural identity	kulturelle Identität
ethnic minority	ethnische Minderheit
race relations	Beziehungen zwischen ethnischen Gruppen
racism	Rassismus
discrimination	Diskriminierung
equality	Gleichberechtigung
equal opportunities	Chancengleichheit
tolerance	Toleranz
integration	Integration
racial tension	Spannungen zwischen ethnischen Gruppen
race riot	Rassenunruhen
(political) asylum	(politisches) Asyl
to apply for asylum	Asyl beantragen
asylum seeker	Asylbewerber(in)
refugee	Flüchtling

Vocabulary in context: Family life in the 21st century is certainly very different from 50 years ago. There is a high percentage of single-parent families, due to both the higher divorce rate and the fact that generally fewer people get married nowadays. In addition to this, the birth-rate has been falling steadily over the last decade or so. This will create new problems in the next few years as there will be a more elderly population and fewer young people to pay the tax that the state will need to support them. A further concern is that the division between rich and poor is growing. There are far too many people in Britain and the US living on the breadline, earning less than the minimum wage and barely having enough money to make ends meet. A recession throughout the western world has meant long-term unemployment for people from all walks of life, from unskilled workers to dynamic young professionals. Many families are reduced to living off social security, and are in debt because of, for example, credit card bills which they are unable to pay off.

It is perhaps unsurprising in these circumstances that crime is on the increase in areas of high unemployment, especially among young people: there is a great deal of juvenile delinquency in these areas. Many crimes involve theft, either mugging people on the street or shoplifting some of the tempting goods that they would love to own but cannot afford to buy. The greatest fear of many parents is that their children will become involved in drugs, as drug-trafficking is often widespread in impoverished areas. Many young offenders, of course, end up in court. If the judge is lenient they may get away with a suspended sentence or community service, where they have to work in an old people's home, for example. However, if they are not first-time offenders, they may well end up with a prison sentence.

Britain and the USA are both multicultural societies, and have been for generations. This does not mean, however, that there is no racial tension there. On the contrary, members of ethnic minorities often have to suffer discrimination instead of tolerance, despite efforts to create equal opportunities in the fields of education and employment.

Cities

metropolis	Großstadt, Weltstadt
conurbation (BE)/ megalopolis (AE)	Ballungsraum
urban	städtisch, Stadt-
urban sprawl	unkontrollierte Ausbreitung einer Stadt
city centre (BE)/ downtown (AE)	Stadtzentrum
inner city	Innenstadt
inner-city school	Schule in der Innenstadt
suburb	Vorort
commuter	Pendler(in)
commuter village/ dormitory suburb	Wohnvorort, Schlafstadt

residential area	Wohngebiet
council housing	Sozialwohnung
housing estate	Wohnsiedlung
tenement	Wohnblock
business centre	Geschäftszentrum
industrial estate	Industriegebiet
pedestrian precinct	Fußgängerzone
shopping centre (BE)/ mall (AE)	Einkaufszentrum

Inner city problems

high cost of living	hohe Lebenskosten
traffic congestion/jam	Stau
rush hour	Hauptverkehrszeit
rush-hour traffic	Berufsverkehr
substandard accommodation	minderwertige Wohnungen
high unemployment	hohe Arbeitslosigkeit
vandalism	Vandalismus
drug abuse	Drogenmissbrauch
gang warfare	Bandenkrieg
car theft	Autodiebstahl
litter	Abfall (auf der Straße)
homelessness	Obdachlosigkeit
begging	Betteln
to sleep rough	auf der Straße schlafen

Vocabulary in context: It goes without saying that cities today are far bigger than 100 years ago. Metropolises such as London or Los Angeles are still spreading, although so-called green belts have been created around London. These are areas of countryside which cannot be built on, the idea being to prevent the urban sprawl from spreading any further. One of the most noticeable features of many new cities, especially in the United States, is the growth of the suburbs. Disliking the litter, pollution, vandalism and high cost of living associated with city centres, those who can afford to do so have moved out to suburban residential areas, preferring to drive to the huge shopping malls outside the city than go downtown to shop. The consequence is that the inner cities, with their substandard accommodation and social problems such as high unemployment, drug abuse and gang warfare, tend to be inhabited by poorer people. Another noticeable feature of cities is the increasing number of homeless people. Many young people run away from home, hoping that they will have better chances in the big city. The reality is that they are often reduced to begging in order to survive, and a frightening number of them have to sleep rough at night.

Work

General terms

job centre (BE)/ employment office (AE)	Arbeitsamt
job market	Arbeitsmarkt
jobseeker	Stellensuchende(r)
job-hunting	Stellensuche
to apply for a job	sich bewerben
(job) application	Bewerbung
applicant	Bewerber
CV (BE, für curriculum vitae)/resumé (AE)	Lebenslauf
job interview	Bewerbungsgespräch
to employ someone	jemanden einstellen
employer	Arbeitgeber
employee	Arbeitnehmer
staff	Belegschaft, Mitarbeiterstab
to resign/quit	kündigen
to fire/sack/dismiss	feuern
to make s. o. redundant	jdn. freisetzen, entlassen
to lay s. o. off	jdn. (vorübergehend) entlassen
trade union	Gewerkschaft
to (go on) strike	streiken

Working conditions

to be self-employed	selbstständig sein
to work freelance	freiberuflich arbeiten
to work part-time	Teilzeit arbeiten
shiftwork	Schichtarbeit
job sharing	Arbeitsplatzteilung
a nine-to-five job	normaler Büro-/Acht-Stunden-Job
flexitime	Gleitzeit
teleworking	Telearbeit
a heavy/light workload	ein hohes/niedriges Arbeitspensum
to meet a deadline	einen Termin einhalten
irregular working hours	unregelmäßige Arbeitszeiten
antisocial working hours	Arbeitszeiten, die wenig Privatleben erlauben
a desk job	Schreibtischtätigkeit
manual work	körperliche Arbeit
a dead-end job	Job ohne Aufstiegschancen
trainee	Auszubildene/r
intern	Praktikant/in
white-collar worker	Angestellte/r
blue-collar worker	Arbeitskraft
public sector	staatliche/öffentliche Unternehmen
private sector	Privatwirtschaft

Working life

maternity leave	Mutterschaftsurlaub
paternity leave	Vaterschaftsurlaub
perks	Vergünstigungen
fringe benefits	Zusatzleistungen
overtime	Überstunden
to get a promotion	befördert werden
a pay rise	Gehaltserhöhung
a bonus	Prämie
job satisfaction	Zufriedenheit im Job
work-life balance	Vereinbarkeit von Berufs- und Privatleben

Work-related buzzwords

globalisation of work	Globalisierung der Arbeit
corporate giant	Großkonzern
downsizing	Stellenabbau, Kündigungswelle
dotcom	Dotcom-Firma (aus E-Mail- oder Internetadressen „.com")
e-commerce	E-Commerce
the new economy	die neue Wirtschaft
recession	Rezession

Vocabulary in context: The current job market does not offer as many opportunities for jobseekers as in the past, and it can take many months to find a good job. There are often hundreds of applicants for a single job vacancy, and prospective employers have to read through the CVs of all these people before they can even decide who to invite to come for a job interview. And even if you have a job, there is no guarantee that you will keep it. In times of recession it is common to make staff redundant, and although the trade unions do their best to protect the workers, for example by organising protest strikes, there is not always very much they can do to help.

The way we work today has also changed: the days when young people started working for one company after leaving school and worked there until they retired are long gone. Of course, it is not only the fact that people are often laid off that makes them change their jobs. The globalisation of work means more mobility, especially within the European Union. As well as this, many people now work freelance or are self-employed, prefering the flexibility of running their own business to working for a corporate giant. Some companies allow their employees to work from home with their computer, teleworking being preferable to having to go into the office every day. Flexitime and job sharing can be of advantage to working mothers in particular, giving them more opportunities to have a family and a career at the same time. The demands of the modern working world, however, mean that many people have antisocial working hours or have to work many hours of unpaid overtime: in times of recession, perks and fringe benefits such as overtime pay tend to be the first to go. Most workers have to put up with these conditions, and are happy if their firms don't go bankrupt as has happened to many dotcoms in the new economy.

Medicine

Medical issues

cloning	Klonen
experiment	Versuch
ethics	Ethik, Moral
to misuse	missbrauchen
genetic engineering	Gentechnik/-technologie
genetic code	genetischer Code
genetic fingerprint	genetischer Fingerabdruck
genetic information	Erbinformation
hereditary disease	Erbkrankheit
bone marrow transplant	Knochenmarktransplantation
handicapped	behindert
abortion	Abtreibung
drug addiction	Drogensucht
STD (sexually transmitted disease)	Geschlechtskrankheit
HIV antibodies	HIV Antikörper
safe-sex campaign	Kampagne für Safersex
AIDS sufferer	AIDS-Kranke(r)
vaccine	Impfstoff

Vocabulary in context: One of the most controversial medical issues of the last few years is that of human cloning. Scientists have carried out experiments to prove that it is possible, but it is the ethics of this procedure that causes the most concern. Some people are afraid that it might be misused to create a race of 'super' human beings. Others, on the other hand, argue that creating an exact genetic copy of a person can help when that person is suffering from a particular disease: for example, if a child needs a very rare bone marrow transplant, a brother or sister with exactly the same genetic code could be used to provide it.

All in all, the field of genetic engineering raises many ethical questions. Undoubtedly it has provided us with vital information about hereditary diseases, but there is also the fear that knowing too much will encourage pregnant women to have an abortion rather than give birth to a child which may be physically or mentally handicapped.

Religion

Catholics	Katholiken
Protestant churches	Evangelische Kirchen
Methodists	Methodisten
Baptists	Baptisten
Jews	Juden
Muslims	Muslime
Hindus	Hindus
Buddhists	Buddhisten
Sikhs	Sikh
Mormons	Mormone
Jehovah's Witnesses	Zeugen Jehovahs

General terms

church service	Gottesdienst
worship	Anbetung, Gottesdienst
churchgoer	Kirchengänger(in)
liturgy	Liturgie
believer	Gläubige(r)
atheist	Atheist(in)
secular	weltlich
state religion	Staatsreligion
religious education	Religionsunterricht
church school	von einer Kirche geleitete Schule
prayer	Gebet
jihad (holy war)	Dschihad (heiliger Krieg)
penance	Buße
holy day	kirchlicher Feiertag

Religious terms and issues in the USA

the Moral Majority	die moralische Mehrheit, das Moralempfinden der Mehrheit
the religious right	die religiösen Rechten (pol.)
the Christian Coalition	die Christliche Koalition (pol.)
fundamentalism	Fundamentalismus
evolution	Evolution
creationism	biblische Schöpfungslehre
the "electronic church"	die „elektronische Kirche"
TV evangelism	Verkündigung des Evangeliums im Fernsehen
TV preacher	TV-Prediger

Vocabulary in context: One can generally say that western society today is more secular than religious-based: the number of churchgoers has decreased dramatically over the last few decades and, although there are still many people who consider themselves to be believers, they rarely attend church services. Church is often limited to christenings, weddings and funerals, and so has a social function rather than a religious one. However, the church still plays an important role in some areas, especially in the south of the USA. Here, the so-called "religious right", or fundamentalists, exercise a strong political influence. Christian fundamentalism is a right-wing, conservative movement based on a literal interpretation of the Bible. It puts a great deal of emphasis on traditional family values, promotes prayer in schools (although America does not have a state religion and this could, therefore, be interpreted as unconstitutional) and advocates the teaching of creationism rather than evolution. The influence of this group can be seen, for example, in Republican politics.

Another unusual characteristic of religion in the USA is the so-called "electronic church", where the media, especially TV and radio, are used to spread the word of God. TV evangelism has, however, attracted criticism, as it is sometimes used to encourage people to donate money. There have been TV preachers who have hit the headlines for using money donated to their church for their own purposes.

The arts

Theatre

fringe theatre	Alternativtheater
stage	die Bühne
backstage	hinter der Bühne
props	Requisiten
scenery	Bühnenbild
costume	Garderobe/Kostüm
lighting	Beleuchtung, die Scheinwerfer
spotlight	Scheinwerfer
setting	Schauplatz

Other performing arts

opera	Oper
ballet	Ballet
classical music	Klassik
orchestra	Orchester
chamber music	Kammermusik
dance	Tanz
puppet theatre	Marionettentheater

The plastic arts

painting	Malerei
oil painting	Ölgemälde
drawing	zeichnen
etching	Radierkunst
watercolour	Aquarell
portrait	Porträt, Bildnis
sculpture	Bildhauerei
a sculpture	Skulptur, Plastik
statue	Statue, Standbild
bust	Büste

carving	Schnitzen/Schnitzerei
exhibition	Ausstellung

Cinema

blockbuster	Kassenschlager
comedy	Komödie
science fiction	Science Fiction
romance	Liebesfilm
weepie	Schmachtfetzen
animation	Zeichentrickfilm
chick flick	Frauenfilm
disaster movie	Katastrophenfilm
period drama	Kostümfilm
screenplay	Drehbuch
new release	neuer Film
remake	Neuverfilmung
director's cut	Version eines Films, mit Szenen, die in der ursprünglichen Kinofassung nicht vorkommen
to dub	synchronisieren
subtitles	Untertitel
soundtrack	Filmmusik
trailer	Vorschau

People associated with the arts

artist	Künstler(in)
actor/actress	Schauspieler(in)
the cast	Ensemble
star	Hauptdarsteller/in, Filmstar
co-star	eine/r der Hauptdarsteller
director	Regisseur(in)
producer	Produzent(in)
painter	Maler(in)
sculptor	Bildhauer(in)
author	Autor(in), Schriftsteller(in)

playwright	Dramatiker(in)
screenwriter	Drehbuchautor(in)
critic	Kritiker(in)

Other terms

rehearsal	Probe
to rehearse	proben
to cast a play/film	ein Stück/einen Film besetzen
to miscast	(eine Rolle) falsch besetzen
to typecast	jmd. auf eine bestimmte Art von Rolle festlegen
portrayal	Darstellung
a review	eine Kritik
rave reviews	glänzende Kritiken
opening night	Premiere
to pan	verreißen
box office	Kasse (in einem Kino oder Theater)
audition	Vorsprechen/Vorsingen
red carpet	Roter Teppich

Vocabulary in context: I never used to enjoy going to the theatre. When I was at school, we often had to watch productions of Shakespeare plays, which I always found much too long, even if the director had given the play a modern setting in an attempt to make it seem more relevant. It made no difference if the props were guns instead of swords, or the cast wore modern costumes instead of 16th century clothes, the story remained the same, as far as I was concerned. But this was before I discovered fringe theatre. The first time I went to the Edinburgh Fringe Festival, I found out how much I enjoyed watching contemporary productions that broke with tradition. There was often a minimum of scenery, and perhaps only a couple of people in the cast, but I loved the fact that the plays themselves were satirical, political, comic, or, often, all three. It was certainly a lot more interesting for me than traditional theatre.

My brother is a huge film fan. He sometimes goes to see two or three films a week, and never misses the new releases by his favourite directors. Whenever he buys a film on DVD he gets the director's cut, if it is available, because he feels that this is the version for real experts. He is interested in all kinds of films, from blockbusters to thrillers, even – occasionally – romantic comedies, although these are not his favourites.

Sport

Athletics

high jump	Hochsprung
long jump	Weitsprung
pole vault	Stabhochsprung
sprint	Sprint
hurdles	Hürdenlauf
relay race	Staffellauf
discus	Diskuswerfen
javelin	Speerwurf
shot-put	Kugelstoßen

Outdoor activities

hiking	Wandern
climbing	Klettern
cycling	Rad fahren
hang-gliding	Drachenfliegen
horse-riding	Reiten

Miscellaneous sports

wrestling	Ringen
archery	Bogenschießen
fencing	Fechten
scuba diving	(Geräte-)tauchen
rowing	Rudern
cross-country skiing	Langlauf
ten-pin bowling	Bowling
martial arts	Kampfsportarten

Sports equipment

oar	Ruder
cue	Billardstock
shuttlecock	Federball
(cricket/baseball) bat	Schläger
(tennis/squash/badminton) racket	Schläger, Racket
golf club	Golfschläger
(swimming) goggles	Schwimmbrille
wetsuit	Tauchanzug
shin pads	Schienbeinschoner
gum shield	Mundschutz

Places where sport is played

court	Platz, Court
golf course	Golfplatz
pitch	(Spiel)feld
track	Laufbahn
boxing ring	Boxring
slope	Piste
ice rink	Schlittschuhbahn, Eisbahn
gym(nasium)	Turnhalle, Sporthalle
stadium	Stadion

People associated with sport

referee	Schiedsrichter(in)
linesman	Linienrichter
umpire	Schiedsrichter (Tennis, Cricket)
goalkeeper/goalie	Torhüter(in)
captain	Kapitän
coach	Trainer(in)
spectator	Zuschauer(in)

Verbs associated with sport

to compete	konkurrieren, teilnehmen
to beat someone	jemanden besiegen
to be defeated	geschlagen sein
to draw	unentschieden spielen
to score	Punkt machen/Tor schießen
to kick	treten/einen Ball schießen
to throw	werfen
to set/break a record	einen Rekord aufstellen/brechen
to coach someone	jemanden trainieren
to jump	springen
to equalise	ausgleichen
to foul	foulen

Vocabulary in context: From a very young age it was clear that Alistair was destined to become a great sportsman. Almost as soon as he could walk he started kicking a ball around, and by the age of nine he was the goalkeeper for his primary school's football team. For two years they beat all the other local primary schools, and Alistair set a new record for the highest number of goals saved in one season.

But it didn't stop there. When he started secondary school, Alistair became interested in athletics. Once again, his talent seemed to know no bounds. No matter whether he did the high jump, long jump, threw the javelin or took part in relay races, he could always be relied on to win. His achievements caught the attention of one of the Olympic team coaches, who was convinced that he would have a good chance of winning a gold medal one day. From then on, Alistair's life became devoted to sport: up for a run in the early morning, training sessions at the gym, rowing to strengthen his arms. He even took up martial arts in order to improve his coordination. But then, to the shock and disappointment of his coach, Alistair decided that enough was enough, and refused to carry on training. When he left school, he got a job in a bank, and, although he still runs and plays football a couple of times a week, he says he prefers to enjoy most kinds of sport as a spectator rather than as a player.

Travel and tourism

General terms

to travel	reisen
travel	das Reisen
a journey	Reise, Fahrt
a (day)trip	(Tages)ausflug
a voyage	lange Reise, oft: Seereise
destination	Reiseziel
How long does the journey take?	Wie lange dauert die Fahrt?
It takes me 45 minutes to get home.	Ich brauche 45 Minuten bis nach Hause.
to have itchy feet	Reiselust/Fernweh haben
to get away from it all	einfach alles hinter sich lassen
off the beaten track	abseits der üblichen Reiseziele

Accommodation and types of holiday

guesthouse	Pension
camp-site	Zeltplatz
self-catering flat	Ferienwohnung
youth hostel	Jugendherberge
cruise	Kreuzfahrt
package holiday	Pauschalreise
backpacking holiday	Individualreise (auch: Rucksackurlaub)

Problems when travelling

the flight was delayed	der Flug hatte Verspätung
the flight was cancelled	der Flug wurde storniert
to be stranded	festsitzen
to miss one's connection	die Verbindung verpassen
a security alert	Sicherheitsalarm
rough sea	hoher Seegang
to be seasick	seekrank sein

to be carsick	Übelkeit beim Autofahren
to get lost	sich verlaufen/verfahren
traffic jam	Stau
to run out of petrol	kein Benzin mehr haben
to break down	eine Autopanne haben
to have an accident	einen Unfall haben
to cause an accident	einen Unfall verursachen

Tourism and connected problems

eco-tourism	Ökotourismus
low-impact	wenig belastend, schonend
mass tourism	Massentourismus
sights	Sehenswürdigkeiten
sightseeing	Besichtigung von Sehenswürdigkeiten
cultural exchange	kultureller Austausch
tourist trap	Touristenfalle
tourist enclave	Touristenenklave
hordes of tourists	Touristenmassen
overpriced	überteuert
to be overrun with	wimmeln von

Vocabulary in context: Now, at the beginning of the 21st century, there are more tourists in the world than ever before. Whether they choose a cheap package holiday, an exclusive round-the-world cruise, or decide to go backpacking somewhere off the beaten track, more and more people are taking the opportunity to escape from their everyday routine and get away from it all.

But is travelling really all that relaxing? Hardly. What with delayed flights, security alerts and traffic jams, the journey alone can be fairly miserable. But what about when you actually reach your destination? A lot of people discover, to their cost, that the place they have chosen to visit is a tourist trap, overrun with hordes of other tourists all trying to visit the same sights. Food and accommodation are overpriced, and the souvenirs look as if they were mass-produced in a factory rather than hand-carved by local artisans.

One alternative is to try eco-tourism. This kind of holiday is more low-impact for the local environment and infrastructure, where people stay in small, locally-run accommodation rather than large, anonymous hotels, and where it is possible for some degree of cultural exchange to take place between the tourists and the local people. However, there are some people who argue that any kind of tourism is unnecessary, and that it would be better if we all just spent our holidays at home.

Describing people's character

Behaviour towards others

broad-minded/ narrow-minded	tolerant/engstirnig
considerate/inconsiderate	rücksichtsvoll/rücksichtslos
envious	neidisch
generous/mean, stingy	großzügig/geizig
good-tempered/bad-tempered	gutmütig/cholerisch, aufbrausend
helpful/unhelpful	hilfsbereit/nicht hilfsbereit
honest/dishonest	ehrlich/unehrlich
hospitable/inhospitable	gastfreundlich/ungastlich
jealous	eifersüchtig
kind/unkind, cruel	freundlich, nett/unfreundlich, gemein
loyal/disloyal	loyal/untreu (auch: nicht loyal)
patient/impatient	geduldig/ungeduldig
reliable/unreliable	zuverlässig/unzuverlässig
selfish/unselfish	egoistisch/selbstlos
sociable/unsociable	gesellig/ungesellig
spiteful	gehässig
tactful/tactless	taktvoll/taktlos
touchy	empfindlich
trustworthy/ untrustworthy	vertrauenswürdig/unzuverlässig

Personal characteristics

ambitious	ehrgeizig
assertive	durchsetzungsfähig
bossy	herrisch
confident	selbstbewusst
creative	kreativ, schöpferisch
determined	entschlossen
down-to-earth	nüchtern, sachlich
easy-going	unkompliziert, gelassen
imaginative	fantasievoll
sensible	vernünftig
sensitive	empfindlich, sensibel
snobbish	snobistisch
vain	eitel

Intelligence, or the lack of it

brainy	gescheit, aufgeweckt
bright	intelligent, gescheit
clever	klug, schlau
smart (AE)	schlau
brainless	hirnlos
silly	blöd
stupid	doof, dumm
thick	blöd, doof

Vocabulary in context: Today, in an exclusive interview, broken-hearted Marianna Harris tells us why she left her film star husband Jamie Jordan. "I just couldn't take it any more," she told Stargazer reporter April Sanderson. "Jamie has always been very ambitious regarding his career: it's no secret that his goal is to win at least one Oscar as Best Actor. To achieve something like that you have to be very confident in your own abilities, and you can't be too sensitive to criticism. But what I loved about Jamie when we first got together was the fact that he was so down-to-earth – you would never have thought that he was a film star because he just seemed like everybody else. He was kind and considerate towards others, and was always completely reliable. I knew that he would keep any promises he made. However, after the success of his film "Mind over Matter", he seemed to change. The public adoration started to go to his head, and he became very vain with regard to his appearance, never leaving the house unless he was perfectly groomed and wearing the latest designer fashions. As well as this, he began to be very cruel to me, telling me about all the women who were in love with him to try and make me jealous. But the final straw came when I found out that he was having an affair with one of his co-stars. If there's one thing I can't accept in a partner, it's dishonesty, which is why I decided to leave him."

> **Merke** **Wortfelder**
>
> Zu diesen Themenbereichen auf Anhieb 20 Wörter zu finden und einen kurzen Text dazu zu verfassen, darf kein Problem sein:
>
> - → *Politics*
> - → *The environment*
> - → *Natural disasters*
> - → *The Media*
> - → *Society today*
> - → *Cities*
> - → *Work*
> - → *Medicine*
> - → *Religion*
> - → *Arts*
> - → *Sports*
> - → *Travel and Tourism*
> - → *Religion*
> - → *People's character*

1.2 Idioms

Below are some idioms which can be used to make your writing more interesting and colourful. The German equivalent is given, and below each phrase there is a sentence to illustrate its use.

Idioms to do with colour

- **to look as black as thunder** – *ein finsteres Gesicht machen*
  The headteacher looked as black as thunder when she saw the vandalism. She was absolutely furious.
- **to be not as black as one is painted** – *nicht so schlecht wie sein Ruf sein*
  Mr Geller is supposed to be a very strict teacher, but once you get to know him you'll find that he's not as black as he's painted.
- **out of the blue** – *aus heiterem Himmel*
  Out of the blue, Tom announced that he was going to spend a year travelling around South America.
- **once in a blue moon** – *alle Jubeljahre einmal*
  Monica isn't very good at keeping in touch. She only phones me once in a blue moon.
- **to feel blue** – *traurig sein/deprimiert sein*
  She's been feeling blue ever since Alex broke up with her.
- **to be green with envy** – *grün vor Neid sein*
  When Nick's friends saw his new Jaguar they were green with envy.
- **to give something the green light** – *grünes Licht für etwas geben*
  They're going to start building a new runway at the airport as soon as the government gives the project the green light.
- **to see red** – *Rot sehen*
  It really makes me see red when people drop litter on the streets.
- **to catch someone red-handed** – *jdn. auf frischer Tat ertappen*
  A passing police officer saw the lights on in the building and caught the burglars red-handed.
- **as white as a sheet** – *kreidebleich*
  The children were as white as a sheet when they got off the ghost train – they were terrified!

→ **a white lie** – *eine Notlüge*
I didn't want to hurt her feelings, so I told a white lie and said I loved her new dress.

Idioms with parts of the body

→ **to be a pain in the neck** – *eine Nervensäge sein*
Pat is a real pain in the neck. He's always asking me to help him when I don't have time.

→ **by the skin of one's teeth** – *um Haaresbreite, mit knapper Not*
She didn't do any work at all, but she still managed to pass the exam by the skin of her teeth.

→ **to be unable to make head or tail of something** – *aus etwas nicht schlau werden*
The guy on the computer helpline used so much jargon that I couldn't make head or tail of what he was saying.

→ **to give someone a piece of one's mind** – *jemandem seine Meinung sagen*
Jane promised to be home by 9, but it's nearly 11 p.m. now. I'll give her a piece of my mind when she gets in!

→ **something makes one's blood boil** – *etwas macht jemanden rasend*
The way they mistreat their dog really makes my blood boil. I'm going to report them to the police.

→ **to turn a blind eye** – *ein Auge bei etwas zudrücken*
We're not really supposed to surf the internet during working hours, but, as long as we meet our deadlines, our boss turns a blind eye.

→ **to give someone the elbow** – *jemandem den Laufpass geben*
Kate got sick of her boyfriend's inconsiderate behaviour and gave him the elbow.

→ **to get something off your chest** – *etwas loswerden*
There's something I want to get off my chest. I was the one who lost your favourite earrings.

→ **to put one's foot in it** – *ins Fettnäpfchen treten*
Jed never thinks before he speaks. He's always putting his foot in it.

→ **to foot the bill** – *die Rechnung begleichen*
When Dylan broke the neighbour's window, his parents were the ones who had to foot the bill.

> **Abi-Tipp: Redewendungen**
>
> Versuchen Sie nicht, Redewendungen wörtlich zu übersetzen –
> dies funktioniert meistens nicht! Es gibt aber in vielen Fällen eine
> entsprechende Redewendung auf Deutsch.

Idioms with animals

- **mutton dressed as lamb** – *sich viel zu jugendlich anziehen*
  My 50-year-old aunt always insists on wearing the latest fashions, but she just looks like mutton dressed as lamb.
- **more fish in the sea** – *es gibt noch andere auf der Welt*
  Who cares if Gillian has left me? There are plenty more fish in the sea!
- **a frog in one's throat** – *ein Frosch im Hals*
  Could I have a glass of water? I've got a frog in my throat.
- **an underdog** – *Außenseiter(in)*
  It's often more interesting to support the underdog than someone who's a sure-fire winner.
- **to kill two birds with one stone** – *zwei Fliegen mit einer Klappe schlagen*
  Since we're going into town anyway we might as well kill two birds with one stone and bring Cindy her books back.
- **straight from the horse's mouth** – *etwas aus erster Hand haben*
  I know the story's true. I heard it straight from the horse's mouth!
- **Don't count your chickens before they are hatched** – *Man soll den Tag nicht vor dem Abend loben.*
  Sharon is sure she's going to get the job, but she shouldn't count her chickens before they're hatched. They might still give it to someone else.

Idioms with food and cooking

- **to sell like hot cakes** – *sich wie warme Semmeln verkaufen*
  The new Robbie Williams album is selling like hot cakes – it's already number one in the charts.

- **to have one's cake and eat it** – *beides gleichzeitig wollen*
  Toby thought he could keep seeing Gina although he was married to Suzie. He just wanted to have his cake and eat it.
- **to be a piece of cake** – *kinderleicht, ein Kinderspiel*
  That exam was no problem at all – it was a piece of cake!
- **to take something with a pinch of salt** – *etwas mit Vorsicht genießen*
  All Colin's stories about how he used to be in a famous rock band should be taken with a pinch of salt.
- **to be (a) chicken** – *feige/ein Feigling sein*
  I don't like fairground rides – I'm far too chicken to enjoy them!
- **to be full of beans** – *putzmunter sein*
  The children are really full of beans. They haven't stopped running around all day.
- **to spill the beans** – *ausplaudern*
  It was supposed to be a surprise party, but someone spilt the beans.
- **to put it in a nutshell** – *es auf den Punkt bringen*
  To put it in a nutshell, it was a wonderful holiday.
- **out of the frying pan into the fire** – *vom Regen in die Traufe*
  I'm not convinced that changing jobs will improve my situation. It might turn out to be a case of out of the frying pan into the fire.

Idioms to do with the weather

- **to be under the weather** – *angeschlagen sein*
  I'm feeling a bit under the weather, so I think I'll stay at home this weekend.
- **a storm in a teacup** – *ein Sturm im Wasserglas*
  It turned out that all the fuss was for nothing. It was just a storm in a teacup.
- **to storm out** – *hinausstürmen*
  Jackie was so furious about the decision that she stormed out of the meeting in protest.
- **to take a raincheck** – *etwas verschieben*
  I'm afraid I don't have time to go for a drink this evening after all. Do you mind if I take a raincheck?
- **to steal someone's thunder** – *jemandem die Schau stehlen*

My sister announced that she was engaged on the same evening that I told the family I'd won a prize. She really stole my thunder.

→ **to make hay while the sun shines** – *das Eisen schmieden, solange es heiß ist*
You should finish the job now, while you have the chance. Make hay while the sun shines!

→ **to throw caution to the wind** – *alle Vorsicht in den Wind schlagen*
He threw caution to the wind and spent all of his savings on a lottery ticket.

→ **to take the wind out of someone's sails** – *jemandem den Wind aus den Segeln nehmen*
I phoned John to give him a piece of my mind, but he took the wind out of my sails by apologising first.

→ **to put the wind up someone** – *jemandem Angst einjagen*
The rumours about possible redundancies have really put the wind up everyone in my office.

→ **it never rains but it pours** – *ein Unglück kommt selten allein*
So your dog's been run over, your bike's been stolen and you've lost your keys? Well, it never rains but it pours!

Idioms to do with nature

→ **to bark up the wrong tree** – *auf dem Holzweg sein*
The police thought they'd found the head of the drugs ring, but it turned out that they were barking up the wrong tree.

→ **to get the wrong end of the stick** – *etwas völlig missverstehen*
Terry got the wrong end of the stick. He thought his boss wanted to fire him, but she actually wanted to promote him.

→ **to beat about the bush** – *um den heißen Brei herumreden*
Come on – don't beat about the bush! Tell me what really happened last night!

→ **to be out of the woods** – *über den Berg sein*
The victims of the bomb attack are recovering slowly, but they are not out of the woods yet.

→ **the grass is always greener on the other side (of the fence)** – *die Kirschen in Nachbars Garten schmecken immer süßer*

It isn't necessarily better to live in the country than in the town, but people often think the grass is greener on the other side.

→ **to be all at sea** – *(ganz) ratlos sein*
We had to admit that we were all at sea: we didn't have a clue what we should do next.

→ **the tip of the iceberg** – *die Spitze des Eisbergs*
Vandalism is just the tip of the iceberg as far as inner city crime is concerned.

→ **to pour oil on troubled waters** – *Öl auf die Wogen gießen*
Tina's really good at dealing with conflicts. She always knows how to pour oil on troubled waters.

Idioms describing people

→ **to have one's heart in the right place** – *das Herz auf dem rechten Fleck haben*
I know Harry can be irritating at times, but his heart's in the right place. He only wants to help.

→ **to be as good as gold** – *ganz brav sein*
The children have been very well-behaved all day. They've been as good as gold.

→ **to be a knight in shining armour** – *ein Retter in der Not sein*
Pete helped me when I was really desperate and didn't know who to turn to. He was my knight in shining armour.

→ **to be a mine of information** – *sehr viel wissen*
If you want to know more about computers you should ask my husband. He's a mine of information when it comes to modern technology.

→ **a know-all** – *ein(e) Besserwisser(in)*
Brendon thinks he's so clever, but he doesn't seem to realise that no-one likes a know-all.

→ **to be a big-head** – *ein(e) Angeber(in) sein*
Shirley is such a big-head. She's always boasting about the tennis medals she's won.

→ **to be as thick as two short planks** – *sehr dumm sein*
He's as thick as two short planks. He just doesn't have the brains you need for the job.

→ **to be a rough diamond** – *ein ungeschliffener Diamant sein*
Jim seems quite bad-mannered at first, but once you get to know him you realise that he's just a rough diamond.
→ **to be one's own worst enemy** – *sich selbst der schlimmste Feind sein*
Lynne is always getting into trouble because she doesn't know when to keep her mouth shut. She's her own worst enemy.
→ **to be quick/slow off the mark** – *schnell/schwer von Begriff sein*
At first I didn't realise that Greg was asking me out. I was a bit slow off the mark there!

Idioms describing relationships

→ **to have the hots for someone** – *scharf auf jemanden sein*
Todd really likes Mandy. He's had the hots for her for months.
→ **to only have eyes for someone** – *nur für jemanden Augen haben*
They are such a sickenly sweet couple. They only have eyes for each other.
→ **to get on like a house on fire** – *hervorragend miteinander auskommen*
I knew that Emily and my sister would get on like a house on fire because they have so much in common.
→ **to (not) see eye to eye** – *mit jemandem einer/geteilter Meinung über etwas sein*
I get on quite well with my brother, although we certainly don't see eye to eye about everything.
→ **to fall out with someone** – *sich (zer)streiten*
Amy has fallen out with her parents. She's not talking to them at the moment.

Idioms connected with problems and their solutions

→ **to be in a tight corner** – *in der Klemme stecken*
We'll be in a tight corner financially if things don't improve soon.
→ **that's all we need** – *das hat gerade noch gefehlt*
Please don't tell me that Mr Jeffreys is now in charge of the project! That's all we need!
→ **to come to a head** – *sich zuspitzen*

Things really came to a head when the rest of the Cabinet demanded the Prime Minister's resignation.

→ **to reach a dead end** – *in eine Sackgasse geraten*
The talks between the government and the trade unions have reached a dead end, with neither side prepared to back down.

→ **to draw the line** – *bei etwas die Grenze ziehen*
I'm prepared to work overtime when there's a lot to do, but I draw the line at working Sundays.

→ **to get one's act together** – *sich am Riemen reißen*
If you don't get your act together very soon you are going to fail your exams and be left without any job prospects.

→ **the tide has turned** – *die Meinung ist umgeschlagen*
It seems that, finally, the tide has turned in favour of the opposition party.

→ **to see light at the end of the tunnel** – *das Licht am Ende des Tunnels sehen*
It's been a long, hard struggle to solve this problem, but we can finally see light at the end of the tunnel.

→ **to sweep something under the carpet** – *etwas unter den Teppich kehren*
Instead of dealing with the situation, those responsible simply swept the problem under the carpet.

→ **to bury the hatchet** – *einen Streit begraben*
After years of conflict, Tom and Marty were forced to bury the hatchet when Tom's son married Marty's daughter.

Idioms connected with numbers

→ **two of a kind** – *aus dem gleichen Holz geschnitzt sein*
My father and my uncle are very much alike: they're two of a kind.

→ **two can play at that game** – *wie du mir, so ich dir*
So you think you can leave me to do all the washing up while you go out with your friends? Well, two can play at that game!

→ **two's company, three's a crowd** – *drei sind einer zu viel*
I'm going to give Tracy and Darren a bit of privacy. As they say, two's company and three's a crowd!

→ **it takes two to tango** – *dazu gehören immer zwei*

It's not fair to blame Charlie completely for the affair. After all, it takes two to tango.

→ **to be in two minds** – *hin- und hergerissen sein*
I'm in two minds about whether to buy the dress or not. It looks fantastic, but on the other hand it's very expensive.

→ **four-letter words** – *Schimpfwörter*
He's so foul-mouthed. Every other word he says is a four-letter word.

→ **six of one and half a dozen of the other** – *Jacke wie Hose*
You're both equally at fault here. It's six of one and half a dozen of the other.

→ **to be in seventh heaven/to be on cloud nine** – *im siebten Himmel sein*
She was on cloud nine when she heard that she'd been offered a place to study medicine.

→ **at the eleventh hour** – *im letzten Augenblick*
The company was about to go bankrupt, but at the eleventh hour they were bought by a larger firm.

→ **twenty-four/seven** – *24 Stunden am Tag, 7 Tage die Woche*
It was such an important project that we worked on it twenty-four/seven until it was finished.

1.3 Recording and learning vocabulary

Organising vocabulary

There are many different ways of organising and recording vocabulary, and it is up to each individual to choose the way that suits them best. Many learners simply write down the new word and its translation, without any context or additional information. However, it has been proved that if the vocabulary is noted down with some degree of organisation, it is easier to remember. Making the vocabulary more visual (see opposite) is also helpful. The words can be arranged in any way that seems logical to the language learner, such as:

words related by topic, e.g. types of animal, types of fruit

words all connected to a particular activity or process, e.g. travelling by plane *(go to the airport, check in etc)*

words with similar meanings, e.g. *pretty, lovely, attractive, beautiful*. Here it is a good idea to note down an example of the use of each word, e.g. a sentence with the word used in context: *She is one of the most beautiful women I have ever seen. Thank you for a lovely evening!*

sets of words, e.g. 'ways of looking': *to stare, to glance, to gaze* etc. Again, it is important to note down an example of how each of these words is used in context.

words that form pairs, e.g. synonyms: *neat and tidy;* or opposites: *buy and sell*

words on a scale, e.g. to describe sound level: *silent; quiet; noisy; ear-splitting; deafening*

word families, i.e. noting down any noun, verb, adjective or adverb forms relating to a particular word, e.g. *to employ; employment; unemployment; employer; employee; employed; unemployed*

collocations (words that can be used in combination with each other), e.g. to *revise for/take/do/pass/fail an exam*

Recording vocabulary – some tips

Use a vocabulary notebook or index cards.

Vocabulary notebook

Notebooks are very flexible. For example, you can start a new page for every new topic, and make use of diagrams. There are several types of these:

→ **tree diagrams**

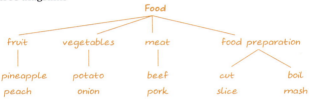

→ **bubble networks**

Below is a bubble network consisting of phrasal verbs with 'put'. As well as different verbs, an example of the context is given in each case:

→ **word forks**

→ For some groups of words it can be useful to **label a picture**, e.g. parts of a car.
→ It is always useful to **write down a sentence** where the word is used in context.

Index cards

These normally have the English word on one side and a translation on the other. The English side of an index card can contain additional information about the word, such as connected noun and verb forms and an example sentence.

> **Abi-Tipp**
>
> → If you cannot remember a particular word when testing yourself, draw a small star in another colour next to it. Do this every time you forget the word. If a word has three stars, this means that this is a word you easily forget and you need to spend more time learning it.
> → Do not forget to go back and revise "old" vocabulary now and again, to check that you still remember it.
> → Do not try to learn too many new words at once. Although the words may be in your short-term memory, it takes lots of repetition and active use of the word for you to really know it.
> → Take your vocabulary notes with you, for example when travelling by bus. Repetition throughout the day is helpful, even if you only spend 10 minutes or so at a time revising words.
> → Write new words on Post-it notes and stick them around your room. In this way you will be constantly confronted with the new vocabulary.
> → Use new words that you have learnt, e. g. when writing essays.
> → Watch a film in English. Many cinemas now show current films in the original English version. DVDs, of course, are perfect for watching films in English.
> → Read a magazine or newspaper in English. All large English-language newspapers and magazines have websites where you can read articles. Choose a topic that interests you and read it, noting any new or useful vocabulary.
> → Try to think in English. Imagine you have to describe certain activities (e. g. driving a car, using the Internet) to someone who has never done it before and only speaks English. How can you explain the procedure involved?

1.4 Getting the most from your dictionary

It is worth investing in a good dictionary, as, when used properly, it is one of the most useful tools a language learner can have.

Tips for using a bilingual dictionary

Choose a dictionary **especially designed for learners** of English such as a school dictionary, the larger the better, as small, pocket dictionaries cannot provide much additional information. And, as the dictionary extract below shows, it is this additional information, particularly the context of a word, that will help you to decide which translation you need.

As many words have several different possible translations, it is important to **read all of the options** and to check carefully whether the word you've chosen really means what you think it means. This can be done by
→ checking the word in a monolingual dictionary or
→ doing a "double search": after selecting a translation in the German-English section of the dictionary, look up the English word again in the English-German section and see which German translations are given there. This should help to make the exact meaning of the word clear.

BEISPIEL: Arbeit mit einem zweisprachigen Wörterbuch
Look at the following extract from a dictionary entry (Pons Großwörterbuch für Experten und Universität) on the word *"Betrieb"*:
Betrieb: 1. (Industrie_) [industrial] company, firm; **ist Direktor Wengel schon im ~ ?** is director Wengel already at work [or in the office]?; **ich muss heute etwas länger im ~ bleiben** I have to work late today 2. (die Belegschaft) workforce 3. kein pl (Betriebsamkeit) activity; **heute war nur wenig/herrschte großer ~ im Laden** it was very quiet/busy in the shop today 4. (Tätigkeit) operation, running; **die Straßenbahnen nehmen morgens um 5 Uhr ihren _ auf** the trams start running at 5 o'clock in the morning; (Ablauf) production process; **etw in ~ nehmen** to put something into operation
The following information can be found:
→ several different translations
→ additional German words to clarify the usage (e. g. „die Belegschaft")
→ collocations (e. g. "to put something into operation")
→ grammatical information (e. g. „kein pl[ural]")
→ sentences with an idiomatic translation of the word in different contexts.

Monolingual learners' dictionary

A monolingual learners' dictionary contains the following information:
- definition → what the word means
- part of speech → e.g. noun, adjective etc.
- for nouns → whether the word is countable [C] or uncountable [U]
- for verbs → whether it is transitive (must have an object) or intransitive (doesn't need an object)
- pronunciation → using the phonetic alphabet
- stress → which syllable is stressed when the word is spoken. This is usually indicated with a small mark before the syllable that is stressed: ba'nana or by using bold type: ba**na**na
- register → whether the word is formal, informal, colloquial or taboo (i.e. words which are considered offensive)
- BE or AE → whether the word is British or American English, including differences in spelling
- example → a phrase or sentence to show how the word is typically used, including the necessary grammar (e.g. *interested: John is very interested in learning how to water-ski.*)

Dictionaries on CD-ROM

It is quick and easy to work with a CD-ROM version of a dictionary on your home computer. These contain all the information provided in a "normal" dictionary, but with the addition of search functions which can save a great deal of time. Many also make use of multi-media functions, such as video clips, and contain exercises and games.

Online dictionaries

There are various dictionary services that can be accessed online, such as http://dict.leo.org or www.dict.cc. These should, however, be used carefully, as the context is not always given. It is a good idea to double-check words if several alternatives are given, e.g. in a monolingual dictionary.

1.5 Coping without a dictionary

When reading a text, especially for the first time, it is not necessary to understand every single word. It is enough to understand the general meaning of the text (= the gist). You will also find that there are several clues in the text that will help you guess the meaning of unfamiliar words.

Context

The other words close to the unfamiliar word (in the same sentence, or in the previous or following sentences) often show us what the word must mean.
→ Example: *Serve the tapioca warm, with sugar or fresh fruit if desired.*
  → Although it is unlikely that you know the word "tapioca", it is clear from the context that it is something to eat, probably a dessert as it is eaten with sugar or fruit.

Your knowledge of a particular situation can tell you what certain words must mean. If, for example, you have seen or read a news report in your own language about the current situation in the Middle East, it will then be easier to read a similar article in English, as you will already know what it is about.

Similarity to other words

Other English words. English contains many compound words, and the separate elements of these can make it fairly easy to guess what the whole word or expression means.

Examples:
→ "answering machine" → what can be answered by using a machine? A telephone. Therefore this is a machine for recording telephone calls when a person is not at home.
→ "sidewalk" → a place to walk at the side of a street.
→ "an all-out strike" → a strike involving everyone in a company: all the workers, who are not in the factory or office, but are outside it, on strike.

Words from other languages. English has a lot of words that are similar to those in other languages, especially Germanic or Latin-based languages. This means that there are many words whose meaning you already know. Example: catastrophe. However, it is important to be careful of → false friends here! Make sure you know what the most common false friends between your language and English are.

Prefixes and suffixes

The prefixes and suffixes used in English also provide useful information about the meaning of words.

Here are some common prefixes:

prefix	meaning	example
anti-	against	anticlimax
auto-	of/by oneself	autobiography
bi-	two, twice	bilingual
co-	together	co-production
dis-	negative, opposite	distrust
ex-	former	ex-boyfriend
il/im/in/ir-	negative, opposite	illogical, immature, inappropriate, irregular
inter-	between	interstate
micro-	small	microscopic
mis-	badly, wrongly	misjudge
mono-	single	monorail
multi-	many	multi-media
over-	too much	overflow
post-	after	postscript
pre-	before	predict
re-	again, back	remake, repay
semi-	half	semifinal
sub-	below	substandard
un-	negative, opposite	unusual
under-	not enough	underpaid

The **suffixes of some adjectives** also indicate the **meaning** of the word:

suffix	meaning	example
-able/-ible	can be done	drinkable
-ful	with a lot of	useful
-ish	approximately	thirty-ish (e.g. 'How old is she?' – 'Thirty-ish.')
-less	without	hopeless

Suffixes tell us **what kind of word** we are dealing with, which can be useful when trying to guess the meaning of a word. For example, if you know the verb 'to employ', and that the suffix '-ment' indicates a noun, then the meaning of 'employment' should also be clear. Here are some common examples of suffixes:

part of speech	suffix	example
noun	-ee	trainee
	-er/-or	swimmer/actor
	-hood	childhood
	-ion/-sion/-tion	production
	-ism	criticism
	-ist	communist
	-ity	mobility
	-ment	arrangement
	-ness	kindness
	-ship	friendship
adjective	-al	magical
	-ive	massive
	-ly	weekly
	-ous	suspicious
	-y	rainy
adverb	-ly	happily
	-wards	forwards
verb	-ify	horrify

Checkliste ## 1 Vocabulary

Vokabeln lernen

- → Wörter beim Aufschreiben logisch gruppieren, z. B. Wörter, die zu einem Thema gehören, Wörter mit ähnlichen Bedeutungen, Synonyme und Gegensätze, Wort-„Familien" usw.
- → Wörter in ein Vokabelheft oder auf Karteikarten schreiben.
- → Ein Vokabelheft kann man auch benutzen, um Wörter bildlich darzustellen, z. B. in Form eines „tree diagram", „bubble network" oder einer „word fork".
- → Schreiben Sie einen Satz, der das Wort enthält, das Sie lernen wollen. Es hilft, wenn man sich Wörter im Kontext merkt.
- → Karteikarten kann man überallhin mitnehmen, um Vokabeln zu lernen oder zu wiederholen, wenn man gerade ein paar Minuten Zeit hat.
- → Versuchen Sie nicht, zu viele Wörter auf einmal zu lernen, und vergessen Sie nicht, alte Vokabeln von Zeit zu Zeit zu wiederholen: Es dauert nämlich, bis Vokabeln im Langzeitgedächtnis „gespeichert" sind!
- → Nutzen Sie moderne Medien (DVDs, Internet usw.), um Ihr passives Verständnis des Englischen zu festigen und zu erweitern.
- → Benutzen Sie die Wörter, die Sie gelernt haben!

Arbeiten mit Wörterbüchern

- → Investieren Sie in ein gutes, großes, zweisprachiges Wörterbuch, das speziell für Schüler und/oder Studenten konzipiert ist.
- → Wenn für ein Wort mehrere Übersetzungsmöglichkeiten angegeben sind, benutzen Sie ein einsprachiges Wörterbuch, um sicherzustellen, dass Sie das richtige Wort ausgewählt haben.
- → Learners' dictionaries enthalten sowohl viele hilfreiche grammatikalische Informationen über die einzelnen Wörter als auch Beispielsätze, in denen das Wort im Kontext erscheint. Solche Infos erleichtern die Suche nach der richtigen Übersetzung.
- → Es gibt auch Wörterbücher im Internet, die kostenlos sind und eine schnelle Hilfe sein können. Aber Vorsicht: oft wird hier keinen Kontext gegeben. Deshalb ist es bei mehreren Übersetzungsmöglichkeiten nach wie vor wichtig, genau zu kontrollieren, dass Sie sich für die richtige entschieden haben.

English grammar – a brief overview

2

Die englische Grammatik besitzt viele knifflige Aspekte, mit denen Nicht-Muttersprachler zu kämpfen haben. Kurze Beispieltexte nach den Zusammenfassungen der verschiedenen Zeitformen zeigen Ihnen, wie diese Formen richtig einzusetzen sind. Dazu kommt ein Überblick über die Verlaufsformen und Partizipien sowie über die häufigsten *phrasal verbs* und *false friends*. Außerdem finden Sie Hilfe bei der Vermeidung von typischen Fehlern.

2.1 Use of the tenses

Simple and continuous forms

The present: The simple and continuous verb forms in English are used in different ways. Listed below are some examples of the main differences:

Use the present simple for:
→ things that are true in general, but not necessarily happening at the time of speaking:
  - Dentists **take care of** people's teeth.
  - Trains **run** on tracks.
→ natural facts and scientific laws:
  - Sharks **live** in the ocean.
  - Water **freezes** at 0° Celsius.
→ routines or regular, repeated actions (often used with adverbs such as always, usually, often, sometimes, occasionally, never etc):
  - Joe **goes** to a football match every Saturday.
  - We often **spend** our holidays in France.

→ permanent situations:
  - The post office **is** opposite the bank.
  - My sister **lives** near Oxford.
→ state verbs, which are not usually used in the continuous form (e.g. be, believe, belong, consist, contain, depend, feel, hate, know, like, love, mean, need, prefer, realise, remember, seem, smell, taste, want):
  - I **like** tea but I **prefer** coffee.
  - This shirt **belongs** to my brother.
→ time clauses after if, when, until, as soon as etc:
  - I'll phone you as soon as I **arrive**.
  - Please let me know if you **wish** to attend the course.

> **Merke** **Schlüsselwörter für die simple-Form**
>
> → *always* → *to contain* → *to realise*
> → *usually* → *to depend* → *to remember*
> → *often* → *to feel* → *to seem*
> → *sometimes* → *to hate* → *to smell*
> → *occasionally* → *to know* → *to taste*
> → *never* → *to like* → *to want*
> → *to be* → *to love* → *if*
> → *to believe* → *to mean* → *when*
> → *to belong* → *to need* → *until*
> → *to consist* → *to prefer* → *as soon as*

Use the present continuous for:
→ actions happening at the moment of speaking or actions incomplete at the time of speaking:
  - "What's Mike **doing**?" "He's **playing** a computer game."
  - Scientists **are working** on the development of alternative energy sources.
→ temporary situations:
  - The police **are diverting** the traffic after a serious accident on Edgware Road.
  - They'**re showing** a lot of old James Bond films at the local cinema this week.

→ changing or developing situations:
- Winter **is coming**: the weather **is getting** colder every day.
- Methods of electronic communication **are becoming** faster and more efficient all the time.

→ irritating habits:
- Emma **is** always **forgetting** to lock the door when she goes out.
- He's always **leaving** his stuff all over the floor – I wish he'd tidy up a bit more often!

Grammar in context: Jack normally goes to work by car, but this week he's going by bike because he wants to try and get fit. He works in the centre of London, in a large financial company. At the moment he only has a desk job, but he feels that it is important to improve his future career prospects, so he's studying at night school for a degree in business administration. On Friday evenings he usually meets up with some friends in one of the bars in the city centre: this week they're trying out a new place that belongs to a Hollywood actor. A lot of trendy new bars like this are opening in London at the moment, whereas, in some parts of the city, the old-style pubs are gradually disappearing. Some people believe that if they close down too many of the old places, it will damage the character of the city.

The past: The differences between the past simple and the past continuous are similar to the differences found in the present tense:

Use the past simple for:
→ permanent or long-term situations in the past:
- I **grew up** in a small village in Yorkshire.
- His family **owned** the land for many generations.

→ routines or repeated actions:
- I **sent** him five text messages yesterday, but he **didn't** reply.
- Neil **played** rugby every weekend when he was younger.

→ completed actions:
- They **finished** the new stadium in time for the World Cup.
- We **had** a great time in France last year.

→ state verbs (see above):
- It **seemed** like a good idea at the time.
- They **needed** a holiday after all their hard work.

→ actions which follow each other in a sequence:
- I **got up**, **had** a shower, **put on** my clothes and **left** the house.
- As soon as I **heard** the news, I **phoned** Simon to congratulate him.

Use the past continuous for:

→ temporary situations:
- Many people **were trying** to flee the city during the bomb raids.
- At that time I **was working** on a fascinating project.

→ activities in progress at a definite time in the past:
- At ten o'clock this morning I **was** still **waiting** for the bus.
- This time last year our company **wasn't doing** very well at all.

→ incomplete actions, often in combination with the past simple to express the idea that one action interrupted another:
- We **were talking** about the match when Tony turned up.
- The thunderstorm started while I **was walking** home.

Grammar in context: Last Saturday I was just finishing lunch when the phone rang. It was my cousin Tim, who told me that he was staying in town for a few days and wondered if he could come and see me. I used to spend a lot of time with Tim when we were children, but his family moved away when he was twelve, and we seldom saw each other any more. So we arranged to meet the following evening. We went to an Italian restaurant together and caught up with each other's news. He told me he was studying chemistry at Birmingham University and hoped to go to America for a year as an exchange student. Anyway, we had a wonderful evening together, and were just leaving the restaurant when an old friend of ours, Julie, walked in the door. So we sat down again, ordered another bottle of wine, and chatted until the restaurant closed.

Last Easter, we spent a few days in London. We had just visited the Tower of London and were standing by the Thames, wondering whether to walk across Tower Bridge or have lunch. Suddenly, a familiar voice said "Hello!" We turned round and were astonished to see our next-door neighbour! He hadn't even told us he was coming to London, and was just walking along by the river when he spotted us. At first he couldn't believe his eyes and asked us what we were doing there. We all agreed that it really is a small world and went to get a coffee together.

Verwendung der simple-Form:	Verwendung der Verlaufsform:
→ allgemeingültige Aussagen → Naturgesetze → Fakten → regelmäßige Handlungen → Dauerzustände → nach Hilfsverben → nach Verben der Sinneswahrnehmung → in Relativsätzen der Zeit → Situationsbeschreibungen → Routinen → wiederholte Handlungen → abgeschlossene Handlungen → aufeinanderfolgende Handlungen	→ passiert jetzt, im Moment → noch nicht abgeschlossene Handlung oder Situation → vorübergehende Situationen → sich ändernde Situationen → sich entwickelnde Situationen → Ausnahme einer gewohnheitsmäßigen Handlung → momentane Handlung, die durch eine andere unterbrochen wurde

Future forms

There is a variety of ways of expressing the future in English. Below are some examples:

Use will/won't for:

→ the future in general, but not things that have already been arranged or decided:
- I wonder if Tom **will be** at the party.
- You probably **won't have** time to do all these exercises.

→ making predictions about the future:
- Tony's pretty sure that he'**ll pass** the exam.
- Over the next 30 years fresh water supplies in some parts of the world **will decrease** dramatically.

→ offers, decisions or promises made spontaneously at the time of speaking:
- It's really hot in here. I'**ll open** the window.
- Don't worry. I **won't tell** anyone your secret.

Use the future continuous for:

→ talking about things that will be happening at a definite time in the future (incomplete actions):
- In a month from today we'**ll be moving** into our new house.

- At this time tomorrow I'**ll be packing** my suitcase for my holiday to Spain – I can't wait!

→ things that are definitely going to happen at some time in the future:
  - I can pick up some more stamps if you like – I'**ll be passing** the post office anyway.
  - Jim **will be arriving** at 5.30 this evening. Let's go and meet him at the station.

Present tenses with future meaning:

→ The present continuous is used to talk about future arrangements:
  - Jamie and I **are having** a party on Saturday – would you like to come?
  - My parents **are flying** back from Mexico next Tuesday.

→ The present simple is used to talk about timetables or programmes in the future:
  - The train **leaves** at 5 a.m. tomorrow, so we mustn't forget to set the alarm clock.
  - "When **does** your course **start**?" "On 1st May."

Use going to for:

→ plans or intentions:
  - I'm **going to get** my hair cut next week.
  - The government is **going to announce** its new tax programme this afternoon.

→ making predictions about the future when there is present evidence:
  - Alison must be really upset. She looks as if she'**s going to cry**.
  - It'**s going to be** a hard year for the retail trade unless consumer spending increases soon.

Use future perfect (simple or continuous) for:

→ actions that will be complete by a certain time in the future:
  - By the end of this month I'**ll have been studying** English for ten years.
  - They'**ll have built** two new motorways and several hotels by the time the Olympic Games begin.

Grammar in context: What does the future hold? Everyone knows that there will be technological and environmental changes in the next few decades, but no-one can say for sure what form these will take. It's clear, for example, that electronic gadgets are going to become smaller, faster and easier to use. Computers will continue to play a vital role in our lives; furthermore, by the end of 2014, the Internet will have existed for 25 years, and there will be a whole generation of adults who have grown up with it.

On the down side, we know that a significant percentage of the world's population will soon be living without fresh drinking water, while others are going to suffer increasingly from natural disasters such as floods. However, even here there is hope that in a few years from now new technology will be predicting such disasters with greater accuracy, making it easier to prevent them.

Some experts argue that we will have done even more damage to our planet by the middle of this century, whereas others predict that, at least in the western world, things are going to improve due to greater awareness of the problems. Certainly the amount of money invested in alternative energy sources is going to increase further in the next few years, to name just one example. Whatever happens, though, we will have to make sure that future generations will still be able to enjoy our world as much as we do.

> **Zukunftsformen** — Merke
>
> **Futur mit will/won't:**
> → Planungen
> → Voraussagen
> → Vermutungen
> → spontane Entscheidungen
> → Versprechen
>
> **will-Futur in der Verlaufsform:**
> → nicht abgeschlossene Handlung oder Situation, die zu einem bestimmten Zeitpunkt in der Zukunft ablaufen bzw. bestehen wird
> → (ziemlich) gesicherte Aussage über ein zukünftiges Geschehen
>
> **Verlaufsform der Gegenwart**
> → Festlegung oder Vereinbarung von zukünftigen Handlungen

> **Einfache Gegenwart:**
> → Zeitplan, Fahrplan, Programm (kann vom Sprecher nicht beeinflusst werden)
>
> **Futur mit „going to"**
> → drückt die Absicht aus, in der Zukunft etwas zu tun
> → Voraussagen über etwas, das (sehr wahrscheinlich) eintreffen (oder: so sein) wird
>
> **Future perfect**
> → Handlungen, die zu einem bestimmten Zeitpunkt in der Zukunft abgeschlossen sein werden
> → mit der üblichen Unterscheidung zwischen simple- und continuous-Formen

The perfect tenses

Perfect tenses are used in a number of different situations in English:

Use the present perfect simple for:
→ things a person has experienced at some time in their life, but without saying exactly when:
  - Jenny **has met** George Clooney.
  - I'**ve been** to the States three times now.
→ recent events, but without mentioning exactly when they took place:
  - Jane **has** just **found out** that she's passed all her exams! She's delighted!
  - I **haven't seen** much of Tom recently. I wonder what he's up to.
→ the results of past actions which can be seen in the present:
  - I know your face, but I'**ve** completely **forgotten** your name, I'm afraid.
  - Oh no! Someone **has broken into** our office and stolen our new computers!
→ situations that started in the past and have continued until now:
  - Lucy is my best friend. I'**ve known** her since we were at school together.
  - We'**ve lived** here for three months now.

2.1 Use of the tenses

- repeated actions or routines that started in the past and have continued up to now:
  - She'**s been** to the gym twice a week for the past year.
  - I **haven't missed** a single episode of "Pop Stars" so far – I'**ve watched** it every week.
- time expressions which indicate unfinished time (today, this week, this month, this year):
  - How much **have** you **spent** on phone calls this month?
  - I **haven't had** a holiday yet this year – I really need one.
- state verbs:
  - This is the most delicious cake I'**ve** ever **tasted**!
  - Anne **has seemed** a bit worried recently – I hope she's OK.
  - **I've** just **remembered** that I need to make a phone call – please excuse me for a few minutes.

The present perfect continuous:

Sometimes there is no real difference in meaning between the simple and continuous forms of the present perfect, especially with the verbs live and work:

- We'**ve lived** in this house for 6 months **or**
- we'**ve been living** in this house for 6 months.

However, the two forms are also used to put emphasis on different things:

- the present perfect continuous emphasizes the activity and the simple form emphasizes the result:
  - I'**ve been searching** for the information on the Internet all morning, but I **haven't had** much luck so far.
  - Please excuse the mess. We'**ve been redecorating** the living room.
  - The living room looks much better now that we'**ve redecorated** it.
- as in other tenses, the continuous form often indicates that an activity is incomplete, whereas the simple form shows that the activity is finished:
  - I'**ve been doing** a lot of revision this weekend because I've got an exam next Wednesday.
  - Well, I'**ve done** my revision. I just hope I remember everything I'**ve learnt**!

→ the continuous form is often used to say how long something has been happening; the simple form is used to say how often something has happened or how many/much of something has been done:
- They'**ve been digging up** the road outside our house for months now.
- How much coffee **have** you **drunk** today?
- My grandmother **has been** in hospital 4 times this year.

→ as in other tenses, we can use the continuous form to indicate that a situation is temporary, and the simple form to say that it is permanent or long-lasting:
- I'**ve been working** on this essay for days now, but I just can't seem to finish it.
- The new drugs **have** greatly **improved** the lives of many cancer patients.

The present perfect and the simple past:
In some situations it can be difficult to decide whether to use the simple past or the present perfect. Here are some pointers:

→ Use the present perfect to talk about things that have happened at an unspecified time in the past, but not with past time expressions that refer to a specific, finished time (ago, yesterday, last week, last month, last year):
- "**Have** you ever **been** to London?" "Yes, several times. I last **went** there about three months **ago**."
- "Jackie **has** just **won** an award!" "Yes, I know. She **phoned** me **yesterday** and **told** me."

NB: "Unfinished" time expressions (see above) cannot be used with the present perfect if they refer to short, completed actions. It also depends on the time when the person is speaking:
- What time **did** you **arrive** here this morning?
- → not: *What time have you arrived…*
- (At 11 a.m.): I **have written** eight e-mails this morning.
  (At 4 p.m.): I **wrote** eight e-mails this morning.

→ Use the simple past if there is no connection to the present:
- Jane Austen **wrote** some of the greatest novels in English literature. *(She is dead so there is no possibility of her writing any more books)*. Compare:

- Michael O'Connor is a journalist. He **has written** several articles for the Times and other papers.

→ Use the present perfect to give new information, but the past simple to continue talking about the situation:
- Ralph Mason, the sailor, **has returned** safely from his solo voyage around the world. He **set off** from Southampton last June, and **arrived** back in England early this morning.

Use the past perfect simple for:

→ events that happened before other past events:
- We missed the bus, so the film **had** already **started** when we got to the cinema.
- Terry phoned a locksmith because he **had lost** his key.

→ Note the use of the past perfect and the simple past in these sentences:
- Sally **told** us the news when Jake arrived. *(She told us after he arrived.)*
- Sally **had told** us the news when Jake arrived. *(She told us before he arrived.)*

Use the past perfect continuous for:

→ events that happened before another past event, the results of which could still be seen later:
- The classroom was in a terrible mess because the children **had been throwing** paper everywhere.
- The garden looked great – Angela **had been digging** up weeds all that afternoon.

→ situations which continued for a while up to a certain point in time in the past:
- I **had been sitting** by the phone all day, waiting for Ben to ring me, but then I gave up and went to bed.
- They **had been planning** the project for months when they finally got the go-ahead.

→ talking about how long an event or activity went on:
- I **had been looking forward** to the party all day.
- He **hadn't been waiting** very long when the tram arrived.

Grammar in context: Sam Nelson interviews Amanda Turner, film star:

SN: How long have you been making films now, Amanda?

AT: I actually made my first film when I was twelve, but I've only been working full-time as an actress for the last three years.

SN: And how many films have you made so far?

AT: My latest film, "Swimming in Paradise", is my 9th to date. As you can see, I haven't had much of a break in the last three years as I've been doing my best to establish myself in the film world.

SN: What has been the proudest moment of your career to date?

AT: Hmm, that's a tricky one – there have been so many things! Obviously, being nominated for a Golden Globe for my role in "As the Night Falls" was a special achievement. But I think I would have to say that the response to the drama "Safe" has moved me the most. Hundreds of people have written to me since the film came out, thanking me for my portrayal of Ella, the young woman who helped refugees to escape from war-torn Somalia. It was a difficult part to play, so it has been very encouraging to know that I have touched so many people with my performance.

SN: Yes, it was a great film. OK, another thing I'd like to ask you is: what is the strangest part you've been asked to play?

AT: (laughing) Oh, that's easy. The film was called "Keep it in the Family", and I had to play three generations of women. It involved a lot of make-up and it was very strange to see myself as an 80-year-old! I've still got a photo of myself in that role, to remind myself of what I might look like one day.

SN: Let's talk about your private life now. What do you have to say about the rumours that you've been dating Zack Zellner, Hollywood's latest heartthrob?

AT: Well, it's true that we've been out a couple of times, but I'm not prepared to say any more than that at the moment. And by the way, just to set the record straight, the story that I decided to become an actress just because of Zack simply isn't true. I had already starred in two films before he even moved to Hollywood.

SN: Amanda, thank you for taking the time to talk to us.

Vergangenheitsformen

Merke

Present Perfect Simple
- → Ereignis oder Handlung in der Vergangenheit ohne genau bestimmte Zeitangabe
- → „just"-Sätze: gerade abgeschlossene Handlungen ohne genau bestimmte Zeitangabe
- → Situationen, die in der Vergangenheit begonnen haben und bis in die Gegenwart reichen
- → Handlungen in der Vergangenheit, deren Ergebnisse für die Gegenwart wichtig sind
- → Wiederholungen bzw. Routinehandlungen, die in der Vergangenheit begonnen haben und in die Gegenwart reichen
- → Zeitangaben von nicht beendeter Dauer (z. B. heute)
- → statische Verben

Present Perfect Continuous
- → der Verlauf, nicht das Ergebnis einer Handlung in der Vergangenheit soll betont werden
- → Handlung in der Vergangenheit ist noch nicht abgeschlossen
- → betont die Dauer einer Handlung (how long …)

Simple Past
- → Ereignis oder Handlung in der Vergangenheit mit genauer Zeitangabe
- → Handlung in der Vergangenheit reicht nicht in die Gegenwart

Past Perfect Simple
- → Situationen, die vor einem Zeitpunkt in der Vergangenheit stattfanden

Past Perfect Continuous
- → Situationen, die vor einem Zeitpunkt in der Vergangenheit stattfanden, um deren Verlauf oder Dauer zu betonen oder weil diese vorzeitige Situation Auswirkungen auf den Zeitpunkt in der Vergangenheit hat

2.2 The passive

The passive in English is formed by the verb 'to be' in the appropriate tense plus the past participle. Below are some examples of the most common forms:

The present (simple and continuous):
- English **is spoken** in hundreds of countries throughout the world.
- The idea **is** currently **being considered** by a committee of experts.

The past (simple and continuous):
- This is where Mozart's house **was situated**, but the building was torn down in the 1960s.
- We couldn't work while the new computer system **was being installed**.

Future forms:
- A new president **will be elected** next month.
- We **are going to be told** what to do when we arrive.
- The exams **will have been marked** by 1st August.

Perfect forms:
- This car **has been tested** for safety.
- When they discovered that their car **had been stolen**, they called the police.

Modal verbs:
- This digital camera **can** also **be used** to make video films.
- Some vegetables **should not be eaten** raw.
- Judging by the language, this book **must have been written** in the 19th century.
- This project **couldn't have been realised** without the support of several local firms.

Grammar in context: Rice is mainly grown in Asia, where it is also eaten every day in most families. On average, over 80 kilos of rice are eaten per person every year throughout Asia as a whole, whereas in Europe less than 10 kilos per person are consumed. Rice was first grown thousands of years ago, and is generally still cultivated using the same methods as back then. Growing rice is, almost literally, a back-breaking job: each individual grain has to be planted separately in the rice field, and the rice growers stand ankle-deep in water, bending overt to plant the seeds.

Rice is very popular in Europe, and is used in many different dishes. These range from the savoury risottos that are served in Italy to the sweet rice dessert so popular in Germany. Here the rice is prepared with milk, and is often served with cinnamon and sugar

The problem for Asian farmers is that too much cheap rice is imported to western countries and they cannot make much of a profit. Of course, until relatively recently very little thought was given to the standard of living of farmers in developing countries. Nowadays awareness is growing, and products such as rice can be bought from fair trade organisations. However, far more people in the west still need to be told what hard work rice production is. If they knew more about it, more fair trade rice would be bought.

> **Passiv**   Merke
>
> Das Passiv wird gebildet aus *to be* in der entsprechenden Zeitform und dem Partizip Perfekt.
>
> | Zeit/Verbform | Aktiv | Passiv |
> | --- | --- | --- |
> | simple present | takes | is taken |
> | present continuous | is taking | is being taken |
> | simple past | took | was taken |
> | past continuous | was taking | was being taken |
> | present perfect* | has taken | has been taken |
> | past perfect* | had taken | had been taken |
> | will-future | will take | will be taken |
> | conditional I | would take | would be taken |
> | conditional II | would have taken | would have been taken |
>
> *hier gibt es keine *continuous form*
>
> Der „Täter" oder „Handlungsträger" wird im Passivsatz oft nicht genannt, weil er nicht wichtig ist oder vorher erwähnt wurde; er wird mit *by* angehängt, wenn er genannt werden soll. Wenn *phrasal verbs* ins Passiv gesetzt werden, bleibt die Präposition beim Verb.

2.3 Irregular English verbs

The most important irregular verbs:

Infinitive	simple past	past participle
be	was/were	been
become	became	become
begin	began	begun
bend	bent	bent
bite	bit	bitten
blow	blew	blown
break	broke	broken
bring	brought	brought
build	built	built
buy	bought	bought
catch	caught	caught
choose	chose	chosen
come	came	come
cost	cost	cost
creep	crept	crept
cut	cut	cut
deal	dealt	dealt
dig	dug	dug
do	did	done
draw	drew	drawn
drink	drank	drunk
drive	drove	driven
eat	ate	eaten
fall	fell	fallen
feed	fed	fed
feel	felt	felt
fight	fought	fought
find	found	found
fly	flew	flown

Infinitive	simple past	past participle
forget	forgot	forgotten
forgive	forgave	forgiven
freeze	froze	frozen
get	got	got (AE: gotten)
give	gave	given
go	went	gone
grow	grew	grown
hang	hung	hung
have	had	had
hear	heard	heard
hide	hid	hidden
hit	hit	hit
hold	held	held
hurt	hurt	hurt
keep	kept	kept
know	knew	known
lay	laid	laid
lead	led	led
leave	left	left
lend	lent	lent
let	let	let
lie	lay	lain
light	lit	lit
lose	lost	lost
make	made	made
mean	meant	meant
meet	met	met
pay	paid	paid
put	put	put
read	read	read
ride	rode	ridden
ring	rang	rung

Infinitive	simple past	past participle
rise	rose	risen
run	ran	run
say	said	said
see	saw	seen
sell	sold	sold
send	sent	sent
set	set	set
shake	shook	shaken
shine	shone	shone
shoot	shot	shot
show	showed	shown, showed
shut	shut	shut
sing	sang	sung
sink	sank	sunk
sit	sat	sat
sleep	slept	slept
slide	slid	slid
speak	spoke	spoken
spend	spent	spent
spit	spat	spat
split	split	split
spread	spread	spread
spring	sprang	sprung
stand	stood	stood
steal	stole	stolen
stick	stuck	stuck
sting	stung	stung
stink	stank	stunk
strike	struck	struck
swear	swore	sworn
sweep	swept	swept
swim	swam	swum

Infinitive	simple past	past participle
swing	swung	swung
take	took	taken
tear	tore	torn
tell	told	told
think	thought	thought
throw	threw	thrown
understand	understood	understood
wake	woke	woken
wear	wore	worn
win	won	won
write	wrote	written

2.4 Use of the gerund

A gerund is a verb which is used as a noun. The form is the same as the "-ing" form of a verb. We use the gerund as follows:

→ **as the subject or object of a sentence:**
- **Swimming** is a good way to get fit. *subject*
- **Shopping** can be stressful. *subject*
- I love **travelling**. *object*
- She doesn't really like **skiing**. *object*

A gerund can have its own object in these types of sentences:
- **Playing** tennis is a good way to get fit.
- **Shopping** for new clothes can be stressful.
- I love **travelling** by plane.
- She doesn't really like **writing** letters.

→ **after some verbs:**
- some common verbs which are **always followed by the gerund**: admit, appreciate, can't help, can't stand, consider, delay, deny, dislike, enjoy, escape, excuse, feel like, finish, forgive, give up, imagine, involve, mention, mind, miss, postpone, practise, put off, resent, risk, suggest, understand

- some common verbs that **can be followed** by the gerund: forget, hate, like, love, prefer, remember, stop, try
- Can you imagine **winning** a trip around the world?
- I've seriously considered **starting** my own business.
- A lot of people find it hard to stop **smoking**.
- I remember **buying** the book, but I've no idea where I put it!

→ **after certain verb + preposition, adjective + preposition or adverb + preposition combinations:**

Here are some common examples of a preposition followed by a gerund:

- They're **interested in finding** out more about the project.
- I **feel like going out** for a meal this evening.
- **As well as speaking** excellent English and French, she also knows a bit of Japanese.
- She was **fed up with doing** the same boring job, so she decided to go back to college to get more qualifications.
- **In spite of working** extremely hard, Stephen still failed the exam.
- We're really **excited about moving** into our new house.
- He **apologised for interrupting** the meeting.
- **How about watching** a DVD this evening?
- **Thank you for inviting** me to your party.
- Andy is **thinking about buying** a new car.
- **Instead of complaining**, why don't you do something about it?
- I think they're quite **keen on taking part** in the play.
- Sophie is very **good at drawing**.
- I've often **dreamt of becoming** a pop star.
- Well, I hope you're happy. You've **succeeded in upsetting** everyone.
- She just stormed out **without waiting** to hear my side of the story.
- **Besides having** a successful career, he helps underprivileged children in his free time.
- He's so boring. He doesn't seem to be **capable of talking** about anything except himself!

→ **as part of some compound nouns:**

- Put your dirty clothes in the **washing** machine.
- Heat up some oil in a **frying** pan.
- We often go to the local **swimming** pool.

- The children played on the **climbing** frame.
- Last year my parents went on a **walking** tour.
- She's so thin because she has an **eating** disorder.

> **Merke**
>
> **Gerund**
> → Funktion im Satz: kann Objekt oder Subjekt eines Satzes sein
> → steht nach einer Reihe bestimmter Verben (s. o.)
> → nach Präpositionen *(I dream of becoming a popstar)*
> → sehr oft in zusammengesetzten Wörtern *(washing machine)*

2.5 Use of participles

The present participle

The present participle is formed by adding "-ing" to the infinitive of the verb. In some cases the spelling has to be changed, e.g.:
→ by leaving off the "e": to have → having
→ by doubling the last consonant: to get → getting

The present participle is used in the continuous tense:
→ He's **making** a phone call.
→ What **were** you **doing** at this time last week?
→ **Will** you be **having** a party on your birthday?

The present participle is used in participle clauses:
→ to give a reason for something:
- **Feeling** hungry, I made myself a sandwich.
  (= I felt hungry and so I made myself a sandwich.)
- **Being** new here, he's not familiar with the procedure.
  (= Because he is new here, he's not familiar with the procedure)
- **Living** in Switzerland, we are used to the high cost of living.
  (= We live in Switzerland and so we know that the cost of living is high.)

→ to say what is or was happening at a particular time:
- Mark is in the living room **zapping** through the TV channels.
  (= He is in the living room and he is zapping …)

- At this time last week we were on the beach, **enjoying** the beautiful sunset.
  (= We were on the beach and we were enjoying the beautiful sunset.)
- There was a long line of people **waiting** to get in to the cinema.
  (= There was a long line of people who were waiting ...)

→ Having (done) can be used to express that one action happens before another action:
  - **Having spent** all our money, we had to walk home.
  - **Having eaten** three bowls of ice-cream, I felt a bit sick.
  - **Having listened** to both sides of the story, the judge gave her verdict on the case.

→ The present participle can be used with while, when and after:
  - Be very careful **when handling** these chemicals.
  - Louise met her boyfriend **while working** in a bar.
  - **After checking in** our luggage, we went through passport control.

The past participle

The past participle is used

...to form various tenses (perfect tenses, the passive):

→ Have you **done** your homework yet?
→ Three o'clock is too late to come round. I'll have **left** by then.
→ English is **taught** in many primary schools nowadays.
→ This project was **funded** by the European Union.

...for participle clauses with a passive meaning:

→ The jewellery **stolen** in the robbery was very valuable.
  (= The jewellery that was stolen ...)
→ The woman **arrested** after the robbery was later released.
  (= The woman who was arrested ...)

Contrast of present and past participles

The past participle is often used to describe how a person feels, whereas the present participle is used to talk about the people or things that caused the feeling.

Compare:
- → The class was **bored** during the long geography lesson.
- → The geography lesson was **boring**.
- → The athlete was **disappointed** that he didn't win a medal.
- → The athlete's performance during the race was **disappointing**.

> **Partizipien** — Merke
>
> **Funktion von Partizipialkonstruktionen:**
> - → verkürzen notwendige Relativsätze: *Pupils who are listening to the teacher will get better marks* → *Pupils listening to the teacher …*
> - → verkürzen adverbiale Nebensätze: z. B.
>   - bei Angaben der Zeit *(while, when, after …)*
>   - bei Angaben des Grundes *(as, since, because …)*
>
> **Present participle:**
> - → gleiche Form wie *gerund (-ing)*
> - → wird in den Verlaufsformen verwendet
> - → hat aktive Bedeutung: *robbers stealing jewellery* → *robbers who are stealing …*
> - → steht bei gleichzeitigen Handlungen: *He sat there watching TV* statt *He sat there and watched TV*
>
> **Past participle:**
> - → bildet Passiv- und Perfektformen
> - → hat passive Bedeutung: *the jewellery stolen by robbers* → *the jewellery which is/was stolen …*
> - → steht bei vorzeitigen Handlungen oder Folge einer vorausgehenden Handlung: *Having spent all our money, we had to walk home*
>
> **Present participle und past participle:**
> Beachte den Kontrast:
> - → Past participle drückt ein Gefühl aus:
>   *The class was bored during the lesson.*
> - → Present participle drückt die Ursache des Gefühls aus:
>   *The lesson was boring.*

2.6 Phrasal verbs

There are a large number of phrasal and prepositional verbs in English, i.e. verbs that are made up of verb + preposition, verb + adverb or verb + particle. Below is a list of some of the most common, in context.

→ **verbs with down:**
- The bus **broke down** in the middle of nowhere, and we had to wait for two hours for a replacement.
- Many small businesses have had to **close down** due to the recession.
- A lot of trees **came down** during last night's storm.
- I really must **cut down** on the amount of coffee I drink – I'm finding it difficult to sleep at night.
- The boat won't be able to go out again until the wind has **died down**.
- I'd better **get down** to writing this essay – I have to hand it in tomorrow!
- The prices of colour printers have really **gone down** in the last few years.
- George is really arrogant. He **looks down** on anyone who doesn't have a university degree.
- That was the most exciting book I've ever read. I simply couldn't **put it down**!
- **Slow down**! I can't understand what you're saying if you speak so fast!
- Dave always **writes down** everything the teacher says.

→ **verbs with on:**
- The children **carried on** talking, even after I asked them to be quiet.
- **Come on**! We'll miss the train if you don't hurry up!
- Annie really doesn't **get on** with her sister – they're always arguing.
- We **got on** the train in Birmingham.
- So Mike is dating Jackie, is he? How long has that been **going on**?
- He just ignored me and **went on** watching TV.
- "Is Liz there, please?" "Yes, **hold on**. I'll get her."

- If you're going to **keep on** complaining all evening, I'm going out.
- When I was younger, the other children used to **pick on** me because I had to wear glasses.
- **Put on** your hat and gloves before you go out.
- They're **taking on** new staff at the local supermarket.
- I'd like to **try on** these shoes in a size 6, please.

→ **verbs with off:**
- The game has been **called off** due to injury.
- **Get off** the bus at the town hall: I live just around the corner from there.
- Be careful: those chemicals **give off** a poisonous gas.
- The police stopped him for cycling at night without lights, but luckily they **let** him **off** with a warning.
- You should do your homework now instead of **putting** it **off** until Sunday evening!
- I'd love to go to New Zealand, but the thought of such a long flight **puts** me **off** a bit.
- Living near the airport means there is a lot of noise from the planes **taking off** and landing.
- My sisters and I always **take** a day **off** work to do our Christmas shopping.
- Why don't you **take off** your coat and sit down?
- His mother **told** him **off** after he broke the window.

→ **verbs with out:**
- The police warned that a dangerous criminal has **broken out** of Holloway Prison.
- Oh no! I've **come out** in a rash! I must be allergic to something in that cake!
- We **eat out** a couple of times a month, usually in a little Chinese restaurant down the road.
- The course leader **gave out** the work sheets to everyone in the seminar room.
- Julie **let out** a scream when she saw Robbie Williams.
- **Look/Mind/Watch out**! You nearly bumped into that man!
- It was so foggy that it was almost impossible to **make out** the road signs.

- We managed to **put out** the fire ourselves, and no serious damage was done.
- We've **run out of** eggs. I'd better get some more this afternoon.
- His latest CD is so popular that it **sold out** within two hours.
- Underlining important words makes them **stand out** when you come to reread the text.
- He **took out** a bank loan to pay for his new car.
- I'm going to **throw out** all the clothes that I don't wear anymore.
- We must have walked 20 km today. I'm **worn out**!
- I'm trying to **work out** how to tell Sandra the news without hurting her feelings.

→ **verbs with up:**
- My parents were killed when I was three years old, so my aunt and uncle **brought** me **up**.
- I hate **getting up** early – I'd rather stay in bed.
- You should **give up** eating sugar if you want to lose weight.
- Martin **grew up** in a tiny village in the countryside.
- I don't like jogging with Susie. She runs so fast that I can't **keep up** with her.
- We often **look up** words in an online dictionary.
- My sister is a wonderful person. I really **look up to** her.
- If you don't know what to write, just **make** something **up**. Use your imagination!
- Jason and Meg often have arguments, but they always **make up** very quickly afterwards.
- There's no need to take a taxi. I'll **pick** you **up** from the station.
- I'll **pick up** a pizza on the way home and we can have it for dinner.
- Stop being so rude! I'm not going to **put up with** it any longer!
- If you're ever in Bath, we'll be glad to **put** you **up** for a few days.
- You'll have to **speak up** when you talk to my grandfather: he's slightly deaf.
- I'm thinking about **taking up** cycling to help me get fit.
- I'd better go now. I've already **taken up** too much of your time.
- By the time John **turned up**, the party was almost over.
- Her dad always **waits up** for her, no matter what time she gets home.

2.6 Phrasal verbs

→ **miscellaneous phrasal verbs:**
- She may **come across** as rather reserved at first, but once you get to know her you see how friendly she is.
- You'll be in trouble if you don't do your homework. Your teacher won't let you **get away with** it.
- My job isn't very well-paid. I barely earn enough to **get by**.
- I've just come to **give** you **back** the book you lent me.
- Her neighbours always **look after** her dogs when she goes on holiday.
- Our company is about to be **taken over** by one of our competitors.
- He's really a bully. He's always **picking on** younger children.

Phrasal Verbs *Merke*

Für die folgenden deutschen Ausdrücke sollten Sie die englischen Entsprechungen kennen. Testen Sie sich selbst: Fällt Ihnen das passende *phrasal verb* ein?

- → (Kredit) aufnehmen
- → etwas übernehmen
- → mit etwas anfangen
- → (Zeit) beanspruchen
- → abfliegen, starten
- → freinehmen
- → aufstehen
- → sich an etwas machen
- → auskommen mit
- → ein-/zusteigen
- → sich vertragen
- → mit etwas durchkommen
- → ausgeben, -teilen
- → aussteigen
- → verschieben
- → jdn. abschrecken
- → sich abfinden mit
- → jdn. aufnehmen
- → ausmachen (Feuer)
- → ausbrechen
- → nachschlagen
- → kümmern um
- → zu jdm. aufsehen
- → erfinden
- → sich versöhnen
- → zurückgeben
- → aufgeben
- → mithalten
- → weitermachen
- → aufbleiben und auf jdn. warten
- → essen gehen
- → absagen
- → auftauchen
- → aufwachsen
- → herumhacken auf
- → sich legen (Wind)
- → etw. einschränken
- → aufpassen

2.7 "False Friends"

English contains many words which appear to be similar to German words, but have a different meaning. These "false friends" often cause confusion, so extra care is needed when using them! Below are some examples of typical mistakes. First the common mistake is pointed out, followed by example sentences in English and German.

→ ***aktuell*** ≠ actual(ly) **current/topical/up-to-date**
- Was ist der aktuelle Stand der Dinge? – What is the current situation?
- I can't believe you're **actually** going to be on TV! – *Ich kann es nicht fassen, dass du wirklich im Fernsehen sein wirst!*

→ ***Annonce*** ≠ announcement **ad(vertisement)**
- Sie gab eine Annonce in der Lokalzeitung auf. – She placed an ad in the local paper.
- The Prime Minister is expected to make an **announcement** about his new tax reform later today. – *Es wird erwartet, dass der Premierminister seine neue Steuerreform heute bekanntgeben wird.*

→ ***bekommen*** ≠ become **get/receive/obtain**
- *Dan bekam ein Auto zum 18. Geburtstag.* – Dan got a car for his 18th birthday.
- My eyes tend to **become** tired if I spend too much time in front of the computer. – *Meine Augen werden oft müde, wenn ich zu viel Zeit vor dem Computer verbringe.*

→ ***blank*** ≠ blank **shiny/bright/clean**
- *Ich putzte das Bad, bis alles blitz-blank sauber war.* – I cleaned the bathroom until everything was shiny and clean.
- *This colourful picture will brighten up any blank wall.* – Dieses farbenfrohe Bild schmückt jede leere Wand.

→ ***brav*** ≠ brave **good/well-behaved**
- *Ich kaufe dir ein Eis, wenn du brav bist.* – I'll buy you an ice-cream if you're good.
- You have to be quite **brave** to be a police officer. – *Um Polizist zu sein, muss man ziemlich tapfer sein.*

→ ***Chef*** ≠ chief **boss/leader**
- *Sein Chef ist extrem faul.* – His boss is extremely lazy.

- She's a **chief executive officer** in a large software firm. – *Sie ist Geschäftsführerin einer großen Software-Firma.*

→ ***eventuell*** ≠ eventual(ly)   **possible(ly)/might**
- *Wir müssen das Spiel eventuell absagen.* – We might have to cancel the match.
- After having asked five people for directions, we **eventually** found their house. – *Nachdem wir fünf Leute nach dem Weg gefragt hatten, fanden wir schließlich ihr Haus.*

→ ***familiär*** ≠ familiar   **family/familial**
- *Ihre familiäre Situation ist sehr schwierig.* – Her family situation is very difficult.
- I've heard of him, but I'm not **familiar** with his books. – *Ich habe von ihm gehört, aber ich kenne seine Bücher nicht.*

→ ***Flur*** ≠ floor   **corridor/hall**
- *Sie hörte Schritte auf dem Flur.* – She heard footsteps in the corridor.
- Pick up your toys! Don't leave them lying all over the **floor**! – *Räum dein Spielzeug weg! Lass es nicht einfach am Boden liegen!*

→ ***Gift*** ≠ gift   **poison**
- *Dieses Putzmittel enthält ein starkes Gift.* – This detergent contains a strong poison.
- I need a **gift** for my sister – she's getting married soon. – *Ich brauche ein Geschenk für meine Schwester, weil sie bald heiratet.*

→ ***Gymnasium*** ≠ gym(nasium)   **grammar school (BE)/high school (AE)**
- *Sie besucht das Rudolf-Diesel-Gymnasium.* – She goes to Rudolf Diesel High School.
- Because it was raining, the children played football in the **gym**. – *Weil es regnete, spielten die Kinder Fußball in der Turnhalle.*

→ ***Handy*** ≠ handy   **mobile (phone) (BE)/cell phone (AE)**
- *Heutzutage ist man per Handy immer erreichbar, egal wo man sich gerade befindet.* – Nowadays, you can always be reached by mobile, no matter where you are.
- *A cell phone is very handy in an emergency.* – Es ist in einem Notfall sehr praktisch, ein Handy zu haben.

→ **_irritieren_** ≠ to irritate   **to confuse**
- *Die viele Informationen irritierten uns eher, als dass sie uns halfen.* – All the information confused rather than helped us.
- Can you please stop tapping your pencil? It's really starting to irritate me! – *Hör bitte auf, mit dem Bleistift zu klopfen. Es fängt an, mich richtig zu nerven!*

→ **_Land_** ≠ land   **country/state**
- *Italien ist ein schönes Urlaubsland.* – Italy is a beautiful country for holidays.
- They sailed for two weeks without once seeing **land**. – *Sie segelten zwei Wochen lang, ohne einmal Festland zu sehen.*

→ **_Mappe_** ≠ map   **folder/schoolbag**
- *Bitte legen Sie die Dokumente in eine Mappe.* – Please place the documents in a folder.
- It's a good idea to take a **map** when hiking in the mountains. – *Es ist sinnvoll, eine Landkarte mitzunehmen, wenn man in den Bergen wandert.*

→ **_meinen_** ≠ to mean   **to think/believe**
- *Was meinst du dazu?* – What do you think about it?
- If you don't know what that word **means**, look it up. – *Wenn du nicht weißt, was das Wort bedeutet, schlage es nach!*

→ **_Menü_** ≠ menu   **set meal**
- *Das Restaurant hat ein billiges Mittagsmenü.* – The restaurant has a cheap set meal at lunchtime.
- Could we see the **dessert menu**, please? – *Könnten wir bitte die Nachspeisekarte sehen?*

→ **_miserabel_** ≠ miserable   **awful/terrible**
- *Das Wetter während unseres letzten Urlaubs war miserabel.* – The weather was awful on our last holiday.
- I'm feeling **miserable**. Frank's just dumped me. – *Ich fühle mich elend. Frank hat gerade mit mir Schluss gemacht.*

→ **_ordinär_** ≠ ordinary   **vulgar/common**
- *Alex ist so ordinär: Er flucht die ganze Zeit.* – Alex is so vulgar: he's always swearing.
- You can cut it with an **ordinary** knife.
  Man kann es mit einem normalen Messer schneiden.

→ **_Pension_** ≠ pension   **guest house**

- *Wir verbrachten eine Woche in einer kleinen Pension an der Küste.* – We spent a week in a little guest house at the coast.
- The state **pension** won't be worth much by the time I retire. – *Die staatliche Rente wird nicht viel wert sein, wenn ich in Rente gehe.*

→ *Politik* ≠ politics **policy**
- *Ich halte nicht viel von seiner Umweltpolitik.* – I don't think much of his environmental policy.
- It is important that young people take an active interest in **politics**. – *Es ist wichtig, dass junge Leute sich aktiv in der Politik engagieren.*

→ *Preis* ≠ prize **price**
- *Alle staunten, als er den ersten Preis gewann.* – Everyone was amazed when he won first prize.
- **Prices** have increased since the introduction of the Euro. – *Die Preise haben sich seit der Einführung des Euro erhöht.*

→ *Programm* ≠ programme **(TV) channel**
- *In welchem Programm läuft der Film?* – What channel is the film on?
- There's an interesting programme on later about Australia. – *Später läuft eine interessante Sendung über Australien.*

→ *Rente* ≠ rent **pension**
- *Mein Vater bekommt eine gute Rente von seiner alten Firma.* – My father gets a good pension from his old company.
- Are the **rents** very high in London? – *Sind die Mieten in London sehr hoch?*

→ *sensibel* ≠ sensible **sensitive**
- *Sie ist wirklich sensibel. Sie weint bei jeder Kritik.* – She's really sensitive. She cries whenever she's criticized.
- It's **sensible** to wear a warm coat in winter. – *Es ist vernünftig, im Winter einen warmen Mantel zu tragen.*

→ *seriös* ≠ serious **respectable/reputable**
- *Ich weiß, dass es sich um eine seriöse Organisation handelt.* – I know that it's a reputable organisation.
- It was a **serious** accident. Several people were badly injured. – *Es war ein schwerer Unfall. Mehrere Leute wurden schwer verletzt.*

- → ***spenden*** ≠ to spend **to donate/give**
  - *Unsere Schule hat viel Geld für die Opfer des Erdbebens gespendet.* – Our school donated a lot of money to the victims of the earthquake.
  - I always seem to **spend** a lot of money when I go on holiday. – *Ich gebe irgendwie immer sehr viel Geld aus, wenn ich in Urlaub fahre.*
- → ***spotten*** ≠ to spot **to mock/tease**
  - *Die Zuhörer haben den Politiker nur verspottet, statt ihm zuzuhören.* – The audience only mocked the politician instead of listening to him.
  - We **spotted** Jane among the crowd of people waiting at the airport. – *Wir bemerkten Jane in der Menschenmenge, die am Flughafen wartete.*
- → ***Strom*** ≠ stream **river/current/electricity**
  - *Der Rhein ist ein mächtiger Strom.* – The Rhine is a mighty river.
  - We ate our picnic next to a nice little **stream**. – *Wir aßen unser Picknick neben einem netten Bächlein.*
- → ***sympathisch*** ≠ sympathetic **likeable/pleasant**
  - *Du wirst Alan mögen – er ist sehr sympathisch.* – You'll like Alan – he's a very pleasant person.
  - My boss wasn't very **sympathetic** when I told him my cat had been run over. – *Mein Chef hatte nicht viel Mitleid, als ich ihm erzählte, meine Katze sei überfahren worden.*
- → ***überhören*** ≠ to overhear **to ignore/fail to hear**
  - *Es war nicht zu überhören, dass sie zornig war.* – You couldn't fail to hear that she was furious.
  - I happened to **overhear** that Helen and Dave are getting married – what a surprise! – *Ich habe zufällig mitbekommen, dass Helen und Dave heiraten – das ist vielleicht eine Überraschung!*
- → ***übersehen*** ≠ to oversee **overlook/miss/fail to notice**
  - *Der Lehrer hat den Fehler übersehen.* – The teacher didn't notice the mistake.
  - Independent observers were sent to **oversee** the first democratic elections in the country's history. – *Unabhängige Beobachter wurden hingeschickt, um die ersten demokratischen Wahlen in der Geschichte des Landes zu überwachen.*

False friends **Merke**

deutsch	englisch	englisch	deutsch
aktuell	current/topical/up-to-date	actual(ly)	wirklich
Annonce	ad(vertisement)	announcement	Bekanntmachung
bekommen	to get/receive/obtain	to become	werden
blank	shiny/bright/clean	blank	leer
brav	good/well-behaved	brave	tapfer
Chef	boss/leader	chief chef	Geschäftsführer Küchenchef
eventuell	possible(ly)/might	eventual(ly)	schließlich
familiär	family/familial	familiar	vertraut
Flur	corridor/hall	floor	Boden, Stockwerk
Gift	poison	gift	Geschenk
Land	country/state	land	Festland, Grundstück
Mappe	folder/schoolbag	map	Landkarte
meinen	to think/believe	to mean	bedeuten
Menü	set meal	menu	Speisekarte
miserabel	awful/terrible	miserable	elend
ordinär	vulgar/common	ordinary	normal
Pension	guest house	pension	Rente
Politik	policy (ways and aims)	politics	Politik (Taktik)
Preis	price (to pay)	prize	Preis (Prämie)
Rente	pension	rent	Miete
sensibel	sensitive	sensible	vernünftig
seriös	respectable/reputable	serious	ernst, gravierend
spenden	to donate/give	to spend	ausgeben
spotten	to mock/tease	to spot	entdecken
Strom	river/current/electricity	stream	Bächlein
sympathisch	likeable/pleasant	be sympathetic	Mitleid haben
überhören	to ignore/fail to hear	to overhear	zufällig mitbekommen
übersehen	to overlook/miss/fail to notice	to oversee	überwachen

2.8 Problem areas of English

There are many aspects of English grammar that cause problems for learners of English, and which result in a number of typical mistakes. Some common examples of these problem areas are highlighted below.

by and until

→ **By** means *no later than*:
- Please hand in your essay by Monday.
- The repairs will be finished by the end of the month.

→ The expression **by the time** is used in examples like these:
- By the time we got her message it was too late to meet up with her.
- They had already finished eating by the time I arrived at the restaurant.

→ **Until** means that an action continues up to a certain time (until is often shortened to till, especially in spoken English.)
- I only have to work until midday today, and then I've got the rest of the day off.
- We waited until she'd finished speaking on the phone before we knocked at her door.

→ **Not until** means *not before*:
- School doesn't start again until 9th September, so I've still got three weeks' holiday.
- You are not leaving this room until you tell me where you were last night!

> **Merke** **Typical mistake**
>
> **wrong:** Please let me know ~~until~~ Monday whether you can come.
> **right:** Please let me know by Monday whether you can come.

for, during and while

→ **For** is used to talk about a period of time, to say how long something happens:
- I lived in Manchester for seven years before moving to Liverpool.

- We had to wait for nearly two hours to go on some of the rides in Disneyland.
→ **During + noun** is used to say when something happens:
  - It was very noisy in the hotel, and I woke up several times during the night.
  - A lot of trees were blown down during the storm.
→ *During* and *while* have a similar meaning, but *during* is followed by a noun, and *while* is followed by subject + verb:
  - The boys talked about football during the meal.
  - The boys talked about football while they were eating.
  - I went to Madame Tussaud's during my stay in London.
  - I went to Madame Tussaud's while I was in London.

> **Typical mistake** — Merke
> *during* cannot be used to say how long something happens:
> **wrong:** The weather was hot and sunny ~~during~~ three weeks.
> **right:** The weather was hot and sunny for three weeks.

so and such

→ **So** is used to make an adjective or adverb stronger:
  - I've been so busy in the last week that I haven't had time to go to the supermarket.
  - Bali is famous because the beaches there are so beautiful.
→ **Such** is also used in front of an adjective or adverb, but only when it is followed by a noun:
  - I didn't know that Annie was such a good singer – she's got a lovely voice!
  - She had such a bad headache that she had to go home early.

> **Typical mistake** — Merke
> **wrong:** We've had ~~so~~ good weather this summer. It's been great!
> **right:** We've had such good weather this summer. Or: The weather has been so good this summer.

used to, to be used to, to get used to

→ **Used to** describes a past habit, or something that was true in the past, but is not true today. It is a regular verb, used in the past tense:
- Ron used to live in New York, but now he lives in Boston.
- When I was younger, I used to go swimming three times a week.

→ **To be used to** (+ -ing) describes something that you are familiar with, that you are accustomed to:
- Most young people nowadays are used to looking for information on the Internet.
- She drove very slowly because she wasn't used to driving on icy roads.

→ **To get used to** (+ -ing) describes becoming familiar with something:
- If you want to be successful in your job, you'll have to get used to working long hours.
- I love living in London, but I can't get used to paying such high prices for food and drink.

NOTE: *to be used to* and *to get used to* can be used in all tenses.

> **Merke** **Typical mistake**
>
> **wrong:** I am used to have very little money.
> It is unclear here what the person who wrote this sentence means, as it is a mixture of two different forms. The sentence could either be:
> **right:** I used to have very little money. (In the past I didn't have much money.) Or: I am used to having very little money. (I don't have much money now, and I am accustomed to this situation.)

yet and already

→ **Yet** is used in questions and negative statements, to talk about things that have (or have not) been done so far:
- "Have you written that report yet?" "Yes, I finished it this morning."
- We can't go. I'm not ready yet.

→ **Already** has a similar meaning to *yet*, but is generally used in positive statements:
- Shall we go and see the new James Bond film this evening? – No, thanks. I've already seen it.
- That's enough! You've already had two helpings of ice-cream!

→ Already can also be used in questions, where it implies that something has been done sooner than expected:
- Is Fiona back from the doctor's already? That didn't take long!
- I've finished my homework. – Already? I hope you haven't made any mistakes!

> **Typical mistake**   Merke
>
> **wrong:** Tom has spent all his money ~~yet~~.
> **right:** Tom has already spent all his money.

Reflexive pronouns

→ **myself, yourself, himself, herself, itself, ourselves, yourselves, themselves**: These pronouns can be used in sentences where the subject and the object are the same, in cases such as these:
- William got out of the bath and dried himself with a big, soft towel.
- The light in the corridor is automatic. It switches itself off after three minutes.
- The first thing I did when I got home was make myself a hot drink.

→ **each other, one another**: There are cases when we use these expressions instead of a reflexive pronoun:
- Patricia and I are good friends. We like each other (I like her and she likes me).
- It was so long since Gerry and Eddie had met that they didn't even recognise one another (Gerry didn't recognise Eddie and Eddie didn't recognise Gerry).

→ **Oneself**, **by oneself** and **on one's own**: A reflexive pronoun can also be used to emphasize the fact that you, rather than another person, did something:

- Would you like to try one of these cookies? I made them myself.
- The reporters were surprised when the film star answered the door herself. They had expected her to have a butler.

→ If you do something **by yourself** or **on your own**, it means you do it alone, without any help:
- Please work by yourselves, without talking to each other!
- Charlotte sat in the corner on her own, reading a magazine.

> **Merke** **Typical mistakes**
>
> Be careful! There are some common cases where a reflexive pronoun is used in German, but cannot be used in English. Study the examples of "German" translations below.
>
> **wrong:** Let's meet ~~us~~ at one o'clock outside the café.
> **right:** Let's meet at one o'clock outside the café.
> **wrong:** There's too much noise in here. I can't concentrate ~~myself~~.
> **right:** There's too much noise in here. I can't concentrate.
> **wrong:** We've known ~~us~~ for 17 years.
> **right:** We've known each other for 17 years.
> **wrong:** There's nothing I like better in the evening than to relax ~~myself~~ in front of the TV.
> **right:** There's nothing I like better in the evening than to relax in front of the TV.
>
> It is easy to mix up *by yourself* and *on your own*:
> **wrong:** Oliver doesn't have any flatmates. He lives ~~by his own~~.
> **right:** He lives on his own. Or: He lives by himself.

Articles

There are several cases when articles are used differently in English than in German, which often give rise to mistakes. Below are some common examples of differences in use:

→ Adding an article:
- My sister ~~is teacher~~.
  My sister is a teacher.
- I've just ~~become aunt~~ for the first time.
  I've just become an aunt for the first time.

→ Leaving out an article:
- Many people have attempted to ~~climb the Mount Everest~~.
  Many people have attempted to climb Mount Everest.
- They go ~~to the church~~ every Sunday.
  They go to church every Sunday.
- He was sentenced to ten months ~~in the prison~~.
  He was sentenced to ten months in prison.
- What time do you normally have ~~the dinner~~?
  What time do you normally have dinner?
- What ~~a wonderful weather~~ we've been having this month!
  What wonderful weather we've been having this month!

Countable and uncountable nouns

→ A **countable** noun is one that can be singular or plural:
- There's **a tree** in our garden.
- Hundreds of **trees** were cut down to make way for the new motorway.

→ An **uncountable** noun only has one form, and cannot be used with an indefinite article (a/an):
- Water was coming in through the hole in the roof.

→ There are many nouns that can be both countable and uncountable. The uncountable noun is used in a general sense, whereas the countable noun refers to specific items. Compare the difference in meaning: a house made of **wood** (the material) and a **wood** (a large group of trees).

→ Although uncountable nouns are not used with an indefinite article, they are often used with "a ... of":
- a cup of tea; a shower of rain; a slice of bread; a piece of information; an item of news; a sheet of paper

→ Some nouns are normally uncountable in English but countable in German. These nouns do not have a plural form and cannot be used with the indefinite article. The following are some common examples:
- accommodation; advice; bread; chaos; furniture; information; luck; luggage; news; progress; traffic; weather; work

uncountable	countable
Coffee is grown in South America.	Would you like **a coffee**? I'm just going to make one.
That vase is made of **glass**.	You'll find the **glasses** in the kitchen cupboard.
Come round this weekend if you have **time**.	They had **a** nice **time** at the theatre.
Plants need **light** to grow.	I knew that someone was at home because there was **a light** on.
I usually go to **work** by train.	Beethoven's 5th Symphony is one of his most famous **works**.
Don't eat too much **chocolate** – it's very fattening!	He gave his girlfriend a box of **chocolates** for Valentine's Day.
He's got a lot of **experience** of working with children.	Climbing Mount Everest was **the** greatest **experience** of my life.
I want to have a shower and wash my **hair**.	My sister came round with her dog. There were dog **hairs** all over the carpet after they left.
Wind can be used as an alternative source of energy.	The east coast is famous for its strong **winds**.

> **Merke** **Typical mistakes**
>
> **wrong:** We asked for some informations about the product.
> **right:** We asked for some information about the product.
> **wrong:** Let me give you an advice.
> **right:** Let me give you some advice/a piece of advice.
> **wrong:** I'm afraid the news are bad.
> **right:** I'm afraid the news is bad.
>
> **Many/much and few/little**
> → *Many* and *few* are used with countable nouns:
>   - Were there many people at the party?
>   - Very few plants grow in the desert.
> → *Much* and *little* are used with uncountable nouns:
>   - There wasn't much traffic, so we got there quite quickly.
>   - Add a little salt and pepper to the soup before serving.

Other typical mistakes

Below are some other examples of mistakes that German learners of English often make:

→ Sandra is a very good friend ~~of me~~.
  Sandra is a very good friend of mine.
→ Clare and ~~her both brothers~~ are having a party on Saturday.
  Clare and both of her brothers ...
  Or: Clare and her two brothers are having a party on Saturday.
→ That's the ~~car from my father~~ over there.
  That's my father's car over there.
→ This is a painting ~~from Picasso~~.
  This is a painting by Picasso.
→ She was able to play the piano perfectly ~~with ten years~~.
  She was able to play the piano perfectly at the age of ten.
→ ~~Where are you born~~?
  Where were you born?
→ My brother is ~~married with~~ a Spanish woman.
  My brother is married to a Spanish woman.
→ I normally drink ~~coffee to breakfast~~.
  I normally drink coffee for breakfast.
→ Shall we watch the match ~~by you~~?
  Shall we watch the match at your house?
→ I need to ~~say you~~ something important.
  I need to tell you something important.
→ Ben never ~~stands up~~ early at the weekend.
  Ben never gets up early at the weekend.
→ I just want to ~~make a photo~~ of this beautiful sunset.
  I just want to take a photo of this beautiful sunset.
→ Could you ~~bring~~ Granny to the station tomorrow morning?
  Could you take Granny to the station tomorrow morning?
→ Sophie can't come out with us this evening because she has to ~~learn~~ for a test.
  Sophie can't come out with us this evening because she has to study/revise for a test.

> **Abi-Tipp**
>
> Um typische Fehler zu vermeiden, braucht man gute Sprachkenntnisse und ein Gefühl für die Fremdsprache. Solche Kenntnisse gewinnt man natürlich nicht über Nacht, sondern müssen erarbeitet werden. Dieses Buch enthält einige Hinweise, wie man Englisch üben kann (z. B. auf Seite 54).

Checkliste 2 Zeitformen

- present simple (I play)
- present continuous (I am playing)
- past simple (I played)
- past continuous (I was playing)
- "will" future (I will play)
- future continuous (I will be playing)
- "going to" future (I am going to play)
- future perfect (I will have played)
- present perfect simple (I have played)
- present perfect continuous (I have been playing)
- past perfect simple (I had played)
- past perfect continuous (I had been playing)
- present simple passive (Football is played in stadiums.)
- present continuous passive (Several matches are being played this afternoon.)
- past simple passive (The last match was played here.)
- past continuous passive (The match was being played.)
- future passive (The match will be played next week. / The match is going to be played next week.)
- future perfect passive (The match will have been played by this time next week.)
- present perfect passive (The match has already been played.)
- past perfect passive (The match had already been played.)
- modal verbs in the passive (The match can/should/must be played next week.)

Understanding Britain and America – important terms

3

Das Thema Landeskunde spielt in der Abiturprüfung eine wichtige Rolle. In diesem Kapitel werden wichtige Begriffe erklärt, die man kennen sollte. Sie stammen aus den Bereichen Politik, Religion, Bildung und Medien und geben einen Überblick über die Geschichte und aktuelle Lage in Großbritannien und den USA.

3.1 Britain

Politics

House of Commons: The lower of the two parliamentary chambers in Britain, where the elected members of the various political parties debate and vote on policy and laws. This is where the first stage of lawmaking takes place.

House of Lords: The upper of the two British parliamentary chambers. Its members are not elected by the people, but are hereditary peers (members of the aristocracy whose title has been passed down through the generations), life peers (people who have been awarded an aristocratic title for the duration of their lifetime, e.g. former leading politicians), Law Lords (judges who sit at the highest court of appeal in Britain) and senior Church of England bishops. New laws must also be passed by the House of Lords before they can come into effect, although today the Lords no longer have the power to reject legislation proposed by the House of Commons, as was the case in the past. Now they can only delay the passing of new laws.

Monarchy: Britain has a monarch as its (now chiefly symbolic) head of state. Although the Queen must sign all new laws before they can come into effect, she can no longer block them or prevent them from becoming law. She meets the Prime Minister once a week to discuss political matters, but does not have the power to actively intervene. Her main role is a representative one, performing ceremonial duties, welcoming foreign heads of state and representing Britain abroad.

Devolution: At the end of the 1990s, Scotland, Wales and Northern Ireland were successful in their campaigns to have their own parliaments. The Northern Ireland Assembly was elected in June 1998, the Scottish Parliament and the National Assembly of Wales in May 1999. While several political decisions are still made in London, these three parliaments were given the power to control aspects of political life that take place at a more local level, such as education, health services, and public transport. The Northern Ireland Assembly has been suspended several times due to breakdowns in relations between the pro-British Unionists and the pro-Irish Republicans. The longest period of suspension to date was from October 2002 to May 2007, after wich the Assembly's full powers were restored.

Scottish independence: For many Scottish people, the mere devolution of their parliament does not go far enough. They want Scotland to leave the United Kingdom and become an independent country. After many years of discussion, a referendum was held in September 2014. A very large number of people voted, 84 % of all those eligible, showing what an important issue this was considered to be. However, those in favour of independence lost. 44.7 % of the voters voted for independence, while 55.3 % voted to stay in the UK.

For the time being, Scotland will remain part of the UK. But for many Scots, the discussion is far from over. Political parties such as the Scottish National Party, the Scottish Green Party and the Scottish Socialist Party are determined to bring about independence as soon as possible, and felt encouraged by the large amount of support for the pro-independence campaign "Yes Scotland".

Some arguments for independence:
- The citizens of Scotland should be allowed to make their own decisions about the future of their country instead of having to go along with policies made in London.
- Scotland would be able to make its own policies on defence and foreign affairs: it could then, for example, decide to leave NATO and to get rid of nuclear weapons in Scottish waters.
- The country has rich natural resources in the form of North Sea oil, which would make it wealthy in its own right.
- Emphasis would be placed on Scottish culture and traditions.
- The country could have more political influence e.g. in Europe: as an independent country, it would be able to have more elected Members of the European Parliament and have its own say in European and world matters.

Some arguments against independence:
- Scotland would have to opt out of the Schengen Area, otherwise it would have to introduce border controls all along the English-Scottish border.
- The North Sea oil resources are not as reliable a source of income as some supporters of independence claim: production levels are dropping on many North Sea oil rigs. Scotland does not have many other natural resources to fall back on, and might find it difficult to encourage other major industries, e.g. IT or manufacturing, to settle there due to the perceived instability of a newly independent country. The revenue that the country makes from tourism would not be enough to sustain it economically.
- Which currency would Scotland use? It would be several years before Scotland was allowed to join the euro and the EU, and an independent Scottish currency would be seen as an uncertain factor on the financial markets. Therefore Scotland would have to keep the British pound at first if it wanted to keep investments and trade up to their current levels.
- Britain's economy is currently strong, which is beneficial to Scotland. Trade opportunities are good, and it is easier for Scottish businesses to win orders as part of the strong UK market. International compe-

tition is tough and will become more so in the coming years, so the support of the British economy as a whole is important for Scottish business.

→ Remaining part of Britain means remaining part of a multi-ethnic and multi-cultural society that enriches Scottish culture. Scottish heritage is important but should not be promoted to the exclusion of other cultures.

→ As part of Britain, Scotland has an international presence, e.g. it has a voice in the EU and NATO, and there are British embassies throughout the world. An independent Scotland would, at least initially, lose this international support; Scottish citizens who ran into trouble abroad and needed the support of their embassy would not necessarily find one nearby.

The Troubles: The name given to the protests, rioting and terrorist campaigns in Northern Ireland which began in 1969 and have still not been completely resolved to this day.

The IRA: The Irish Republican Army, or IRA, is the militant branch of Sinn Fein, the Northern Irish Catholic political party which campaigns for Northern Ireland to become part of the Republic of Ireland again. The IRA has been responsible for many terrorist attacks, both in Northern Ireland itself and on the British mainland. Many decades of peace talks, which for years had little or no effect on the situation, seem to be gradually paying off, and treaties such as the 1998 "Good Friday Agreement" have led to talks about disarmament of the IRA and an end to the campaign of terror. However, as the political disagreements surrounding the suspension of the Northern Ireland Assembly show, there is still a long way to go.

Britain and Europe

Britain and Europe versus Britain and the USA: Britain's attitude to continental Europe has always been mixed. As an island, it is physically separate from a large part of the continent, and, due to its colonial past, it has developed close relationships with many non-European countries. In particular, it has a strong relationship with the USA. The two countries are united by a common language, and have often supported each other in international affairs. They were allies during the First and Second World Wars, and this mutual support has, on the whole, continued since then. During the 1980s, the Thatcher and Reagan governments worked together, and were in agreement on matters such as nuclear weapons. The British government under Tony Blair backed George Bush's Gulf War in the 1990s, providing direct military assistance for the conflict. On the other hand, Britain has to accept that it is geographically a European country, and that it makes sense to maintain close economic and political ties to the rest of the continent. It would not make sense for Britain to cut itself off politically and economically from Europe.

Post-war Britain: After the Second World War, Britain's global position changed significantly. Its economy had collapsed and it had to rely on financial aid from the USA and Canada. It suffered severe shortages of everything from housing to food and basic commodities. In addition to this, many of its overseas territories were demanding independence; the next couple of decades would see the end of the British Empire. Instead, the USA and the USSR took over as the new world powers. The rest of Europe was in a similar position, and, like Britain, would take many years to recover from the destruction caused by the war. Furthermore, the continent was divided ideologically into the western countries, supported by the USA, and the eastern bloc, supported by the USSR. The latter group "disappeared" behind the Iron Curtain for the next few decades. The western European countries began to consider forms of closer cooperation, in order to prevent a repetition of the two wars that had affected the first half of the 20th century so significantly.

Britain and the European Community: The European Economic Community (EEC) was founded by France, Italy, West Germany and the Benelux countries in 1957. Britain's first attempts to join, in the 1960s, were blocked by the French President de Gaulle, as he felt that Britain's strong ties to the USA would mean a lack of commitment to Europe. Britain finally joined the European Community (EC), as it was now called, in 1973, although many Britons were against this. As a result, a referendum on membership was held in 1975, in which two-thirds of the voters chose to stay in the EC. In 1991, the Maastricht Treaty was signed, creating the single European market. However, Prime Minister John Major ensured that Britain would have the right to opt out of the single currency when the time came. This meant that Britain was one of just 3 European Union states, along with Denmark and Sweden, not to change its currency to the euro when it came into usage in 2002.

Eurosceptics: Many British politicians are against the country's membership of the EU. They are "sceptical" about the benefits that it brings, feeling that many European laws do not apply to Britain or have a negative effect on it, e.g. certain agricultural and economic policies. They are strictly against Britain ever joining the single currency and believe that its financial contributions to the EU are too high. Recent economic controversies, such as the financial aid provided to bankrupt Greece and the refugee crisis that began in 2015, have only helped to increase support for the idea that Britain should leave the EU altogether. One of Prime Minister David Cameron's election promises in 2015 was to hold a referendum on Britain's EU membership, perhaps as soon as 2016.

Social institutions

National Health Service: Founded in 1948, the National Health Service (NHS) provides all residents of Britain with free medical care. All working adults pay into this system with their 'national insurance' contributions. Although this revolutionary system worked well in the beginning, in recent years it has been hit with the same sorts of problems that face state health insurance schemes throughout Europe: costs are too high, and the system is coming under pressure from an increasingly elderly population. Today all working adults have to pay towards their medical treatment (e.g. for medication), although a consultation with a doctor is still free.

The dole: An informal name for unemployment benefit. Unemployed people receiving this money are said to be "on the dole".

Social benefits: A range of benefits are available in Britain to needy people. Child benefit is given to all families with children; and new mothers are entitled to maternity benefit. Other financial aids include income support for people on low wages, disability living allowance and carer's allowance for people with disabilities and those who look after them at home, and winter fuel payment for people who need help with their heating costs. However, the coalition government under David Cameron has introduced an increasing number of benefit cuts since coming to power, often seeming to target the most vulnerable members of society. As a result, the gap between rich and poor in Britain is increasing significantly. One way in which this can be seen is the growing number of people who rely on food banks, places where people can go to get emergency food if they have no other way of feeding themselves and their families.

Religion

Church of England: This is the official state religion of Britain, also referred to as the Anglican Church. The monarch is the official head of the Church of England, and appoints the high-ranking members of the clergy, such as the Archbishops of Canterbury and York, on the Prime Minister's advice. The Church of England is not separate from the state, as senior bishops are automatically members of the House of Lords, and therefore actively take part in political affairs.

"Cultural Christianity": Although over 70% of Britons officially describe themselves as Christians, a far smaller percentage attend church services on a regular basis. This is especially true of Anglicans. In fact, surveys have shown that a considerable percentage of people in Britain do not believe in God, yet still say that they have an affiliation to a particular religion, because their family has always belonged to that religion and they therefore see it as part of their cultural heritage. This is referred to as "cultural Christianity", which means that religion has little to do with faith, but instead forms part of a person's cultural and social identity. The social aspect in particular can be seen in the fact that many people still choose to have a church wedding and to have their children christened even if they do not normally go to church. In so doing, they are carrying on a tradition rather than expressing their spirituality.

Issues affecting the Church of England: The Anglican Church has had to deal with a number of controversies in recent years. One such issue is the question of women priests. In 1994 the first women were ordained to the priesthood in the Church of England, although protests against this move were still widespread. However, nowadays one in five Anglican priests are women. The debate then moved on to the question of women bishops. After several years of discussion, the General Synod, the Church's governing body, finally approved the necessary legislation in November 2014. The first woman bishop, Libby Lane, was consecrated in January 2015.

Another widely debated topic is the question of whether people who are openly homosexual, rather than homosexual but celibate, should be ordained as priests and bishops. Connected to this issue is the matter of blessings for same-sex couples as the equivalent to a marriage ceremony. Opinion is split on these two points, both within the Church of England and in the other Anglican Churches throughout the world. While some members accept homosexuality, others completely reject any tolerance of it, and strongly protest against the ordination of gay people.

Education

Primary school: For children aged between 5 and 11.

Secondary school: For pupils aged 11 and above. Children must attend school until the age of 16, although it is possible to stay on until they are 18.

Comprehensive schools: Most pupils in state education attend this kind of secondary school. It is more or less the equivalent to a combination of a German Gymnasium and Realschule, as the pupils are of mixed ability. All pupils have the opportunity to stay on at school until they are 18 and do A-levels. As well as purely academic subjects, a number of vocational courses are available.

Grammar schools: A few still exist in the state system. In order to get in, children have to pass an entrance exam. Most of the subjects taught are academic ones.

Private schools: Approximately 8% of British schoolchildren attend private schools. Traditionally an upper-class method of education, these schools have seen a growing number of children from middle-class families in recent years, whose parents are dissatisfied with the low education standards and violent behaviour of some pupils at state schools. Private schools tend to have smaller classes and therefore higher teaching standards.

Public schools: Despite the name, these are, in fact, private schools for pupils aged between 13 and 18, very often boarding schools. Many of these are very famous (e.g. Eton and Harrow), and have a reputation of being extremely elitist, of being where the powerful people in Britain send their children. In the past it was certainly true that most leading politicians, for example, had been to public school. It is expected that most public school pupils will go on to university, often Oxford or Cambridge.

Independent schools: These are former grammar schools which took the option of leaving the state school system rather than becoming comprehensive schools. Independent schools are fee-paying, and they do not have to follow the National Curriculum.

The National Curriculum: This is the name for the official teaching programme that all state schools have to follow (for pupils aged 5–16). The subjects that have to be taught and the standards expected from each age group are set down. Core subjects include English, maths and science subjects; compulsory subjects include history, geography and modern languages; other subjects, such as drama, may also be taught if the school has the appropriate resources.

GCSEs: The General Certificate of Education (GCSE) is taken by all British pupils at the age of 16. Each pupil takes a number of different subjects, normally between 6 and 9, and normally including English and maths. The final mark is a combination of an exam taken at the end of Year 10 and coursework done throughout the year. Unlike in Germany, each GCSE subject is assessed separately, instead of there being an overall mark. That means if, for example, a pupil takes 9 subjects, passes 7 and fails 2, he has 7 GCSEs.

BTECs and OCR Nationals: These are vocational qualifications in a range of subjects such as art and design, business, health and social care or sport. They are usually studied by pupils over 16, but can also be taken by 14- to 16-year-olds in combination with GCSEs. They have replaced the old GNVQ qualification.

A-levels: Short for Advanced Level, these are exams that are taken at the age of 18, and are required for university entrance. Like with GCSEs, each subject is assessed separately; pupils normally take 3 subjects.

Higher education: Britain has approximately 200 universities, plus other institutions of higher education such as vocational colleges. The first degree programme at university is a Bachelor degree (e.g. Bachelor of Arts), and takes either 3 or 4 years, depending on the subject. The students studying for a Bachelor degree are called undergraduates. People who then wish to continue their university education can do a post-graduate degree, first a Masters, and then a PhD (a doctorate). In comparison to Germany, graduates with a Bachelor degree are very flexible in their choice of career. Many companies and institutions offer graduate-level entry programmes, which means that people with a degree can start working there at a higher wage than a school-leaver, and are trained on the job. For some companies, it is not very important what the subject of the degree is, although obviously it helps to have studied something which is relevant to the job in some way.

The **financial aspect** of studying in Britain has been a subject of controversy in recent years. In the past, tuition was free, and grants (for accommodation, books etc) were freely available to those who were less well-off. However, this system became too expensive to maintain and nowadays students have to pay for their tuition, fees that have continued to increase since their introduction in 1998 and are currently at a rate of approximately £ 9,000 per year. This is, of course, in addition to living costs, books and other materials. People who cannot afford to pay for this out of their own pocket can take out a student loan, which has to be repaid once the graduate is earning £ 21,000 a year or more. In today's economic climate, graduates cannot be sure of getting a good job after they leave university, and many young people dislike the idea of starting their working lives with large debts, especially when they have no way of knowing how long it will take them to pay them off. Many people argue that tuition fees discriminate against poorer people, turning universities into institutions primarily for the middle and upper classes, who are more likely to be able to afford to go there. In addition to this, student loans are often a factor when a young person is deciding whether to go on to higher education after leaving school. Critics of the system point out that highly qualified professionals are essential if Britain is to remain competitive on the international markets, and the fewer university graduates the country has, the fewer such professionals there will be.

The media

The BBC: The BBC (British Broadcasting Corporation) is the state broadcasting service in Britain, with 5 national radio stations, several local radio stations, 2 terrestrial television channels plus digital channels. The BBC is partly funded by the television licence fee that each household with a television has to pay; there are no advertisements.

ITV: Short for Independent Television, this is a commercial channel, consisting of 15 regionally based television companies. These produce programmes for the area in which they are located, although many of these programmes are shown nationwide.

Tabloids: The term "tabloid" implies a certain type of newspaper which is more informal and sensational in style than the more serious newspapers. The name comes from the small format newspaper, and the layout is characterised by large headlines, short articles and lots of pictures. The emphasis of the content tends to be on human interest stories and celebrity news. Some well-known tabloids (also known as "popular" or "gutter" press) are *The Sun* and *The Mirror*.

Quality papers: These include papers such as *The Times, The Guardian, The Telegraph and The Independent*. The format is large (also known as "broadsheets"), and the style of reporting is more serious, with in-depth, wide-ranging coverage of national and international news.

3.2 The British Empire and the Commonwealth

The reign of Elizabeth I: The foundations for the first British Empire were laid during the reign of Queen Elizabeth I (1588–1603). During the 16th century, Europeans began to explore the wider world. These included English explorers such as Francis Drake, who sailed round the world in 1588, and Walter Raleigh, who explored the Americas between 1578 and 1595. However, it was not until the beginning of the 17th century that any long-term English colonies were founded. The greatest motivation behind this colonization was economics: England wanted to establish foreign trade routes to bring wealth to the home country. The colonies were to provide cheap raw materials (such as cotton, silk, opium, salt and tea from eastern Asia) and were also seen as new sources of trading partners. Trading companies such as the East India Company (founded in around 1600) and the Virginia Company of London (1606) were established to make the most of these new opportunities.

The first colonies:
- the West Indies (Jamaica, the Bahamas, Bermuda)
- India (although it was not ruled directly by Britain until 1858, by which time the East India Company was so well-established that it practically ruled the country)
- Canada (Newfoundland, Hudson Bay)
- parts of North America
- Gibraltar

The North American colonies: The first permanent colony on North American soil was Jamestown, established in 1607 and run by the Virginia Company of London. This was followed by the Plymouth colony, founded by the Puritans in 1620 in present-day Massachusetts. Also known as the Pilgrims, this group had left Britain in order to practise their religious beliefs in a distant place where there was no danger of persecution. The Plymouth colony was the starting point for the other New England colonies, which spread out from Boston and the surrounding areas. The area around what would become New York attracted immigrants from England and Europe who wished for religious and political freedom; Pennsylvania was founded in 1681. The southern colonies, on the other hand, were where cotton and tobacco were produced, crops that generated a great deal of wealth for England. These colonies were also the place where the slave trade was introduced to North America; slaves were already a well-established source of income in the English Caribbean colonies.

The loss of the Thirteen Colonies: By 1733, there were 13 British colonies in the east of North America, stretching from New Hampshire in the north to Georgia in the south. From the 1760s, the citizens of these colonies grew more and more dissatisfied with the fact that they were governed by distant Britain. A particular point of contention was that the colonies had to pay taxes to Britain but were not allowed to have a seat in the British Parliament, and therefore had no-one to represent their interests. In the course of the next few years, there were an increasing number of protests against Britain, such as the Boston Tea Party in 1773, in which a large shipment of tea was thrown into Boston Harbor as an act of resistance. In 1774, the British sent soldiers to restore order, and the resulting conflict led to the American Revolutionary War, or War of Independence, from 1775–1783. Although the war was still going on at the time, the Continental Congress declared independence from Britain in 1776, signing the Declaration of Independence and turning the former colonies into states. Eventually, in 1783, the Treaty of Paris was signed, making the new states completely separate from Britain.

The Second Empire: The loss of the North American colonies was a severe blow to Britain, causing the government to look to other parts of the world for the expansion of its overseas territories. This expansion began at the end of the 18th century, and between 1815 and 1914 was so successful that it was said that the sun never set on the British Empire. In other words, the empire was spread so extensively throughout the world that it was always daytime somewhere.

Canada: Newfoundland was Britain's first North American colony, founded in 1583. In the 17th century, several French colonies were also established there, most of which were passed over to Britain after the Treaty of Paris in 1763. In the 19th century, the Canadian provinces gradually united and became self-governing, except in matters concerning international relations, for which they still had to rely on the British Parliament. In 1867, Canada became a British dominion, dominions being free nations that retained the British monarch as head of state. The country remained a dominion until 1953; today it is a Commonwealth realm with the British monarch as its constitutional monarch and head of state.

Australia: James Cook discovered the eastern coast of Australia in 1770 and claimed it for Britain. In 1788, the first British settlers arrived on the "First Fleet" of ships. Most of them were criminals, as Australia was to be a penal colony. Gradually, as more British settlers arrived, they spread across the country, especially after gold was discovered there in the 1850s. In 1901, the separate Australian colonies formed a federation and became a dominion of the British Empire in 1907. During the First and Second World Wars, Australians fought on the side of the British and their allies, and many were killed overseas instead of being able to defend their own country. In 1942, the Australian government adopted the Statute of Westminster that ended most of the constitutional links between Australia and Britain; in 1986, the Australia Act was passed, after which Britain no longer played any role in the Australian government. However, although Australia now has much closer ties with its neighbours on the Pacific Rim, it remains part of the British Commonwealth. A referendum was held in 1999 to decide whether Australia should become a republic; the majority voted against, so for now the British monarch remains head of state.

New Zealand: In 1788, New Zealand was claimed by the British as part of New South Wales in what would become Australia, becoming a separate colony in 1841. It was proclaimed a dominion in 1907 as it was now self-governing, and became independent in 1953. Like Canada and Australia, it is still a Commonwealth realm with the British monarch as head of state.

India: Thanks to the East India Company, by the 19th century India was already well-established as an important trading post. The British government became increasingly involved in the Company's business, and gradually the territories controlled by the Company came under the rule of the British Crown. Matters came to a head in the mid-19th century after the Indian Rebellion, which started with a mutiny of sepoys, Indian soldiers employed by the East India Company's army. The rebellion spread through central India, threatening the Company's power there. Large numbers of people were killed on both sides before the rebellion could be stopped; afterwards, the British government disbanded the Company and made itself the direct ruler of India as set down in the Government of India Act of 1858. This Act established the British Raj, or rule, which lasted from 1858 to 1947. During this time, the country was governed by a British governor-general; Queen Victoria was crowned Empress of India in 1858. As in other British overseas possessions, the citizens of India became more and more dissatisfied with the situation of being ruled by a foreign power. The protests grew stronger, including the passive resistance to British rule led by Mahatma Gandhi in the 1920s. India finally became a federal republic in 1950.

Africa: At the height of the Empire, Britain occupied territories in Africa from South Africa to Egypt, as well as some north-western parts of the continent. Cecil Rhodes, a British mining magnate who also founded the territory of Rhodesia (now called Zimbabwe), wanted to build a "Cape to Cairo" railway link. This would connect the southern part of the continent with its rich mineral resources (such as diamonds in South Africa) with the Suez Canal in the north, which was of huge strategic importance as a shortcut from Europe to eastern Asia. The railway was never built, but Britain almost achieved control of an unbroken line of territories from north to south. As elsewhere, the African territories began to develop a sense of national pride and to demand independence. Some colonies, such as Egypt after World War I, were granted independence for economic reasons, i.e. to ease the financial strain on Britain. All Britain's remaining African colonies had gained independence by 1968, except Southern Rhodesia, which was self-governing. The path to independence was not always easy or peaceful, but was often the result of uprisings by the native population.

The foundation of the Commonwealth: In 1926 and 1930, Imperial Conferences were held in London. These granted full autonomy to the dominions of Australia, New Zealand, Canada, Newfoundland, Ireland and South Africa. All dominions were given full equality in the 1931 Statute of Westminster, which established the Commonwealth of Nations as an association of these newly independent states. The independent nations were now able to reject any laws passed by the British government and make their own laws regarding domestic matters. Other former colonies, such as Pakistan, which had become republics, did not recognise the British monarch as their head of state. Such countries joined the Commonwealth at a later stage, accepting the monarch as the symbolic head of the Commonwealth but not of their own country. Economic ties played an important role in the early days of the Commonwealth: although the various countries were no longer governed by Britain, they did not wish to lose out on lucrative trade. Moreover, these former colonies had several things in common: they shared a language and culture, as well as certain values such as democracy and human rights. The Commonwealth countries maintain close ties, coming for events such as the Commonwealth Games, comparable to the Olympic Games and also held every four years. In addition to this, there are various institutes, professional associations, societies and university exchange programmes for member countries, as well as programmes promoting agriculture, engineering, health and education.

The Commonwealth today: The ties between the former British colonies are no longer as strong as they once were, and the future of the Commonwealth is doubtful in the long term. Although it has been able to encourage democracy in some countries, it does not have any real power when it comes to sanctions. From time to time, countries have been suspended from the Commonwealth as a protest against human rights violations, e.g. Nigeria between 1995 and 1999, but this does not really have much practical effect. Furthermore, member states have the right to leave the Commonwealth at any time, since membership is voluntary. This happened, for example, in the case of Zimbabwe, which was suspended in 2002 for its human rights violations and undemocratic government; instead of making the changes demanded of it, the country left the Commonwealth the following year. In many cases, the former colonies have changed so much that they now have little in common with each other, so the traditional sense of solidarity among these states has been lost. New economic ties have been formed, e.g. with the USA or among the Pacific

Rim countries, so the Commonwealth states no longer rely completely on Britain for trade. However, some institutions are still going strong, such as the Commonwealth Games, the latest of which are being held in Glasgow in 2014.

The remains of the Empire: Today, there are still 14 British Overseas Territories "left over" from the Empire. These are: Gibraltar, Akrotiri and Dhekelia (on Cyprus), the Turks and Caicos Islands, the Cayman Islands, the British Virgin Islands, Anguilla, Montserrat, the Pitcairn Islands, Ascension Island, Saint Helena, Tristan da Cunha, the British Indian Ocean Territory, the Falkland Islands, South Georgia and the South Sandwich Islands, and the British Antarctic Territory. British sovereignty of some of these territories is a matter of contention with their neighbouring countries, the most notable examples being Gibraltar and the Falkland Islands. Spain claims sovereignty of Gibraltar, but its citizens have twice voted against this, most recently in 2002. The Falkland Islands were invaded by Argentina in 1982, as a result of which the British government sent a navy taskforce to reclaim the islands. A 10-week military conflict followed, at the end of which Argentina surrendered and the Falklands returned to British control. However, Argentina has never given up its claim on the territory and still believes that the islands should be handed back to Argentine control.

3.3 USA

Politics

The Constitution: Written in 1787, eleven years after Britain's American colonies got their independence, this document was to form the basis of the new nation that would become the United States of America. Among the important concepts set down in the Constitution were the separation of powers, the system of checks and balances, and federalism.

The **separation of powers** means that the country is governed by three different branches: Congress (for making laws), the President (executive branch) and the Supreme Court (the judicial branch).

The **system of checks and balances** means that each of the three governmental branches mentioned above has a certain amount of control over the other two. In other words, no branch can act independently of the others, which prevents any of them from becoming too powerful.

Federalism means that the state governments share power with the national government, and have the right to decide certain things themselves at state level. Again, the idea is that power-sharing will stop one institution from having complete supremacy over the other.

The Bill of Rights: In 1791 the first 10 amendments were added to the Constitution, collectively known as the Bill of Rights. These amendments set down important civil rights, such as freedom of speech and freedom of religion.

Congress: As in Britain, the parliament in the USA is split into two chambers: the Senate and the House of Representatives. Each chamber has equal power, and all decisions made in one chamber have to be approved in the other before they can come into effect.

Supreme Court: As the highest court in the United States, the Supreme Court makes the final decisions on legal matters, including selected appeal cases which have already gone through the Courts of Appeal and State Supreme Courts. Another important role that it plays is to decide whether certain laws or government actions are unconstitutional (the Judicial Review).

Political lobbies: The National Rifle Association: The NRA is a non-profit organisation which promotes the legal use of guns and protects the right of US citizens to own them. Its activities include training programmes for gun owners and lobbying politicians to oppose gun control measures. It is quite successful in this, as it receives a huge amount of financial backing from members. However, repeated incidents of, for example, school children taking their parents' guns and running amok at their school mean that the gun control debate will continue.

International affairs

Dollar diplomacy: An informal name for the kind of economic imperialism practised by the United States since the end of the 19th century. By pouring money into foreign countries, the US has been able to command a large amount of economic and political influence there.

The Roosevelt Corollary: This proposal, made in 1904, was essentially one of the first examples of the US as the "world's police force". It declared that America could step in to stop any conflicts in Latin America which it considered to be an example of "chronic wrongdoing".

The Truman Doctrine: This was originally a programme started after World War II (in 1947) to help anti-Communists in Turkey and Greece. In later years it was extended so that the US could give aid to any countries which in their opinion were under threat from communism during the Cold War. It was this policy which led, among other things, to America's involvement in the Vietnam War.

The Marshall Plan: This programme, started in 1947, was also known as the European Recovery Program, and financed a large part of the rebuilding of Europe after the Second World War. One idea behind it was to make sure that western Europe, at least, was rebuilt to a democratic, capitalist pattern rather than a communist one.

9/11: The informal term for September 11, 2001, when terrorists from the radical Al-Qaida organisation hijacked four American planes and flew them into the World Trade Center, New York, and the Pentagon. This event marked the start of an anti-terrorist campaign which, less than two years later, had already included wars in Afghanistan and Iraq.

Axis of evil: The name given by the Bush administration to states such as Iraq, Iran, North Korea and Syria, which according to them are involved in the production of weapons of mass destruction with the intention of carrying out further terrorist attacks against the USA and their allies.

Rogue states: According to the US government, a rogue state is a country that supports terrorism and threatens its neighbours, pays no attention to international laws, denies its citizens human rights, wants to own weapons of mass destruction, and hates the USA and everything it stands for. Therefore, countries that are part of the "axis of evil" are, by definition, also rogue states.

Crime and punishment

Capital punishment: In the USA, the death penalty is still used to punish serious crimes such as murder. Most of the individual states (38 out of 50) have the legal option of applying the death penalty, although many of them have not executed anybody for many years. Others, however, such as Texas, execute a relatively large number of the people on death row in the state. The method of execution varies, although nowadays the most common method is the lethal injection. The use of the death penalty is extremely controversial, with emotional arguments on both sides. Those in favour of capital punishment believe that it is a deterrent that discourages people from committing violent crimes. They also think that anyone who takes a life does not deserve to live, and that the victim's loved ones will be comforted by the fact that the murderer has suffered the same fate. The opponents of the death penalty claim that it has not been proved to act as a deterrent, and that the system is unfair as people without enough money to pay for good legal representation are far more likely to be sentenced to death than those who can afford a good lawyer. They also argue that people have been executed who were later found to be innocent, and, as long as there is any danger of this happening, the death penalty should be abolished. However, it does not seem likely that this will happen in the USA any time soon.

Drug-related crimes: Drug abuse and drug trafficking are considered to be among the most serious crimes in the US, and the penalties attached to them are high. However, some states have now decriminalized the consumption and possession of a small amount of marijuana. It is also a crime for young people to buy and consume alcohol: in many states the legal drinking age is as high as 21.

Social issues

The American Dream: The "American Dream" is a concept that has attracted many people to emigrate to the United States. It is based on the idea that in the States everyone is free and equal, no matter what their race, political viewpoint, religion or social status is; that everyone has the opportunity to improve their financial situation; and that it is possible for people to become whatever they want to be, as long as they work hard enough. However, there are large discrepancies between the "dream" and reality. Belonging to an ethnic minority can be a huge disadvantage in many areas; some religious groups (e.g. Muslims after September 11, 2001) have to suffer discrimination; and there is a wide gap between rich and poor.

The "melting pot": In the past, the term "melting point" was often used as a metaphor for the way in which immigrants would become part of American society, i.e. although there were people from many different backgrounds, they would all somehow "melt" together to become Americans. In reality, however, this assimilation has not always worked. It tended to be easier for immigrants who came to the US up to the middle of the 19th century to adapt to and become part of American society, as most of them were white, northern European Protestants, and so the cultural gap was not so wide. However, immigrants who arrived from the end of the 19th century onwards have not always been accepted into this society, as there were far more cultural differences to overcome. Today many people prefer to identify themselves by their origins, (e.g. "Asian-American"), rather than call themselves straightforward "Americans". Nowadays, therefore, experts often refer to the "salad bowl" or "mosaic" theory instead of to the "melting pot": this means that there are many individual elements that make up the whole society, while still keeping their separate identities.

The Civil Rights Movement: This consisted of several groups which, from the early 20th century onwards, campaigned to put a stop to discrimination against America's black population. One of the most famous of these groups was the Southern Christian Leadership Conference. Its leader, Martin Luther King, Jr., encouraged peaceful campaigning for civil rights and the end of black segregation through boycotts (e.g. of buses where whites and blacks had to sit separately) and peaceful demonstrations. 1963 he led the famous march to Washington, D.C., a peaceful demonstration in which over 200,000 people from all over the US took part. It was here that he made his famous "I have a dream" speech, in which he spoke of his hopes that one day people of all races would live together on equal terms.

The assassination of Martin Luther King in 1968 was, in some ways, a turning point, after which more effort was made to integrate people of ethnic minorities. This included, for example, schemes in which white children were "bussed" to schools in black areas and vice versa. Perhaps the greatest example of how times have changed was the election of Barack Obama in November 2008 as the country's first African-American president. His election was seen by many as a sign that people can achieve whatever they want in America, despite their ethnic background.

Social welfare

Support for needy citizens: Traditionally, in the USA it is not seen as the government's job to provide social benefits for its citizens. Instead, the role of supporting the needy has often been taken on by churches and charitable organisations. The Protestant work ethic that is still part of the American mentality creates the attitude that people should be responsible for their own welfare. Although there have been social benefit programmes in the USA since the 19th century, there is a resistance to simply handing out cash relief, especially to people who are capable of working. It was not until the Great Depression of the 1930s that the government came to accept that people were not poor because they were lazy, but that instead the large number of people living below the poverty line was a consequence of the widespread unemployment at the time. Therefore, President Roosevelt passed the Social Security Act in 1935 as part of the "New Deal". This provided needy people with unemployment and old-age benefits.

Healthcare pre-2010: Before 2010, no US citizen was obliged to have health insurance. People either had to take out private insurance or had a health insurance plan covered in part or in whole by their employer (which, of course, they lost as soon as they stopped working for that employer). There were two healthcare programmes: Medicare provided money for the elderly and some disabled people; Medicaid was for those on low incomes. However, neither system covered all medical costs. In addition to this, not all people on low incomes were eligible for Medicaid. As a result, the citizens least likely to have medical insurance were those on low incomes or people from ethnic minorities, which was often the same thing. Private insurance was extremely expensive; moreover people who, for example, had a chronic medical condition often found it difficult to find an insurance company willing to take them on. If someone needed medical treatment but was not insured, he or she had to pay for it out of their own pocket. Anyone who was seriously ill or, for instance, needed an urgent operation, could very quickly find themselves facing debts they had no way of repaying. The alternative was to simply leave the condition untreated, an option from which some people never recovered.

Obamacare: One of Barack Obama's election promises during his first presidential campaign was the reform of the US healthcare system. In March 2010, the Patient Protection and Affordable Care Act (ACA), colloquially known as "Obamacare", was passed. The various provisions of the Act will be introduced gradually, and it will take until 2022 until all of the provisions are up and running.

As of January 2014, American citizens must have health insurance; otherwise they have to pay extra tax. Subsidised health insurance is now available; in addition to this, citizens can use the new "Health Insurance Marketplace" to find the best insurance deal for their needs. Improvements to basic healthcare and, in particular, to preventative healthcare, will be made, the idea being that this will save money in the long term by treating patients before their condition becomes serious, and therefore expensive to treat. Another radical change is that it will be more difficult for health insurance companies to cancel patients' policies or refuse to cover a pre-existing illness.

Resistance to Obamacare: There was a great deal of resistance to the new healthcare Act, especially from the Republican Party. Their objections include the fact that higher earners will have to pay more taxes. They also dislike the idea that obliging people to take out insurance cover or pay an exemption fee means taking away their personal freedom to decide what they want. The Republicans did all they could to stop the law from being passed, and continue in their attempts to block or change the Act. If the next US president is a Republican, it is clear that some parts of the law may be changed.

Religion

The Puritans: The Puritans belonged to the second main group of original settlers who came from England (in 1629, 9 years after the Pilgrims) because they had not been free to practise their religious beliefs in their home country. They themselves enforced the practice of these beliefs very strictly in the colonies that they founded. Their legacy can still be seen today in certain attitudes in the US:

→ they regarded America as a "promised land" which God had given to them, and felt that they were a special people chosen by God. This connection between religion and patriotism still exists for many Americans.

→ WASPs: (White Anglo-Saxon Protestants) no longer make up the largest ethnic group in America in terms of numbers, but they still command a great deal of political, economic and social influence.

→ The Protestant work ethic, which means hard work, self-discipline, and the importance of not wasting money, forms the backbone of the American attitude to work. Material wealth plays an important role: the Puritans saw it as a gift from God for people who had earned it.

Christian fundamentalism: A Protestant movement whose followers believe in a literal interpretation of the Bible. Among other things, its followers:
- want prayer in schools
- are against teaching evolution in schools as anything other than an "unproven belief", and want equal emphasis to be placed on teaching creationism, which states that the world was created in six days, as written in the Bible.
- place great emphasis on traditional family life and family values
- are against, among other things, sex outside marriage, abortion, feminism and homosexuality.

Some conservative Christian groups even have an influence on politics, especially at local level, generating support for those politicians who vote in accordance with Christian values.

The "electronic church": In the southern states in particular, fundamentalists make use of TV and radio to preach their beliefs to a wider audience. "TV evangelism" is well-known for its fund-raising as well as preaching, its critics believing that making money, rather than spreading the word of God, is the main goal of these TV shows.

Education

Public education: Unlike in Britain, public education in America means state education. Another difference between the two countries is that there are no national educational programmes: each state is free to design its own curriculum and education policies. One obvious example of this is the teaching (or not) of evolution in some states (see above).

Elementary school: Pupils attend elementary school from the age of 5 or 6 to 10 or 12 (depending on the state).

High school: The equivalent of a British comprehensive school, where pupils of all abilities learn together. Both academic and vocational subjects are taught. There is also a certain amount of focus on what is involved in being a good citizen and playing an active role in the local community.

Examinations: There are no national standards laid down for school exams; once again, these matters are decided in the individual states. However, pupils who wish to continue on to higher education have to take the SAT (Scholastic Aptitude Test), a nationally recognised exam which determines if the pupils have a necessary standard of education to go to college.

Higher education: There are many universities in America, from the famous, exclusive "Ivy League" universities (including Yale, Princeton and Harvard) to a number of small, private ones. Technical colleges offer vocational courses, normally lasting two years. Junior or community colleges either offer technical or professional-based programmes, or serve as a preparation for university.

The **financial aspect** of higher education in the US is an important one: all colleges are fee-paying, and costing an average of to $30,000 a year for tuition alone. Although scholarships are available (e.g. sports scholarships), the costs mean that most students are from well-to-do backgrounds.

Homeschooling: Around 4% of American pupils do not go to school, but instead are "homeschooled", i.e. taught at home by their parents. Although, on the face of it, this is not a large percentage, the number of children being schooled at home has increased by approximately 75 % since 1999; the number is expected to keep rising. The most common reason given for homeschooling is parents wanting to give their children a certain kind of religious instruction. In other cases, parents are worried that the schools available locally are too dangerous (e.g. because of drugs or violent pupils), or they are not satisfied with the academic standards available. Each state has different regulations for homeschooling; in some, but not all states, the person teaching the children needs a qualification, and pupils have to attend lessons for a certain number of days per year. Some states also set down a curriculum that must be followed, whereas in other parts of the country teachers are free to choose what to teach.

3.4 English as a world language

The spread of English: In the late 16th and early 17th centuries, English started to really come into its own. This was when English began to replace Latin as the language of official documents in England. More and more books were published in English, and spellings and usage became more standardised. This process was significantly helped by the publication of the King James Bible, or Authorized Version, in 1611. The existing English translations of the Bible were completely reworked to produce this new standard version, one that is still in use today. It was also the age of Shakespeare, who took the possibilities of the English language to a new level, inventing new words and phrases that greatly enhanced and expanded the language.

In the early 17th century, the first North American colonies were established by English migrants. From the 18th century, immigrant groups from other countries followed, many of which often spoke nothing but their native tongue. However, by the time the Thirteen Colonies declared their independence from Britain in 1776, there was never any question that English would become the official language of the new nation. Both the Declaration of Independence and the Constitution were written in English, and are among the great documents in the language. From the 19th century onwards, new immigrants were expected to learn English, and nearly all of them did. In many cases, their children, born in the USA, never learnt their parents' native language.

After the loss of the Thirteen Colonies, Britain began to expand its overseas territories in other parts of the world. This, of course, increased the spread of English as it was adopted as the official language in places as far apart as India, Australia and Kenya. Not only was English used for general communication, but it became the language used to deal with governmental, administrative, legal, educational and cultural matters. Naturally, this was not always seen as a positive development. One of the ideas behind colonisation was the importance of bringing British culture and values to other nations. There was often little acceptance of other cultures on the part of the colonists, who believed it was good for the natives to be "civilised" by their British superiors. This contributed to the resentments that ultimately led most of the former British overseas possessions to demand their independence. However, after the break-up of the Empire, English was perhaps the most important legacy that the former rulers left. Particularly among the upper and professional classes in these countries, an excellent command of English is still seen as an essential part of a good education and as an aid to a good career. In fact, many high-ranking politicians and other influential figures in the former colonies went to university in Britain, particularly to Oxford or Cambridge, before returning to their native country and playing important roles there. One example is the Burmese politician and human rights activist Aung San Suu Kyi, who has a degree from Oxford.

Post-colonial literature: From the mid-20th century onwards, as European colonisation gradually came to an end, a new literary genre, post-colonial literature, arose. Writers from former European colonies, including the British ones, began to write books that discussed the colonial experience and reflected on its effects on their society, culture and national identity. Many of these authors write in English, and their works are an important contribution to our understanding of the colonial experience from the point of view of the colonised. They also consider the problems caused by a clash of cultures and the search for identity, especially for those authors whose families moved to the country of their former rulers, hoping for a better life for their children. These children are caught between two cultures, feeling British rather than, for example, Pakistani, yet also feeling the need to respect their parents' values. These are just a few of the after-effects of colonialism. Some of the most significant English-speaking writers in this genre include Salman Rushdie, J.M. Coetzee, Doris Lessing, Hanif Kureishi, Ngugi wa Thiong'o and Michael Ondaatje.

The influence of the USA: Just as the influence of Britain on world affairs was diminishing in the wake of the end of the Empire, the influence of the USA began to rise. Today, it can be said that a large proportion of global English originates in the States rather than in Britain. This began after World War II, when the USA emerged as one of the new world powers. A lot of their influence was political, e.g. their input in the rebuilding of Western Europe after the war. They wanted to help these countries to grow strong economically and therefore resist the rise of Communism. Western Europe, suffering from the after-effects of the war, received America's help gratefully and embraced the values it was promoting.

However, the real spread of American English did not come through politics, but rather through the world of entertainment. The influence of Hollywood had always been strong, and, with the rise of television, American TV shows also became increasingly popular. Shown in Britain, they began to influence the way the British spoke, as a result of which British English took on more and more Americanisms. Needless to say, many Britons disapproved of this "corruption" of their language, but in the long term there was little they could do to stop it. British English has now been enriched by many American words and expressions. Due to the large number of American films and television programmes shown in Britain, the British are generally able to understand Americans very well. The opposite is not necessarily true: until fairly recently, not many British films and TV programmes were shown in America, and British colloquialisms were often not understood there. In addition to this, nowadays it is very often American rather than British English that is used, for example, for international business, as it is felt that it is more likely to be understood by people who do not speak English as a first language.

English as lingua franca: Today, English is truly the world language. Whenever people with different native tongues have to deal with each other, it is highly likely that they will use English as their default language. English is used in several important fields of international affairs. For example, English is the language of civil aviation, as it is safer if pilots and air traffic controllers have one common language in which they can communicate, reducing the risk of misunderstandings. Likewise, English plays a vital role in international research and development, with a large number of academic and scientific papers being published in that language. Many universities in non-English-speaking countries offer individual courses or even whole degree programmes in English to encourage more international students to apply. There are still more than 60 countries in the world that use English as their language of government, even if it is not spoken by the majority of their citizens.

When it comes to international entertainment, a good grasp of English is almost unavoidable. A large percentage of the world's biggest, most popular movies are in English. In addition to this, anyone wanting to really succeed in the world of pop music had better make sure their songs are in English if they really want to reach a wide audience. The BBC World Service is one of the most trusted sources of information throughout the world, as it is seen as providing unbiased information about issues that certain governments may wish to conceal from their citizens. In the field of tourism, hotel staff and others who rely on holidaymakers for their livelihood need to have at least some command of English. In many parts of the world, English is seen as essential for improving one's career opportunities.

The disadvantage for native speakers of English is, of course, that there is little encouragement for them to learn other languages. Many have no desire to do so, presuming that "everyone speaks English" and that they will be able to get by without speaking anything else. For example, the number of pupils and students in Britain choosing foreign language options has dropped significantly in recent years. Learning a language is seen as difficult, and probably unnecessary. However, as learning to speak another language also involves learning about other people and cultures, anyone with this attitude will miss out on a great deal. It seems unlikely, though, that another language will take over the position in the world held by English any time soon.

Checkliste 3 USA und Großbritannien

Testen Sie sich selbst:

Können Sie zu jedem Stichpunkt etwas sagen?
- → A-levels
- → African colonies
- → Australia
- → BBC
- → American Dream
- → American War of Independence
- → Axis of evil
- → Bill of Rights

Checkliste

- Boston Tea Party
- British Overseas Territories
- Canada
- Church of England
- Commonwealth
- Comprehensive schools
- Constitution
- Devolution
- Dollar diplomacy
- East India Company
- Elementary school
- Examinations
- Federalism
- First Fleet
- Gibraltar
- High school
- Homeschooling
- House of Lords
- India
- ITV
- Marshall Plan
- Monarchy
- National Health Service
- New Zealand
- Primary school
- Public education
- Puritans
- Rogue states
- Secondary schoo
- Single European currency
- Supreme Court
- Tabloids
- The Thirteen Colonies
- Truman Doctrine
- British Empire
- BTECs
- Cape to Cairo
- Civil Rights Movement
- Commonwealth Games
- Congress
- Cultural Christianity
- Dole
- Dominions
- Electronic church
- Eurosceptics
- Falkland Islands
- First colonies
- Fundamentalism
- Grammar schools
- Higher education
- House of Commons
- Independent schools
- IRA
- Lobbies
- Melting pot
- National Curriculum
- National Rifle Association
- Obamacare
- Private schools
- Public schools
- Quality papers
- Roosevelt Corollary
- Separation of powers
- Social benefits
- System of checks and balances
- The Pilgrims
- The Troubles

4 Textanalyse

Es gibt viel zu bedenken bei der Analyse eines Textes. In diesem Kapitel erhalten Sie anhand konkreter Beispiele einen Überblick über die wichtigsten Begriffe und stilistischen Mittel. Außerdem gibt es viele praktische Tipps zum Thema „Wie soll ich überhaupt eine Textanalyse angehen?". Am Ende des Kapitels zeigen Prüfungsbeispiele mit Musterlösungen, wie Textanalysen konkret aussehen können.

4.1 Wie man an eine Textanalyse herangeht

Generelle Tipps

Dies sind einige Vorschläge, wie man an die Aufgabe herangeht, einen Text zu analysieren.

Lesen Sie einmal schnell den ganzen Text durch, um einen generellen Eindruck zu erhalten, wovon der Text handelt.

Lesen Sie sich sorgfältig alle Fragen durch, damit Sie wissen, nach welcher speziellen Information Sie suchen müssen, wenn Sie den Text noch einmal durchlesen.

Schenken Sie der **Überschrift** oder dem **Titel** besondere Aufmerksamkeit. Beides verschafft Ihnen meistens einen ersten Eindruck vom Inhalt des Textes.

Achten Sie auch besonders auf die **Quelle des Textes** (sie ist in der Regel am Ende angegeben). Oft, besonders bei Sachtexten, lässt sie Rückschlüsse auf das Zielpublikum zu.

Lesen Sie alle **Fuß- oder Endnoten**, die der Text hat, denn sie können Vokabelerklärungen oder Zusatzinformation enthalten. Dies hilft Ihnen beim Verstehen des Textes.

4.1 Wie man an eine Textanalyse herangeht

Versuchen Sie die **Schlüsselwörter** des Textes zu **identifizieren** (Tipps, wie man dies macht, finden Sie auf → Seite 208). Diese sollten Ihnen auch dabei helfen, die Kernaussagen des Textes zu erkennen.

Lesen Sie den Text noch einmal sorgfältig durch und achten Sie dabei besonders auf Inhaltspunkte, die in den Fragen erwähnt werden. Unterstreichen oder markieren Sie alle Wörter und Phrasen, von denen Sie denken, dass sie für die Beantwortung signifikant sind.

Die Fragen

Lesen Sie die Fragen immer **mit großer Sorgfalt** durch und unterstreichen (oder markieren) Sie dabei alle wichtigen Wörter.

Beachten Sie, dass die Fragen normalerweise so angeordnet sind wie die **Reihenfolge der Textteile**, die man zum Beantworten der Frage benötigt.

Lesen Sie alle Fragen durch, ehe Sie anfangen, diese zu beantworten, und überlegen Sie sich sorgfältig, nach genau welcher Information in jedem Fall gefragt wird. Dies hilft Ihnen zu vermeiden, die gleiche Information bei mehr als einer Frage anzubringen.

Achten Sie auf die **Anzahl der maximalen Punkte**, die Sie pro Frage erreichen können. Es ist offensichtlich, dass bei einer Frage mit vielen Punkten eine längere Antwort von Ihnen erwartet wird als bei einer Frage mit nur wenigen Punkten.

Versuchen Sie, möglichst genau **die verlangte Wortzahl** zu erreichen.

Wie man die Fragen beantwortet

Soweit möglich, sollten Sie **eigene Worte** bei der Beantwortung verwenden. Damit zeigen Sie, dass Sie sowohl den Text als auch die Frage an sich verstanden haben. Anstatt einfach Wörter und Phrasen aus dem Text zu kopieren, sollten Sie Synonyme oder andere grammatikalische Strukturen verwenden. Nehmen Sie folgende Beispiele:

→ *The Prime Minister had a great deal of difficulty in ...* → *The Prime Minister had several problems with ... (Synonyme)*

→ *Inner cities are considered to be problem areas by the government because ...* → *The government thinks that inner cities are problem areas because ...* (andere Struktur + Synonym)

Wiederholen Sie in Ihrer Antwort nicht die Frage. Damit kopieren Sie diese nur, beantworten sie aber nicht (selbst wenn Sie diese paraphrasieren). Dadurch können Sie dem Prüfer den Eindruck vermitteln, dass Sie nicht wissen, was sie schreiben sollen.

→ Beispiel: *Why are so many British people still sceptical about the idea of having closer ties with the rest of Europe?*
  → ~~*So many British people are still sceptical about the idea of having closer ties with the rest of Europe because they believe ...*~~ = *false*
  → *One reason for British scepticism about Europe may be that ...* = *correct*

Um Ihre Meinung zu veranschaulichen, können Sie ein paar **Zitate in Ihre Antwort einflechten** – übertreiben Sie es aber nicht dabei! Um das Zitat zu kennzeichnen, müssen Anführungszeichen, die im Englischen immer oben sind (" "), benutzt werden.

→ Beispiel: *The protagonist is referred to as being "a loner", which explains why he does not want to join the others on the excursion to the waterfall.*

Schweifen Sie nicht ab, sondern bleiben Sie beim Thema. Beantworten Sie die Frage so präzise wie möglich, ohne unnötig ins Detail zu gehen.

Die Überschrift oder der Titel

Der Titel eines Textes gibt uns oft schon eine erste Vorstellung darüber, wovon der Text handelt.

→ Beispiel: Ein Zeitungsartikel mit der Überschrift *We are what we eat* sagt uns, dass der Text etwas mit Essen zu tun hat und mit dessen Wirkung auf Menschen.

Der Titel eines Textes kann aber auch doppeldeutig sein, also ein Wortspiel (*pun*). Dass eine Überschrift mehrdeutig ist, wird klar, nachdem man den ganzen Text gelesen hat.

→ Beispiel: Ein Artikel, der berichtet, dass Mahatma Gandhi einen Hungerstreik begonnen hat, um gegen die Zustände in Indien zu protestieren, wurde mit *Hungry for justice* betitelt. Wenn man den Text liest, findet man heraus, dass die Überschrift sowohl wörtlich gemeint war – Gandhi wurde durch seinen Kampf um Gerechtigkeit hungrig – als auch metaphorisch: *to be hungry for something* bedeutet *etwas sehr stark wollen*.

Das Zielpublikum

Schenken Sie der Textquelle immer besondere Beachtung. Stammt der Text aus einer Zeitung, Zeitschrift, Enzyklopädie, Anzeige, Umfrage, Rede, einem Roman oder Gedicht? Die Textquelle gibt Ihnen eine ungefähre Vorstellung, wer das Zielpublikum ist. So ist zum Beispiel eine Zeitung eher an erwachsene Leser gerichtet, Anzeigen können sich aber auch mehr an Jugendliche richten. Die Texte können verschiedenen Magazinen entstammen, von eher allgemeinen Nachrichtenmagazinen bis zu solchen, die ein spezielles Publikum haben – etwa Menschen, die sich besonders für die Umwelt interessieren.

Die **Sprachebene** eines Textes kann uns auch Hinweise auf das Zielpublikum geben. So werden ein informeller Ton oder Umgangssprache oft beim Versuch verwendet, junge Leute anzusprechen.

4.2 Sprachstile

Es ist wichtig, den **Stil** zu erkennen, den der Autor im Text benutzt hat.

Hier sind ein paar Beispiele für förmliche, informelle oder neutrale Ausdrücke, die dieselbe Grundbedeutung haben. Versuchen Sie, der Liste weitere Wörter hinzuzufügen, wenn Sie neue Wörter nachschlagen.

formal	neutral	informal
to converse	to talk	to chat
offspring	children	kids
clothing/garments	clothes	gear/kit/clobber
lavatory	toilet	loo
thank you	thanks	ta
goodbye	bye	see you
acceptable	all right	OK
much/many	a lot of/lots of	loads of/tons of
to appear	to seem	to look like

Förmliche Texte verwenden in der Regel keine Zusammenziehungen wie *she's,* sondern eher *she is*.

Beim **informellen Sprachgebrauch** werden oft Abkürzungen verwendet, wie *TV* oder *telly* für *television*; *bike* für *bicycle*.

Hier sind ein paar Beispiele für geschriebene Sprache im Gegensatz zu gesprochener Sprache:

written	spoken
frequently	often
moreover	and
to address someone	to speak to someone
to regret something	to be sorry about something
to consume	to eat/drink
to purchase	to buy
to participate	to take part
therefore	so

Abi-Tipp: Stilsicher

→ Wenn Sie einen Text zu Hause vorbereiten, ist es eine gute Idee, ein einsprachiges Lernwörterbuch oder ein gutes zweisprachiges Wörterbuch zu benutzen, um Wörter nachzuschlagen. Diese Wörterbücher zeigen nämlich an, ob ein Wort eher formal, umgangssprachlich oder Slang ist.

→ Wenn Sie sich neue Wörter aufschreiben, notieren Sie sich auch, ob das Wort eher gehoben oder umgangssprachlich ist, denn dies hilft Ihnen dabei, ein Gefühl für den Ton und Stil eines Textes zu entwickeln.

→ Wenn Sie selbst einen Text in einer Fremdsprache verfassen, ist es am besten, Slang zu vermeiden, außer Sie sind sich absolut sicher, was das Wort bedeutet und in welchem Kontext es gebraucht wird!

Slang ist eine sehr informelle Sprachform, die normalerweise nur im gesprochenen Sprachgebrauch vorkommt. Slang kann aber manchmal auch in Anzeigen oder Boulevardzeitungen *(tabloid newspapers)* vorkommen. Teilweise wird Slang als sehr anstößig empfunden, z. B. die Bezeichnung *birds* für *women*. Ein gutes Wörterbuch wird Ihnen darüber Auskunft geben. Hier sind einige Beispiele für Slangwörter:

neutral	slang
money	dosh/bread/brass/readies
a stupid person	prat/wally/jerk (can be offensive)
drunk	legless/off his head/pissed (can be offensive)
food	grub/nosh

Der Ton eines Textes kann ernst oder humorvoll sein, es ist daher wichtig, darauf zu achten, ob der Autor Stilmittel wie **Ironie**, **Sarkasmus**, **Wortspiele** oder andere verwendet. (Definitionen für gebräuchliche → Stilmittel finden Sie auf Seite 135). Der Stil eines Textes kann sehr unterschiedlich sein. Sehen Sie sich folgende Beispiele genau an:

BEISPIEL: Verschiedene Stile
Förmlicher Schreibstil:

We regret to inform you that we are currently unable to offer you a position in our firm appropriate to your qualifications. However, we will keep your application on file and will contact you should a suitable opening arise.

Informeller Schreibstil:
Dear Mike,
It was great to hear from you! Thanks a million for sending the photos – they're great! Can't wait to see you on the 18th!

Anleitungen:
To start the program, insert the disk into the disk drive and press any key.

Förmlicher Stil (mündlich):
"I have a dream that my four little children will one day live in a nation where they will not be judged by the colour of their skin, but by the content of their character. I have a dream today." (Speech by Martin Luther King, Jr., 1963, Washington, D.C.)

Informeller Stil (mündlich):
"Well, I was just queuing up at the cashpoint the other day when along comes Becky. You'll never believe it, but she's dumped Paul and now she's going out with that prat Tony!"

Literarischer Stil:
"There was music from my neighbour's house through the summer nights. In his blue gardens men and girls came and went like moths among the whisperings and the champagne and the stars." (F. Scott Fitzgerald, The Great Gatsby*)*

Humorvoller Stil:
"Bashfully I dropped my shirt onto the sand and stood naked but for my sagging trunks. Glenn, never having seen anything quite this grotesque and singular on an Australian beach, certainly nothing still alive, snatched up his camera and began excitedly taking close-up shots of my stomach." (Bill Bryson, Down Under*)*

4.3 Stilistische und rhetorische Mittel

Im Folgenden sind stilistische und rhetorische Sprachmittel aufgelistet, die in literarischen, aber auch in Sachtexten Texten oft verwendet werden.

Alliteration *(alliteration)* ist die Bezeichnung für den Gleichklang des Wortanfangs benachbarter Wörter, durch die Wiederholung des ersten Lauts (normalerweise eines Konsonanten) oder einer Lautgruppe. Sie markiert die betonten Silben eines Textes und hebt die Wortbedeutung hervor, besonders wenn man den Text laut vorliest.
→ Beispiel: *a short, sharp shock*

Anapher *(anaphora)* bezeichnet die Wiederholung eines Wortes oder einer Phrase jeweils am Anfang aufeinanderfolgender Sätze oder Teilsätze. Diese Wiederholung dient dazu, die Aufmerksamkeit des Lesers auf dieses Wort oder diese Phrase zu lenken.

Eine **Anekdote** *(anecdote)* ist eine kurze Geschichte über einen interessanten oder lustigen Vorfall. Sie wird oft benutzt, um als Beispiel ein Argument in einer Diskussion zu unterstreichen.

Bei einer **Antithese** *(antithesis)* benutzt ein Autor einander entgegengesetzte oder kontrastierende Wörter, um eine Aussage zu pointieren.
→ Beispiel: *She didn't learn to read and write until she was 25. These skills finally brought her out of the **darkness** of ignorance into the **light** of knowledge.*

Ein **Klischee** *(cliché)* ist eine Phrase, die so oft benutzt wurde, dass die Aussagekraft der ursprünglichen Bedeutung verloren gegangen ist. Klischees werden oft in sehr stilisierten Texten (wie Balladendichtung oder Märchen) verwendet oder auch in ironischer Form, um hervorzuheben, dass etwas nicht originell ist.
→ Beispiel: *He kissed her **rosy-red lips**.*

Die **Klimax** *(climax)* eines Textes ist der wichtigste Punkt, der Höhepunkt. Eine Reihe von Ereignissen innerhalb der Geschichte baut sich zum entscheidenden Moment oder Schlüsselerlebnis *(key incident)* auf, was oft besonders aufregend oder auch schockierend sein kann. Dieser

Moment wird in der Regel durch sprachliche Mittel (Wechsel der Zeit, des Rhythmus etc.) besonders gestaltet. Das Hinführen auf diesen Höhepunkt erzeugt innerhalb der Geschichte eine sich stetig steigernde Spannung.

Als **Konnotation** *(connotation)* bezeichnet man die Vorstellungen oder Emotionen, die durch ein Wort hervorgerufen werden, obwohl sie nicht immer ein Teil der tatsächlichen Wortbedeutung sind. Sie kann benutzt werden, um bestimmte Ideen zu implizieren, ohne dass man sie direkt ausspricht. Wenn man einen älteren Text interpretiert, kann sie uns eine Vorstellung davon geben, welche Assoziationen die Menschen in der Vergangenheit mit Wörtern hatten, die heutzutage nicht mehr relevant sind.

→ Beispiel: *connotations associated with the colour **white** include **purity**, **innocence** and **virginity**.*

Als **Euphemismus** *(euphemism)* bezeichnet man einen „harmlosen" Ausdruck, der ein entsprechendes anderes Wort ersetzt, das tabuisiert ist oder als unhöflich oder Angst erregend gilt.

→ Beispiel: ***to use the little girls'/boys' room*** *instead of* ***to go to the toilet***.

Übertreibung *(exaggeration)* wird benutzt, um etwas als größer, besser oder schlechter darzustellen, als es wirklich ist. Sie wird häufig benutzt, um einen komischen Effekt zu erzeugen oder um etwas zu dramatisieren.

→ Beispiel: *I've told you **a million times** not to exaggerate!*

Tropen/Bildhafte Figuren *(figurative images)* in einem Text zeichnen ein Bild davon, wie etwas ist, benutzen dabei Wörter gerade nicht in ihrer direkten Bedeutung (und üblichem Kontext). Die bildhaften Figuren werden benutzt, um einen Text poetischer zu machen.

→ Beispiel: *The city was covered in a thick **blanket** of snow.*

Eine **Rückblende** *(flashback)* kann es in Romanen, Dramen und Filmen geben. Die Handlung kehrt zu einem Punkt der Geschichte zurück, um vergangene Ereignisse zu zeigen. Die Rückblende wird oft benutzt, um bestimmte Aspekte der Handlung zu erläutern, indem der Hintergrund oder Ausgangspunkt bestimmter Ereignisse gezeigt wird.

Bei einer **Hyperbel** *(hyperbole)* übertreibt ein Autor eine Aussage, um diese hervorzuheben.
→ Beispiel: *She cried **oceans** of tears.*

Bildliche Sprache *(imagery or figures of speech)* benutzt eher symbolische Darstellungen von Ideen als wörtliche. Unter → Metapher *(metaphor)*, → Personifikation *(personification)*, → Vergleich *(simile)* und → Symbol *(symbol)* finden sich Beispiele.

Ironie *(irony)* bezeichnet die Diskrepanz zwischen der Verwendung eines Wortes und dessen tatsächlicher Bedeutung. Sie wird oft benutzt, um witzig zu sein oder Ärger auszudrücken.
→ Beispiel: *A suite in the five-star Palace Hotel can be had for the **bargain** price of only $ 9,000 per night.*

Eine **Metapher** *(metaphor)* ist ein Ausdruck, der eine Person, ein Objekt oder eine Idee mit etwas anderem vergleicht, ohne ein Vergleichswort (z. B. wie) zu benutzen. Dieser übertragene Sinn wird verwendet, um Aussagen lebendiger erscheinen zu lassen.
→ Beispiel: *New York City is **a jungle.***

Onomatopöie *(onomatopoeia)* bezeichnet die Lautmalerei, das heißt, die Wörter sollen klingen wie das, was sie repräsentieren.
→ Beispiel: *a snake **hisses**; the crowd **booed** when the referee disallowed the goal.*

Ein **Oxymoron** *(oxymoron)* ist die Verbindung zweier Worte, die sich anscheinend widersprechen. Dieser Widerspruch zwischen den Worten dient dazu, besondere Aufmerksamkeit auf die Aussage zu lenken.
→ Beispiel: ***loneliness** in a **crowded** room.*

Ein **Paradoxon** *(paradox)* besteht aus zwei Aussagen, die sich scheinbar widersprechen und daher zuerst unmöglich oder lächerlich wirken, bei genauerer Betrachtung aber sehr wohl Sinn ergeben.
→ Beispiel: *The film star lived his private life in the public eye.*

Von **Personifikation** *(personification)* spricht man, wenn Objekten oder abstrakten Ideen Verhaltensmerkmale zugeordnet werden, die man normalerweise mit Menschen verbindet. Wie auch sonst in der Verwendung

von bildlicher Sprache wird die Personifikation dazu benutzt, die Aussage lebendiger erscheinen zu lassen.
→ Beispiel: *The table **groaned** under the weight of all the food and drink.*

Ein **Wortspiel** *(pun)* kann bei einem Wort gemacht werden, das mehr als eine Bedeutung hat oder mit zwei Wörtern, die gleich klingen und/oder gleich geschrieben werden, aber unterschiedliche Bedeutungen haben. Es wird meistens humoristisch verwendet.
→ Beispiel: Die erste Zeile eines Zeitungsartikels lautete: *"Undertakers made a **grave** mistake when they buried a man in the wrong cemetery." A **grave** is the hole in the ground where a dead person can be buried; the adjective **grave** means **serious**.*

Wiederholung *(repetition):* Wenn Worte oder Phrasen innerhalb eines Textes mehrfach wiederholt werden, dient dies dazu, Aufmerksamkeit auf deren Aussage zu lenken.

Sarkasmus *(sarcasm)* ist der Ironie ähnlich, wird aber mit der Intention verwendet, die Gefühle einer anderen Person zu verletzen.
→ Beispiel: *"Well, you certainly made a great job of cooking the dinner", Molly said to Pete when he served burnt potatoes and underdone meat.*

Satire *(satire)* wird benutzt, um Leute oder deren Ideen auf amüsante Weise zu kritisieren. Der Zweck einer Satire ist es, den Leuten zu zeigen, was an einer bestimmten Situation falsch ist.
→ Beispiel: Der Roman *Animal Farm* von George Orwell ist eine politische Satire.

Ein **Vergleich** *(simile)* vergleicht ein Objekt mit einem anderen, um ein lebendiges Bild zu zeichnen, verwendet dabei im Gegensatz zur Metapher aber ein Vergleichswort.
→ Beispiel: *Why are you in such a bad mood? **You're like a bear with a sore head.***

Ein **Symbol** *(symbol)* ist ein bildhaftes Zeichen, das benutzt wird, um eine Eigenschaft oder eine Idee zu repräsentieren. Es wird benutzt, um Texte poetischer zu gestalten; so wurde beispielsweise der *Fuchs* in der Literatur oft als Symbol für Schläue und Gerissenheit genutzt.

Untertreibung *(understatement)* ist das Gegenteil einer Hyperbel, d.h. etwas wird als weniger ernst oder wichtig dargestellt, als es in Wirklichkeit ist. Auch die Untertreibung wird benutzt, um eine Aussage besonders hervorzuheben, oft zu komischen Zwecken.

→ Beispiel: *Sylvia is not a bad swimmer. She won a gold medal at the last Olympic Games.*

> **Stilmittel** — Merke
> - → *alliteration*
> - → *anaphora*
> - → *anecdote*
> - → *antithesis*
> - → *cliché*
> - → *climax*
> - → *connotation*
> - → *euphemism*
> - → *exaggeration*
> - → *figurative images*
> - → *figures of speech*
> - → *flashback*
> - → *hyperbole*
> - → *imagery*
> - → *irony*
> - → *metaphor*
> - → *onomatopoeia*
> - → *oxymoron*
> - → *paradox*
> - → *personification*
> - → *pun*
> - → *repetition*
> - → *sarcasm*
> - → *satire*
> - → *simile*
> - → *symbol*
> - → *understatement*

4.4 Die Analyse literarischer Texte

Grundlegende Termini

Im Folgenden finden Sie einige Definitionen, die bei der Analyse oder Beschreibung literarischer Texte nützlich sind.

Der **Erzähler** *(narrator)* ist die Person, die den Roman oder die Kurzgeschichte erzählt. Der Erzähler darf nicht mit dem Autor verwechselt werden! Auf → Seite 141 wird näher auf die verschiedenen Arten der Erzählperspektive eingegangen.

Die **Geschichte/Handlung** *(plot)* eines Romans, einer Kurzgeschichte, eines Dramas oder Films ist der Handlungsverlauf, die Bezeichnung für die Ereignisse, die stattfinden.

Prosa *(prose)* bezeichnet die Art zu schreiben, die in Texten wie Romanen und Zeitungsartikeln verwendet wird. Der Text ist kontinuierlich und normalerweise in Abschnitte eingeteilt.

Das Gegenteil von Prosa ist die **Versform** *(verse)*, wie sie etwa in der **Lyrik** *(poetry)* verwendet wird.

Die **Protagonisten** *(protagonists)* sind die Hauptpersonen eines Romans, einer Kurzgeschichte oder eines Dramas.

Der **Schauplatz** *(setting)* eines Romans, einer Kurzgeschichte, eines Dramas oder Films ist Ort und Zeit der Handlung. So ist zum Beispiel der Schauplatz der Romane von Jane Austen das England des frühen 19. Jahrhunderts.

> **Merke — Grundlegende Termini**
> - narrator
> - poetry
> - plot
> - prose
> - protagonist
> - setting
> - verse

Die Erzählperspektive *(narrative perspective)*

Wenn man einen Erzähltext analysiert, ist es wichtig, dass man die **Erzählperspektive** identifizieren kann und dass man darüber nachdenkt, was für einen Einfluss sie auf den Leser hat. Man sollte dabei keinesfalls den Fehler begehen, zu denken, dass der Erzähler die gleichen Ansichten und Einstellungen hat wie der Autor: Der Erzähler ist ebenfalls eine fiktionale Figur und ein Teil der Geschichte. Hier sind einige typische Formen von Erzählperspektiven:

Ich-Erzähler *(first-person narrator)*: Eine der handelnden Personen gibt die Geschichte aus ihrer Sicht wieder. Dies kann zur Folge haben, dass die Geschichte aus einem Blickwinkel erzählt wird, der nicht „zuverlässig" ist (man spricht dann von einem ***unreliable narrator***), und dass der Leser zwischen den Zeilen lesen oder die geschilderten Reaktionen anderer Figuren berücksichtigen muss, um sich ein Gesamtbild zu verschaffen.

Personale Erzählperspektive *(third-person narrator)*: Die Geschichte wird in der dritten Person geschildert, meist aus dem Blickwinkel verschiedener Figuren, ohne dass ein Ich-Erzähler die Geschehnisse interpretiert. Durch diese variable Perspektive erfährt der Leser, wie die Figuren die unterschiedlichen Ereignisse der Geschichte erleben.

Auktoriale Erzählperspektive: Hierbei wird unterschieden zwischen

→ **Allwissender Erzähler** *(omniscient narrator)*: Der Erzähler hat eine uneingeschränkte Perspektive *(unlimited point of view)*, das heißt, er hat einen Einblick in alle handelnden Personen und Ereignisse. Dies gibt dem Leser den Eindruck, dass er alles über die Gefühle und Gedanken der Figuren weiß.

→ **Beschränkte Erzählperspektive** *(observer narrator)*: Ein persönlicher Erzähler, der außerhalb der Ereignisse steht, die er beschreibt, schildert die Handlung aus seiner Sicht. Diese ist natürlich eingeschränkt *(limited point of view)*, da sie die Gefühle, Emotionen und Motivationen der handelnden Personen meist nur schlecht oder sogar gar nicht kennt. Der Leser muss daher vorsichtig sein und darf sich nicht ausschließlich auf die Beobachtungen dieses Erzählers verlassen, um zu einem vollen Verständnis der Ereignisse zu gelangen.

Erzählweise *(ways of narrating)*

Es gibt verschiedene Möglichkeiten für einen Erzähler, die Handlung wiederzugeben. Einige typische Beispiele finden sich hier:

Berichtende Erzählweise *(telling)*: Der Erzähler berichtet über die verschiedenen Ereignisse und Figuren, gibt dazu Kommentare ab und erlaubt sich manchmal sogar Interpretationen. Der Leser kann dadurch zum Beispiel etwas über den Charakter einer handelnden Person erfahren oder die Position des Erzählers.

→ Beispiel: *He had changed since his New Haven years. Now he was a sturdy straw-haired man of thirty, with a rather hard mouth and a supercilious manner. Two shining arrogant eyes had established dominance over his face and given him the appearance of always leaning aggressively forward. Not even the effeminate swank of his riding clothes could hide the enormous power of that body – he seemed to fill those glistening boots until he strained the top lacing, and you could see a great pack of muscle shifting when his shoulder moved under his thin coat. It was a body capable of enormous leverage – a cruel body. (F. Scott Fitzgerald,* The Great Gatsby*).*

Szenische Erzählweise *(showing)*: Die Ereignisse werden dem Leser direkt präsentiert, der dadurch den Eindruck hat, dass er ein Zeuge dieser Ereignisse ist. Dies wird normalerweise durch die Wiedergabe von Dialogen erreicht. Der Leser muss daher die Gefühle und Motivationen der Figuren aus dem ableiten, was sie sagen.

→ Beispiel: *The following Wednesday morning, Robyn found herself back in Vic Wilcox's office, rather to her own surprise, and certainly to Wilcox's, to judge from the expression on his face as Shirley ushered her in. "You again?" he said, looking up from his desk.*
Robyn did not advance into the room, but stood just inside the door, stripping off her gloves. "It's Wednesday", she said. "You didn't send a message telling me not to come." "I didn't think you'd have the nerve to show your face in this place again, to tell you the truth." "I'll go away, if you like," said Robyn, with one glove off and one on. "Nothing would please me more." (David Lodge, Nice Work*)*

Innerer Monolog *(interior monologue)*: Es ist dem Leser möglich, direkt die Gedankengänge und Gefühle einer der handelnden Personen zu erleben, so als befände er sich im Kopf der Figur. Der Leser erhält dadurch eine komplett subjektive Sicht der Ereignisse, dies hilft ihm aber oft dabei, die Figur besser zu verstehen.

→ Beispiel: *But for that mark, I'm not sure about it; I don't believe it was made by a nail after all; it's too big, too round, for that. I might get up, but if I got up and looked at it, ten to one I shouldn't be able to say for certain; because once a thing's done, no one ever knows how it happened. Oh! dear me, the mystery of life; the inaccuracy of thought! The ignorance of humanity! To show how very little control of our possessions we have – what an accidental affair this living is after all our civilisation – let me just count over a few of the things lost in one lifetime [...]* (Virginia Woolf, The Mark on the Wall)

Bewusstseinsstrom *(stream of consciousness)*: Dieser reflektiert die sprunghaften Gedankengänge, die Gefühle, Emotionen und Assoziationen, die es im Kopf einer Figur gibt, sowohl die bewussten als auch die unbewussten. Dies wird meistens durch einen → inneren Monolog erreicht, aber einen, der sogar ohne Satzzeichen auskommt, also ein langer Strom von Gedanken ist.

→ Beispiel: *Yes because he never did a thing like that before as ask to get his breakfast in bed a couple of eggs since the City Arms hotel when he used to be pretending to be laid up with a sick voice doing his highness to make himself interesting to that old faggot Mrs Riordan that he thought he had a great leg and she never left us a farthing all for masses for herself and her soul greatest miser ever [...]* (James Joyce, Ulysses)

Charakterisierung *(characterisation)*

Es ist wichtig, dass man sich zu der Art und Weise, wie die Protagonisten eines Textes dargestellt werden, äußern kann.

Hier finden Sie einige Beispiele:

→ **Typisierte Figuren *(flat characters)*** sind meist stereotyp gezeichnet, ihre Darstellung ist sehr einfach und einseitig. Oft wird nur eine einzige Eigenschaft dieser Figur gezeigt, zum Beispiel: Eine Person ist nur komisch, ein „Erzbösewicht" oder ein typischer *"bad guy"*.

- **"Runde" Figuren *(round[ed] characters)*** sind komplexe Figuren mit vielen verschiedenen Eigenschaften. Der Leser erfährt von den unterschiedlichen Aspekten des Charakters der Protagonisten im Laufe der Handlung. Oftmals ist auch eine Entwicklung oder eine Veränderung festzustellen, wenn der Protagonist von den Ereignissen der Geschichte betroffen ist.
- **Äußere Charakterisierung *(external characterisation)*** bedeutet, dass der Leser vom Erzähler oder von anderen Figuren der Geschichte Informationen über die Eigenschaften einer speziellen handelnden Person erhält. Das kann natürlich bedeuten, dass diese Information unzuverlässig oder unvollständig ist und der Leser diese Information noch interpretieren muss, weil die Figur, von der die Information stammt, nur ihre persönliche Meinung ausdrückt.
- **Innere Charakterisierung *(internal characterisation)*** bedeutet, dass der Leser etwas über die Eigenschaften einer speziellen Figur herausfindet, indem er interpretiert, wie die Person handelt oder was sie über sich selbst sagt, z. B. während eines inneren Monologes.

Eigenschaften verschiedener Texte

Wenn man mit unterschiedlichen literarischen Texten arbeitet, ist es wichtig, zu wissen, was deren Hauptmerkmale sind. Im Folgenden finden Sie einen Überblick über die geläufigsten literarischen Textarten.

Ein **Roman** *(novel)* ist ein längeres fiktionales Prosawerk, normalerweise in Form einer langen Geschichte. Er hat normalerweise eine komplexe Handlung, eine größere Anzahl an Figuren und spielt an verschiedenen Orten über einen längeren Zeitraum hinweg. Es gibt verschiedene Unterkategorien des Romans, wie zum Beispiel *romantic, historical, fantasy, science fiction, crime, thriller.*

Eine **Fabel** *(fable)* ist eine kurze Geschichte mit einer Moral. Oftmals sind die handelnden Figuren Tiere. Die Handlungen der Figuren dienen dazu, bestimmte Arten von menschlichem Verhalten zu reflektieren und sollen den Leser zum Nachdenken bringen, damit er etwas aus den dargestellten Ereignissen lernt.

Ein **Märchen** *(fairy tale)* ist eine Geschichte, in der Gutes belohnt und Böses bestraft wird. Viele Märchen sind sehr alte und ursprünglich oft mündlich überlieferte Geschichten wie zum Beispiel: *Snow White and the Seven Dwarves* (Schneewittchen). Sie haben meistens einen typischen Anfang *"Once upon a time…"* und ein typisches Ende *"… and they lived happily ever after."*

Eine **Legende/Sage** *(legend)* ist eine Geschichte, die über Generationen hinweg erzählt wird. Protagonisten sind meistens Heilige, historische Figuren oder Volkshelden, wie Robin Hood oder König Arthur und die Ritter der Tafelrunde. Es ist eine Erzählung über Ereignisse im Leben der Protagonisten, von denen manche auf Tatsachen beruhen (sofern welche bekannt sind), während der Rest passend zur Figur erfunden ist.

Eine **Kurzgeschichte** *(short story)* ist ein kurzes Erzählwerk, das meist unvermittelt in die Handlung einsteigt. Die meisten Kurzgeschichten haben nur eine geringe Anzahl an Figuren und wenige Ereignisse und sind um ein zentrales Motiv geschrieben oder um eine Situation, die typisch für den Protagonisten ist. Im ersten Fall wird die Handlung Stück für Stück entwickelt und gipfelt meist in einer Klimax, im zweiten Fall ist das zentrale Thema ein Porträt des Charakters des Protagonisten. Zwei weitere Varianten sind „Lokalkolorit"-Kurzgeschichten *(local color stories)*, die im Amerika des 19. Jahrhunderts geschrieben wurden und regionale Dialekte und Eigenschaften von Einheimischen darstellen (z.B. Geschichten von Mark Twain) und Geschichten mit einem überraschenden Ende *(surprise ending stories)*, bei denen die Handlung eine nicht vorhergesehene Wendung in letzter Minute nimmt (z.B. einige Kurzgeschichten von Roald Dahl). Andere Kurzgeschichten haben ein offenes Ende *(open ending)*, sodass es dem Leser überlassen bleibt, sich den Ausgang der Geschichte auszumalen.

Ein **Gedicht** *(poem)* ist ein Text, der normalerweise nicht in Prosa, sondern in Versform verfasst ist. Es ist oft in Strophen *(stanzas)* eingeteilt, kurze Abschnitte mit einer festgelegten Anzahl an Verszeilen. Natürlich gibt es eine große Zahl unterschiedlicher Gedichte, sie haben aber alle einige oder alle der folgenden Eigenheiten:

- **Reime** *(rhyme):* Viele Gedichte haben ein bestimmtes Reimschema, das beschreibt, wie sich die Verszeilen miteinander reimen (z. B. aabb; abab).
- **Rhythmus** *(rhythm):* Die meisten Gedichte sollen laut vorgelesen werden und folgen daher einer bestimmten Betonung, dem Metrum *(metre)*, welches das Gedicht rhythmisch fließen lässt. Einige Gedichte sind in **Strophen** *(stanzas)* unterteilt, also Gruppen von (z. B. vier) Verszeilen.
- **Blankvers** *(blank verse):* Dies ist ein reimloser Vers, der besonders gerne von Shakespeare verwendet wurde.
- **Symbolische Sprache** *(symbolic language):* Viele Gedichte benutzen bildliche Sprache, was für den Leser bedeutet, dass er das Gedicht genau interpretieren muss, um herauszufinden, was der Autor sagen will.

Drama *(drama/play)* ist ein Werk, das auf einer Bühne gespielt werden soll. Auch hier gibt es wieder sehr unterschiedliche Formen, aber die meisten Dramen bestehen aus einem oder mehreren Akten *(acts)*, die wiederum in verschiedene Szenen *(scenes)* aufgeteilt sein können. Die meiste Information über die Figuren wird durch Dialoge geliefert. Der Autor *(playwright)* kann zwar im Text *(script)* Zusatzinformationen zu den Figuren und ihren Handlungen in den Bühnenanweisungen *(stage directions)* unterbringen, diese werden aber nicht als Teil der Aufführung gesprochen. Es liegt daher zu einem großen Teil am Regisseur *(director)*, den Text und die Bühnenanweisungen zu interpretieren, um dann zu entscheiden, wie das Stück aufgeführt werden soll. Das ist der Grund, warum es von den gleichen Dramen so viele unterschiedliche Aufführungen gibt. Ein gutes Beispiel dafür sind Interpretationen von Shakespeare-Stücken. Es ist heutzutage eher selten, dass eines von Shakespeares Werken in Kostümen aus der Tudor-Zeit gespielt wird. Stattdessen werden Kostüme und Bühnenbild aus einem anderen Zeitalter gewählt, z. B. könnte eine Produktion von „Macbeth" im Golfkrieg spielen. Dadurch kann der Regisseur den Zuschauern vermitteln, dass die Botschaft des Stückes auch heutzutage noch Relevanz hat.

Analyse literarischer Texte

narrative perspective
- first-person narrator
- unreliable narrator
- third-person narrator
- omniscient narrator
- unlimited point of view
- observer narrator
- limited point of view

ways of narrating
- telling
- showing
- interior monologue
- stream of consciousness

poetry
- rhyme
- rhythm
- blank verse

characterisation
- flat characters
- round(ed) characters
- external characterisation
- internal characterisation

literary genres
- novel
- fable
- fairy tale
- legend
- short story
- poem
- drama/play

4.5 Examples of text analysis

Literary texts

Unten finden Sie Auszüge aus zwei literarischen Texten, danach Fragen zum Text mit Hinweisen, wo bzw. wie die Antworten zu finden sind und anschließend eine Musterantwort. Beachten Sie, dass es wichtig ist, so weit wie möglich die eigenen Worte beim Beantworten der Fragen zu benutzen, um zu zeigen, dass Sie den Text verstanden haben.

PRÜFUNGSBEISPIEL 1: *"About a Boy"*
The novel is about an unlikely friendship that develops between Marcus, a twelve-year-old schoolboy, and Will, a thirty-six-year-old man who, since he has a lot of money, doesn't have to work and simply spends his days having fun. In the extract, Marcus has recently started at a new school.

He got to school early, went to the form room[1], sat down at his desk. He was safe enough there. The kids who had given him a hard time yesterday were probably not the sort to arrive at school first thing; they'd be off somewhere smoking and taking drugs and raping people, he thought darkly. There were a
5 couple of girls in the room, but they ignored him, unless the snort of laughter he heard while he was getting his reading book out had anything to do with him.
What was there to laugh at? Not much, really, unless you were the kind of person who was on permanent lookout for something to laugh at. Unfortunately,
10 that was exactly the kind of person most kids were, in his experience. They patrolled up and down the school corridors like sharks, except that what they were on the lookout for wasn't flesh but the wrong trousers, or the wrong haircut, or the wrong shoes, any or all of which sent them wild with excitement. As he was usually wearing the wrong shoes or the wrong trousers, and his haircut
15 was wrong all the time, every day of the week, he didn't have to do very much to send them all demented.
Marcus knew that he was weird, and he knew that part of the reason he was weird was because his mum was weird. She just didn't get this, any of it. She was always telling him that only shallow people made judgements on the basis
20 of clothes or hair; she didn't want him to watch rubbish television, or listen to rubbish music, or play rubbish computer games (she thought they were all rubbish), which meant that if he wanted to do anything that any of the other kids spent their time doing he had to argue with her for hours. He usually lost, and she was so good at arguing that he felt good about losing. She could explain why
25 listening to Joni Mitchell and Bob Marley (who happened to be her two favourite singers) was much better for him than listening to Snoop Doggy Dogg, and why it was more important to read books than to play on the Gameboy his dad

had given him. If he tried to tell Lee Hartley – the biggest and loudest and nastiest of the kids he'd met yesterday – that he didn't approve of Snoop Doggy Dogg because Snoop Doggy Dogg had a bad attitude to women, Lee Hartley would thump him, or call him something that he didn't want to be called. It wasn't so bad in Cambridge, because there were loads of kids who weren't right for the school, and loads of mums who had made them that way, but in London it was different. The kids were harder and meaner and less understanding, and it seemed to him that if his mum had made him change schools just because she had found a better job, then she should at least have the decency to stop all that let's-talk-about-this stuff.

He was quite happy at home, listening to Joni Mitchell and reading books, but it didn't do him any good at school. It was funny, because most people would probably think the opposite – that reading books at home was bound to help, but it didn't: it made him different, and because he was different he felt uncomfortable, and because he felt uncomfortable he could feel himself floating away from everyone and everything, kids and teachers and lessons.

[1] classroom

from *About a Boy*, Nick Hornby (Victor Gollancz, 1998), copyright © Nick Hornby, 1998

Musteraufgabe: *Explain the narrative perspective of the text.*

Hier wird nach der Erzählperspektive gefragt. Wir wissen, dass es sich um einen Erzähler in der dritten Person handelt, weil *he, she, they* benutzt wird, statt *I*. Der Leser erfährt, wie die Hauptfigur, Marcus, die hier beschriebenen Ereignisse erlebt und beurteilt: Er sieht diese sozusagen durch die Augen von Marcus, was bedeutet, dass es sich um eine begrenzte Ansicht (*limited point of view*) handelt. Weil wir Marcus' Gedankengang klar folgen können, können wir auch von einem inneren Monolog (*interior monologue*) reden und als Beweis dafür ein paar Beispiele seiner informellen, jugendlichen Sprache nennen.

Musterantwort: *The text is told from the point of view of Marcus, a twelve-year-old schoolboy. It is a third-person narrative, and there is a limited point of view here, as the reader sees the events described through Marcus' eyes. In fact, the extract is a kind of interior monologue, as we are clearly able to follow his train of thought. The language is informal and colloquial, e.g. "kids", "weird", "to send them all demented", reflecting the speech of a boy of his age.*

Musterfrage: *Why does Marcus get to school early?*

Als erstes muss man die Stelle im Text finden, in der steht, dass er früh in die Schule geht.

Hinweis: Die Fragen werden normalerweise in der gleichen Reihenfolge gestellt, in der die notwendigen Informationen für die Antworten im Text erscheinen. In der ersten Zeile kann man lesen, dass Marcus früh zur Schule geht, und im Laufe des Absatzes werden die Gründe dafür genannt: dass er sich dort vor den Kindern, die ihm Schwierigkeiten gemacht haben, sicher fühlt.

Musterantwort: *Early in the morning, before school begins, Marcus can be more or less alone in his classroom, and therefore feels safe from the children who have given him "a hard time", as they are unlikely to get to school before they absolutely have to be there. He does not want to draw attention to himself, and by sitting quietly in the almost empty classroom he can avoid most of his fellow pupils.*

Musteraufgabe: *Find a stylistic device in the second paragraph and explain its function.*

Siehe oben die Erklärungen und Beispiele verschiedener → Stilmittel – es ist wahrscheinlich notwendig, einige Beispiele zu lernen. Hier handelt es sich um einen Vergleich (*simile*), was an der Verwendung von „like ..." zu erkennen ist. Die anderen Schüler werden mit Haifischen verglichen, die immer auf der Suche nach Kindern sind, die auf irgendeine Art und Weise anders sind. Es ist auch wichtig, die Wirkung dieses Vergleichs zu erläutern, was in diesem Fall nicht schwierig zu erraten ist: Haifische sind Tiere, vor denen die meisten Menschen Angst haben, also wird der Vergleich benutzt, um Marcus' Angst vor seinen Mitschülern widerzuspiegeln.

Musterantwort: *In the second paragraph there is a simile: "They patrolled up and down the school corridors like sharks". It is used to compare the other children to dangerous animals, who are not, however, on the lookout for something to eat, but for something or someone who is different in some way, because they are wearing the "wrong" clothes or because they do not fit in. This comparison clearly shows how threatened Marcus feels by the other children. For him, walking along the school corridors is like swimming in shark-infested waters: the danger of being "attacked" is always present.*

Musterfrage: *In what ways does Marcus consider himself to be an outsider, and how does he feel about this?*

Bei solchen Fragen kann es hilfreich sein, die relevanten Passagen oder Phrasen im Text zu unterstreichen. In diesem Fall suchen wir nach Informationen zu Marcus' Aussehen und Charakter, Punkte, die er als Beispiele für sein Anderssein erwähnt; es gibt im ganzen Text einige Beispiele. Außerdem müssen wir nach Hinweisen auf seine Gefühle in dieser Situation suchen. Zum ersten Teil finden wir Beispiele zu Marcus' Aussehen (z. B. ab Zeile 14) und Freizeitaktivitäten (z. B. ab Zeile 21), die ihn als Außenseiter kennzeichnen. Ab Zeile 18 können wir lesen, dass Marcus seine Mutter als Teil seines Problems betrachtet. Seine Gefühle in dieser Situation sind leicht zu erraten, aber natürlich ist es notwendig, dafür auch Beweise im Text zu finden: ab Zeile 41 findet man sie.

Musterantwort: *Marcus knows that one reason he is an outsider is because of his appearance. His clothes are usually unfashionable, as is his haircut. Because of this, he is constantly laughed at and teased by the other children at his school. Another reason is that he is not allowed to watch the same television programmes, listen to the same music, or play the same computer games as most other children of his age, which means that he has little in common with them. A third reason is that he enjoys reading books, which most of his classmates do not seem to do. Marcus feels "uncomfortable" because he knows he is different from the other children and cannot relate to them very well. They do not share the same topics of conversation. He feels distanced from the world around him, that he is "floating away from everyone and everything". He is also aware that part of his problem is that his mother is "weird", which reflects on him. She is always able to make him see her point of view, so in some ways he accepts her arguments. However, he knows that this understanding of her attitude towards certain things will not help him deal with the other children at school.*

Musterfrage: ***What impression does the reader get of Marcus' mother?***
Der Absatz, der mit Zeile 17 beginnt, enthält einige Informationen zu Marcus' Mutter. Es ist wichtig zu erwähnen, wie sie ihn behandelt, was ihre Motivation dazu ist und was dies für eine Wirkung auf Marcus hat. Daraus kann sich der Leser ein Bild der Mutter machen. Wie immer ist es wichtig, Beweise im Text für alle Aussagen zu finden.

Musterantwort: *Marcus's mum wants him to be an individual, rather than just do what all the other children do. She does not want him to waste* *his time watching television or playing computer games, but instead to read books. She encourages him to think about the sort of music he listens to and the attitude of the singers. However, we get the impression that, although she wants to help Marcus, she does not really understand the needs of a twelve-year-old. It may be true that only "shallow people" judge others by their appearance, but she does not seem to see that he suffers at school because of this, and that he might be happier if he was more like the others. She is obviously very good at explaining her point of view, as Marcus admits that he does not mind losing arguments with her, but she does not seem to take his point of view into account.*

Musterfrage: *Why is Marcus suffering more at his new school than at the one in Cambridge?*

Diese Frage ist relativ leicht anhand von Fakten im Text zu beantworten. Ab Zeile 32 wird seine alte Schule in Cambridge erwähnt und mit der Schule in London verglichen. In der Musterantwort werden zwei kurze Zitate aus dem Text gegeben, um den Punkt klarer zu machen. Wie aber oben schon erwähnt, sollte man das Benutzen von Zitaten nicht übertreiben!

Musterantwort: *At the school in Cambridge, Marcus did not feel so much like an outsider, as there were lots of other children there who did not really fit in, either, and who also had "weird" mothers. However, in London the other children are very different: they are "harder and meaner and less understanding". In other words, they are less tolerant of the fact that he does not conform, and he suffers a lot more as a consequence.*

PRÜFUNGSBEISPIEL 2: *"Touching the Ground"*

The narrator, Bobo, is from a white family who moved to Africa in the early 1970s. They lived in Zimbabwe, Malawi and Zambia, in times of civil war and racial tension. Bobo has been driving through her parents' tobacco plantation on her motorbike, and has accidentally knocked down a local child. The child's father invites her into their hut.

And this is how I am almost fourteen years old before I am formally invited into the home of a black African to share food. This is not the same as coming *uninvited* into Africans' homes, which I have done many times. As a much younger child, I would often eat with my exasperated nannies at the compound
5 (permanently hungry and always demanding), and I had sometimes gone into the labourers' huts with my mother if she was attending someone too sick to

come to the house for treatment. I had ridden horses and bikes and motorbikes through the compounds of the places we had lived, snatching the flashes of life that were revealed to me before doors were quickly closed, children hidden behind skirts, intimacy swallowed by cloth.

I am aware suddenly of watching my manners, of my filthy, oil-stained, and dust-covered skirt, of my dirty hands. I turn my dirty fingernails into the palms of my hands and duck out of the heat into the soft, dark, old-smoke-smelling hut. I blink for a few moments in the sudden dim light until shapes swim out of the greyness and form into four small stools crouched around a black pot on a ring of stones. The father is pointing to a stool. *"Khalani pansi,"* he says. "Please, sit here."

I sit on the small smoothly worn stool, my knees drawn up above my hips.

The father crouches at the far end of the hut and shouts an order. The mother leans over the fire. She bends at the waist, gracious and limber. Her baby is suckling at an exposed breast. The woman pounds at the pot on the stones where hot *nshima* is bubbling and steaming, letting out burps of hot breath as it cooks. A smaller pot is emitting fiery gasps of greasy fish.

A girl child comes into the hut, tottering under the sloshing weight of the basin of water that she balances on her head. She stops when she sees me and looks likely to drop her burden and run.

The father laughs and points to me.

The girl hesitates. The father encourages.

The girl lowers the basin from her head and holds it in front of me. I see that I am to wash my hands. I rinse my hands in the water, shake the drops at my feet and smile at the little girl, but still she stands there, the muscles in her thin, knobbly arms jumping under the pressure.

"Thank you." I smile again.

The whole family is watching me. *"Zikomo kwambiri,"* I try, smiling in general at everyone, for lack of knowing what else to do. The smell of the food and the heat it is giving off while cooking makes me sweat.

The mother hands me a plate. She spoons food.

"Thanks," I say when the plate is just covered, making a gesture of sufficiency.

Her large spoon hovers between her pot and my plate.

"No, really," I say, "I had a late breakfast."

The mother glances at her husband. He nods, barely, and she lets her spoon drop back into the pot. Carefully she covers the leftover food.

"Isn't anyone else going to eat?"

The father shakes his head. "No, please … Thank you."

The children are watching me hungrily. The toddler has started to cry, weakly, plaintively, like a small goat. The mother absently pats the boy, nurses the baby, rocks and rocks, staring at me. The father swallows. "Eat," he says. He sounds desperate. I sense that it is only through the greatest exertion of will that my spectators don't fall on the food on my plate in a frenzy of hunger.

"It looks delicious."

I make a ball of *nshima* with the fingers of my right hand, the way I had been taught to do as a small child by my nannies. I insert my thumb into the ball, deep enough to make a dent in the dense hot yellow porridge. Onto the dent, as if onto a spoon, I scoop up a mouthful of the fish stew.
55 Almost before my mouth can close around the food, the young girl (who has not left my side) offers me the water and I see that I must wash my hands again. I am conscious of the groaning, sometimes audible hunger pangs that ripple through the hut. The food, which is sharp and oily in my mouth, has been eagerly anticipated by everyone except for me. I know that I am eating part of a
60 meal intended for (I glance up) five bellies.
I have a long meal ahead of me.

Alexandra Fuller, *Don't Let's Go to the Dogs Tonight. An African Childhood*, Picador, 2002

Musterfrage: *What is the narrative perspective of the text and what effect does it have?*
In diesem Text gibt es eindeutig eine Ich-Erzählerin, und diese beschreibt das Ereignis, wie sie es damals erlebte. Aus diesem Grund ist die Erzählweise *showing* (siehe oben). Der Leser hat das Gefühl, das Ereignis mitzuerleben. Hier ist auch die benutzte Zeit erwähnenswert: Obwohl die Geschichte irgendwann in der Vergangenheit spielt, wird sie in der Gegenwart erzählt. Wichtig ist natürlich auch, die Wirkung dieser Tatsache darzustellen: Dass die Verwendung der Gegenwartsform dem Leser die Geschichte viel näher bringt.

Musterantwort: *The story is told as a first-person narrative, as Bobo describes an incident from her childhood. The way of narrating here is "showing" rather than "telling". The narrator tells the story in the present tense, which gives it a sense of immediacy, and helps the reader to imagine that he or she is really experiencing this incident, too.*

Musteraufgabe: *Compare Bobo's feelings on entering this family's hut to her attitude towards going into Africans' homes as a young child.*
Für diese Frage ist es erforderlich, Bobos Einstellung in der Vergangenheit mit der hier beschriebenen Situation zu vergleichen. Der erste Absatz enthält Beispiele für ihre frühere Einstellung. Die Adjektive *exasperated* (Zeile 4) und *demanding* (Zeile 5) sagen viel über das Verhältnis zwischen ihren Kindermädchen und ihr aus: Die Kindermädchen waren wegen Bobos ständigen Forderungen verärgert, während sie, als weißes Mädchen, verlangen kann, mitgenommen zu werden. Es ist unverkennbar, dass sie auch eine Position der Macht genoss, als sie ihre Mutter

begleitete. Ab Zeile 11 wird die aktuelle Situation beschrieben, und der Kontrast ist deutlich zu erkennen: Weil sie jetzt eingeladen wurde, wird ihr plötzlich bewusst, dass sie sich anständig benehmen muss, etwas, das ihr als Kind niemals eingefallen wäre.

Musterantwort: *When she was young, Bobo often forced her African nannies to take her into their homes to get something to eat, although they were reluctant to take her. She also accompanied her mother from time to time to help a sick person. She had always gone into these homes as a member of a ruling class, someone who considered that she had a right to be there, no matter what the owners of the home might have thought. In this situation, however, she is an invited guest, and we can see that she suddenly realises the difference, because she feels that she has to have good manners, and be as neat and clean as if she were visiting people of her own class. She feels the need to show respect.*

Musterfrage: *How, in Bobo's experience, do most Africans react to white people in their compound?*

Es wird nach der allgemeinen Reaktion von Afrikanern auf Weiße gefragt und nicht nach dem speziellen Ereignis, worum es hier hauptsächlich geht. Deshalb beziehen wir uns wieder auf den ersten Absatz, der den Hintergrund zu diesem Ereignis darstellt. Dabei ist aber zu beachten, dass man nicht etwas aus der zweiten Frage wiederholt. Zeilen 9–10 sind hierfür relevant, weil sie die Reaktionen von Leuten beschreiben, die im *compound* leben.

Musterantwort: *Most Africans living in the compounds did not seem to want white people to know anything about their lives, but rather to keep themselves to themselves. Whenever Bobo passed by, they would close their doors and hide their children, protecting their families from the eyes of a white person.*

Musterfrage: *How does this particular family react to Bobo?*

Um diese Frage zu beantworten, sollte man im Text nach Beispielen von Reaktionen einzelner Familienmitglieder suchen. Es gibt drei Personen, den Vater, das Mädchen und die Mutter, deren Reaktionen man hier beschreiben kann. Es wäre auch wichtig, als Zusammenfassung die Gastfreundlichkeit zu betonen, die die Familie Bobo trotz ihres Hungers entgegenbringt.

Musterantwort: *The father of the family is polite and welcoming, and invites Bobo to come in and sit down. Later, he encourages her to eat. The little girl almost seems afraid of her at first, but is encouraged by her father to approach Bobo with the water. It is difficult to judge the mother's reaction to this unexpected dinner guest, but she obeys her husband and serves Bobo food. The family shows her hospitality, although they are obviously hungry and it is therefore not easy for them to share their food.*

Musteraufgabe: *Find two examples of personification in the text and explain their function.*

„Personifikation" bedeutet, dass Tieren oder Gegenständen menschliche Züge verliehen werden. In den Zeilen 22–23 wird das kochende Essen anhand von Personifikationen beschrieben (hier kann man natürlich die relevanten Stellen direkt aus dem Text zitieren). Die Funktion dieses Stilmittels muss auch verdeutlicht werden, was natürlich im Text nicht direkt erwähnt wird. Deshalb ist etwas Interpretation notwendig, wobei in diesem Fall eine Interpretation nicht sehr schwierig ist. Es wird beschrieben, dass das Essen „rülpst" und „keucht": Es scheint fast zu leben, was das Erlebnis noch intensiver erscheinen lässt, aber nachdem diese Körperfunktionen nicht angenehm sind, dient die Personifikation als Darstellung der für die Erzählerin unangenehmen Situation.

Musterantwort: *Personification is used twice in the text when the narrator describes the cooking food. The nshima is said to be "letting out burps of hot breath as it cooks" (Zeile 22), and there are "fiery gasps of greasy fish" (Zeile 23) coming from another pot. The food is described very vividly here, almost as if it is alive. This emphasizes the intensity of the situation for Bobo, and, as 'burps' and 'gasps' are not particularly pleasant bodily functions, the description helps to illustrate the fact that she is not at ease here.*

Musteraufgabe: *Describe Bobo's feelings while having this meal.*

Es ist klar, dass die Erzählerin nicht unbedingt explizit sagt, wie sie sich in dieser Situation fühlt, aber man kann ihre Gefühle aus dem Text heraus rekonstruieren. Um dies zu tun, muss man nach Beispielen ihrer Taten und Reaktionen suchen und ihre Gefühle dabei interpretieren. Man kann Beweise dafür finden, dass sie sich in dieser Situation einerseits geehrt, andererseits aber auch ziemlich unwohl fühlt: Es ist natürlich wichtig, auch hierfür konkrete Beispiele aus dem Text zu nennen.

Musterantwort: *On the one hand, she is aware that it is an honour for her to be invited to have some food with this family, as we can see from the fact that she wishes to be clean and polite. On the other hand, she clearly feels uncomfortable when she realises how hungry the family are and that, out of politeness, she has to eat some of their dinner. This is shown by the fact that she takes the minimum amount of food possible, and that she doesn't want to be the only one who is eating. Her discomfort can be seen in the way in which she describes having to sit in the middle of a hungry family who are watching every mouthful she takes. She has the feeling that it is very hard for them not to eat the food from her plate. Her comment "I have a long meal ahead of me" (Zeile 61) indicates the difficulty of her situation: she has no choice but to go through the long ritual of eating this food, as she does not want to offend her hosts.*

Musterfrage: *Why might the author have entitled this scene "Touching the Ground"?*

Manchmal werden Sie gebeten, den Titel eines Textauszugs zu erklären (→Seite 130). In diesem Fall ist es offensichtlich, dass der Titel nicht viel über den Text aussagt, bevor man ihn gelesen hat. Erst nach aufmerksamem Lesen des Textes kann man eine Interpretation wagen. Bei solchen Fragen gibt es nicht unbedingt nur eine einzige korrekte Antwort, sondern es können verschiedene Interpretationen zutreffen, man muss sie allerdings aus dem Text heraus begründen, wie im folgenden Beispiel.

Musterantwort: *The title might refer to the fact that, for the first time, Bobo is confronted with the reality of everyday life for most Africans. She sees for herself that they are poor and do not have enough to eat, whereas before she either took them for granted (e.g. when she went to the compound with her nannies) or simply did not think about it. The Africans she came across in the compound wanted to have their privacy, and she passed by their homes without ever trying to discover what went on inside. But now, instead of floating past in a world of her own, she comes in contact with (touches) what is underneath (the ground).*

Non-literary texts

Der Text, den Sie analysieren müssen, kann natürlich genauso gut ein Sachtext sein. Unten finden Sie zwei Beispiele dafür, auch diese mit Erläuterungen und Musterantworten.

PRÜFUNGSBEISPIEL 1: *"Rome, AD ... Rome, DC?"*

They came, they saw, they conquered, and now the Americans dominate the world like no nation before. But is the US really the Roman empire of the 21st century?

Tom Wolfe has written that America today is "now the mightiest power on earth, as omnipotent as ... Rome under Julius Caesar."

But is the comparison apt? Are the Americans the new Romans? The most obvious similarity is overwhelming military strength. Rome was the superpower of its day, boasting an army with the best training, biggest budgets and finest equipment the world had ever seen. No-one else came close. The United States is just as dominant – its defence budget will soon be bigger than the military spending of the next nine countries put together, allowing the US to deploy its forces almost anywhere on the planet at lightning speed. Throw in the country's global technological lead, and the US emerges as a power without rival.

But there the similarities only begin. Today's Americans seem to have learnt a lot from the Romans about how imperial business should be done.

Lesson one would be a realisation that it is not enough to have great military strength: the rest of the world must know that strength – and fear it, too. The Romans used the propaganda technique of their time – gladiatorial games in the Colosseum – to show the world how hard they were. Today 24-hour news coverage of US military operations – including video footage of smart bombs scoring direct hits – or Hollywood shoot-'em-ups at the multiplex serve the same function. Both tell the world: this empire is too tough to beat.

The US has learned a second lesson from Rome: realising the centrality of technology. For the Romans, it was those famously straight roads, enabling the empire to move troops or supplies at awesome speeds. It was a perfect example of how one imperial strength tends to feed another: an innovation in engineering, originally designed for military use, went on to boost Rome commercially. Today those highways find their counterpart in the information superhighway: the internet also began as a military tool, and now stands at the heart of American commerce. In the process, it is making English the Latin of its day – a language spoken across the globe.

However, Rome's greatest conquests came not at the end of a spear, but through its power to seduce conquered peoples. As Tacitus observed in Britain, the natives seemed to like togas, baths and central heating – never realising that these were the symbols of their "enslavement". Today the US offers the people of the world a similar cultural package, a cluster of goodies that remain reassuringly uniform wherever you are. Today we have Starbucks, Coca-Cola, McDonald's and Disney, all paid for in the contemporary equivalent of Roman coinage, the global hard currency of the 21st century: the dollar.

There are some large differences between the two empires, of course – starting with self-image. Romans revelled in their status as master of the known world, but few Americans would be as ready to brag of their own imperialism. Indeed, most would deny it. But that may come down to the US's founding myth. For America was established as a rebellion against empire, in the name of freedom and self-government. Raised to see themselves as a rebel nation, they can't quite accept their current role as master.

One last factor that scares Americans from making a parallel between themselves and Rome is that the Roman empire declined and fell. The historians say that this happens to all empires; they all follow a path from beginning to middle to end. Anti-Americans like to believe that an operation in Iraq might be proof that the US is succumbing[1] to the temptation that ate away at Rome: overstretch. But it's also possible that the US is simply moving into what was the second phase of Rome's imperial history, when it grew frustrated with indirect rule through allies and decided to do the job itself. Which is it? Is the US at the end of its imperial journey, or just beginning its most ambitious voyage? Only the historians of the future can tell us that.

[1] to succumb to something: to no longer oppose it, to give in to it

Adapted from: Jonathan Freedland, 18/09/2002, *The Guardian*, © *Guardian*

Musterfrage 1: *Who are the target readers of this text?*

Bei Sachtexten wird man oft nach dem Zielpublikum gefragt (→ Seite 131). Um solche Fragen zu beantworten, ist natürlich ein gewisses Maß an Hintergrundwissen (Landeskunde) notwendig. Vom Ende des Textes wissen wir, dass es sich um einen Artikel aus dem *Guardian* handelt; wenn man weiß, dass dies eine seriöse britische Zeitung ist, kann man ohne Probleme die Zielleserschaft identifizieren.

Musterantwort: *This text is taken from a newspaper article in The Guardian, one of the serious British newspapers. Therefore we can generally say that the target readers are professional people who are used to reading political comments like this and considering several different sides of an issue.*

Musterfrage 2: *Find two stylistic devices and explain why they are used.*

Wie oben schon erwähnt, muss man sich mit den verschiedenen Stilmitteln und ihren Funktionen vertraut machen (→ Seite 135). Es ist hilfreich, beim zweiten Durchlesen des Textes (nachdem man auch alle Fragen durchgelesen hat) Beispiele von Stilmitteln, die einem auffallen, zu unterstreichen, um sie dann leicht wiederzufinden. In diesem Text gibt es beispielsweise in den Zeilen 12 und 51 Stilmittel, deren Verwendung auch relativ leicht zu begründen ist.

Musterantwort: *Line 12: "at lightning speed" is a metaphor. It is used here to express the fact that, because it invests so much money into its army, America is able to send troops all over the world unbelievably quickly.*
Line 51: "the temptation that ate away at Rome" is a personification. Here it is used to say that, piece by piece, the Roman empire got smaller until it disappeared altogether, in the same way, for example, as someone eats a sandwich: bite by bite the sandwich gets smaller until it is gone.

Musteraufgabe 3: *Describe two ways in which, from a military point of view, America is similar to Ancient Rome.*

Dies ist eine rein sachliche, sich auf den Text beziehende Frage, für deren Beantwortung anschauliche Beispiele im Text (ab Zeile 6) genannt werden. Bei solchen Fragen kann man allerdings sehr leicht in Versuchung kommen, Passagen aus dem Text einfach abzuschreiben. Sie werden aber mehr Punkte sammeln, wenn Sie ihre eigenen Worte benutzen. Vergleichen Sie die Musterantwort unten mit dem Originaltext.

Musterantwort: *According to the article, one obvious similarity is that the Americans, like the Romans, have more military power than any of their contemporaries. This is because they also invest a great deal of money in training their armies to make them the best in the world, and back up this training with the latest equipment. Another similarity, which is connected to military strength, is that the USA is aware of the importance of showing this strength to the rest of the world, so that other countries will be afraid of them. The Romans had gladiators who were the best, most fearsome fighters in the world at the time; today the media makes it easy for America to spread its message of military superiority. Every military action in which the US is involved is shown, almost simultaneously, around the world, and everyone can see how powerful they are.*

Musteraufgabe 4: *Explain the significance of technology for these two states.*

Eine weitere sachliche Frage. Die Zeilen 23 bis 31 enthalten einige Informationen, mit deren Hilfe man diese Frage beantworten kann. Achten Sie darauf, dass Sie sich beim Beantworten von sachlichen Fragen auf die

Information im Text beschränken und nicht anfangen, Zusätzliches hineinzuinterpretieren.

Musterantwort: *Both America and Rome discovered that technology originally developed for military use can also be put to commercial use, and that, through this, their position in the world will become even stronger. The Romans built good-quality, straight roads for their armies to march along, which, of course, also increased the opportunities for trade. In the case of America, it was the internet: originally it was only used by the army, and now it is a "street" that has revolutionised the way in which millions of people all around the world do business. This development has greatly benefited the American economy, as well as helping to spread the influence of the US by spreading their language. Two thousand years ago, people throughout the Roman empire spoke Latin; today those who wish to be a part of the modern world have to speak English.*

Musterfrage 5: *What is meant by Rome's "power to seduce conquered peoples"?*

Bei solchen Fragen muss man eine Phrase erklären und eventuell auch interpretieren. Hier ist nicht viel Interpretation nötig, weil die Phrase (Zeile 33) anhand des Textes leicht zu erklären ist. Man muss nur beschreiben, inwiefern die Römer besiegte Nationen „verführten" und wie diese darauf reagierten.

Musterantwort: *According to the text, it was not only Rome's military power which made their empire so successful, but the new technology and goods that they brought with them to the countries that they took over. Soon countries all over the Roman empire were able to enjoy amenities like baths, or central heating in their homes, and usually welcomed the positive changes to everyday life that the Roman occupancy had brought about. After a while, these people forgot that they only had such things because their country had been invaded and conquered by outsiders. This was, of course, another reason why the Roman empire was so successful: after a while, the natives of the conquered countries were actually glad that they were there.*

Musteraufgabe 6: *Explain the phrase "reassuringly uniform".*

Wie bei Frage 5 muss auch hier eine Phrase (Zeile 37) erklärt werden. Hier ist allerdings ein bisschen Interpretation nötig: Das Wort "uniform" ist nicht schwierig zu erläutern; das Wort "reassuringly" muss aber interpretiert werden, das heißt, man muss erklären, dass die Uniformität von amerikanischen Produkten in der Welt hier als etwas Positives dargestellt wird, weil sich die Leute aufgrund dieser Gleichförmigkeit wohlfühlen.

Musterantwort: *The author uses this phrase to talk about the symbols of American predominance that can be seen all over the world today. These American exports, such as fast food restaurants or Coca-Cola, are the same throughout the world, i.e. they are "uniform". However, for many people this is not seen as something negative; on the contrary, the fact that these products are the same everywhere is seen as "reassuring", something that makes people feel at home wherever they go, as they know the product and know what to expect.*

Musterfrage 7: *Why don't the Americans want to compare themselves directly to the Romans?*

Diese Frage kann sowohl mit sachlicher Information aus dem Text als auch durch eine Interpretation beantwortet werden. Wenn Sie die relevante Stelle (ab Zeile 41) dazu lesen, werden Sie eventuell feststellen, dass es ein paar Wörter gibt, die Sie nicht kennen (z.B. *revelled, brag, founding myth*). Hier ist es wichtig, den Gesamtsinn zu betrachten, den man auch entschlüsseln kann, wenn man das eine oder andere dieser Wörter nicht kennt. (→ Kapitel „Vocabulary", Seite 51 für weitere Hinweise dazu). Die meisten Punkte in der Musterantwort basieren auf Aussagen im Text; nur der letzte Satz geht mehr in Richtung Interpretation, dabei handelt es sich um eine logische Schlussfolgerung aus den Angaben des Texts.

Musterantwort: *One reason why the Americans don't like this comparison is that, according to their history, they were the ones who had to fight for freedom against an oppressive ruler, in their case the British. While the Romans were proud of the fact that they ruled the world, the Americans are not quite as comfortable with this image, as it does not really go with the idea of ruling other nations as they themselves were once ruled. Another important factor is that the Roman empire eventually declined, and finally ceased to exist. According to historians, this is something that has happened* *to all empires in the past. Americans do not like the idea that one day their own nation may no longer be powerful and dominant, as it is today.*

Musterfrage 8: *Does the author of the text believe that the American empire is on the decline?*

Für diese Frage müssen wir nach der Meinung des Autors suchen, die am Ende des Textes zu finden ist. Beim Lesen wird klar, dass der Autor nicht genau weiß, ob das „Kaiserreich" USA im Untergang begriffen ist oder nicht. Deshalb ist es notwendig, genau wie es der Autor tut, beide Seiten des Arguments zu erwähnen.

Musterantwort: *The author is not sure whether this is the case or not. History shows that one of the reasons for the fall of the Roman empire was that it went too far: it "overstretched" itself by trying to become too powerful. On the other hand, it is possible that America is just at another stage of its development as an empire and, like Rome, it wants to take more direct control of certain countries over which it has power. The author concludes that we will only know if the end of the American empire has now come at some point in the future: at the moment, it is impossible to say.*

PRÜFUNGSBEISPIEL 2: *Of course all white people are racist*

When the head of the crown prosecution service[1] said he believed almost all British people were racist, he was widely condemned. It was a moment of political correctness gone mad, commentators said. But one thing no-one seems to have paused to consider was the possibility that he was right. In fact, what about this theory: all white people are racist.

I don't mean that this is always intentional. But racism is a combination of prejudice and power. And sadly prejudice is a deeply ingrained human trait.

Globally, white people are the dominant group, and in politics, economics, the media and all aspects of society, this power is used every day. It starts from the top and filters down to white people everywhere.

At the highest level, when President Bush tells Palestinians a different leader must take the place of the man they elected, he's treating them as second-class human beings. When the leaders of western economic powers deny fair trading terms to African countries, they are doing exactly the same. And the images of these pathetic victims help fuel more stereotypes about their "inferior" status.

The actions of those in power create a constant drip[2] of negative images which seep[3] into the national consciousness. Why is it that every time a TV news report mentions unemployment or crime statistics you are almost guaranteed to see a black face? Black and Asian people are seen far less on reports about the health service, for example, where they make up a high proportion of nurses and doctors. Do you question it each time? Has this negative imagery become normalised in your own mind?

Only last week, a train crash in Tanzania which killed 200 people received only a brief mention in the media. What impression does this give about the value of black life?

But the media are not entirely to blame. It is a chicken-and-egg situation in which editors know that their readers care less for non-white lives – they see the evidence in their sales – and so devote less time and effort to covering them. Some "non-racists" like to pretend that racial differences don't exist – they even proudly claim not to notice skin colour. This is nonsense. Claiming to be "colour blind" is as ridiculous as suggesting you wouldn't notice a person's gender. What's important is what you do, not what you see.

It is naive to believe that the long history of racial distortion – which goes back to the days of slavery and colonialism – has not had a lasting effect on the individual subconscious. We receive messages almost from birth, and as children's thought processes develop, they build up a bank of stereotypes. A black man and a white man walking down the street: Which one is the doctor? Which one is good at sport? Which one does drugs?

White people need to accept that they will always make assumptions, however subconscious, which are influenced by a racial society and which help to form their opinions. It would be a lie to deny this. Institutional racism is now an accepted term, but it's not the "institutions" themselves which are racist: it's their staff that continue the overall inequalities with their actions. Before you get rid of personal racism, you have to admit that it exists.

As a black man, I admit that I suffer from prejudices of my own. I cannot be racist, however, because in the global order I do not belong to the dominant group. If I were to mistreat a white person, the weight of this country's white power structure would come down against me. As many black people have found out, this does not work the other way round.

And how could I be racist anyway? I assure you, some of my best friends are white.

[1] crown prosecution service: an independent legal group that decides whether cases brought by the police should go to the courts

[2] drip: to fall in small drops, like water

[3] seep: to move or spread gradually from one place to another

Adapted from: Joseph Harker, 03/07/2002, *The Guardian*, © *Guardian*

Musterfrage 1: *What does the author think are the causes of racism?*

Um diese Frage zu beantworten, muss man natürlich nach einer ersten Äußerung des Autors zum Thema Rassismus suchen. Nachdem, wie oben schon erwähnt, die Fragen meistens in der gleichen Reihenfolge wie die Antworten im Text erscheinen, fängt man am Anfang an und findet schon ab Zeile 6 relevante Informationen dazu. Man kann hier gut Schlüsselwörter aus dem Text zitieren, sollte diese Zitate aber nicht alleine stehen lassen.

Musterantwort: *The author's opinion is that racism is caused by "prejudice" and "power". This means that, on the one hand, white people have a deep, subconscious feeling that they are worth more than people of other races, or that, for example, black people are more likely to commit crimes. As well as this, the fact that white people play the leading role in our society can be seen everywhere you look: from politics (there are very few black politicians) to society in general. This may also make white people think that they are superior.*

Musterfrage 2: *What are some of the different ways in which white people are seen to be "dominant" over other races?*

In der Frage wird direkt aus dem Text zitiert, deswegen ist der logische Anfangspunkt die Zeile, in der das Zitat vorkommt (Zeile 8). Es sollte klar sein, dass Sie zu dieser Frage etwas anderes schreiben müssen als zu Frage 1: Dort wurde nach den Ursachen des Rassismus gefragt, und man konnte erwähnen, dass beispielsweise Weiße oft die Machtpositionen in der Gesellschaft besetzen, z. B. als Politiker. Erst in dieser Frage wird aber nach einem konkreten Beispiel dieser Macht gefragt. Wenn man daher zuerst alle Fragen durchliest, läuft man weniger Gefahr, Informationen wiederholen zu müssen.

Musterantwort: *There are examples of this dominance at all levels of society. One example is western leaders, such as the president of the United States, telling other countries how they should be run. This shows a complete lack of respect for the decisions made by the people of those countries. A further example is the way in which the west treats African countries. They refuse to trade fairly with them, which confirms their position of power, since the Africans are not strong enough to fight back.*

Musterfrage 3: *According to the author, what role do the media play in portraying racist images?*

Um diese Frage zu beantworten, muss man nach konkreten Beispielen für die Rolle der Medien in der Förderung des Rassismus suchen. Die Zeilen 16–25 enthalten einige relevante Informationen. Man sollte erwähnen, wie Schwarze und Weiße in den Medien dargestellt werden und was für eine Wirkung diese Darstellung hat.

Musterantwort: *It seems that the media strengthen the idea that people from ethnic minorities are inferior, because it always seems to show them in a negative light. Black people appear on reports about unemployment or crime, but seldom on reports about, for example, the health service, although there are a lot of black doctors and nurses. Big disasters in African countries are hardly mentioned in the British press, which the author considers to be a sign that the death of black people is not seen as very important in Britain. He thinks that this constant stream of negative images becomes normal after a while, until nobody thinks about it any more.*

Musterfrage 4: *What is meant by "a chicken-and-egg situation" (line 26)?*

Es ist möglich, dass Sie die Redewendung "*Which came first, the chicken or the egg?*" (Was war zuerst da, die Henne oder das Ei?) nicht kennen. Trotzdem ist es aus dem Kontext heraus möglich, die Bedeutung zu erraten, nämlich eine Situation, bei der man nicht genau feststellen kann, was Ursache und was Wirkung ist. Hier handelt es sich um die Tatsache, dass Menschen aus ethnischen Minderheiten weniger in den Medien vorkommen, weil weniger Interesse an ihrem Leben besteht; andererseits wäre ein möglicher Grund für diesen Mangel an Interesse die Tatsache, dass es eben so wenig Information über sie in den Medien gibt.

Musterantwort: *A "chicken-and-egg situation" is one where it is impossible to tell what the cause of a particular situation is and what the effect of this is. It comes from the old saying: "Which came first, the chicken or the egg?" Here it means that the media produce fewer reports about people from ethnic minorities because they believe fewer people are interested in reading such reports. However, if more reports of this kind were written, it is possible that more people would be interested in reading them after all.*

Musterfrage 5: *In the author's view, are white people honest about racism?*

Bei dieser Frage muss man gezielt nach der Meinung des Autors zu diesem Punkt suchen. Die Zeilen 29–38 liefern Beispiele; man kann sich auch zusätzlich auf die Zeilen 39–44 beziehen.

Musterantwort: *The author does not think that many white people are honest enough to admit that racism exists. It is impossible not to notice the colour of another person's skin, and so we are automatically influenced by someone's race. White people cannot help having certain opinions of other races, even if they are not conscious of this, and their behaviour reflects these opinions (for example, the way black people are treated in some institutions). The author believes that you can only stop racism if you first admit that it exists, but that many white people do not want to admit this.*

Musterfrage 6: *What subconscious images of people of different races do we have?*

Das Wort "*images*" wird im Text nicht explizit benutzt, aber der Autor redet von gewissen Einstellungen, die ins Unterbewusstsein gehen (Zeilen 33–38). Hier ist es entscheidend, etwas kulturelles Hintergrundwissen über existierende Stereotypen einzubringen.

Musterantwort: *It is very common to stereotype people according to their race, because of the messages that we get from society. For example, it is typical to think of white people as having a profession, such as a doctor, whereas it is often assumed that black people are naturally good at sport. We are also more likely to associate black people with crimes such as drug-taking.*

Musterfrage 7: *What is the author's viewpoint on being black and being racist?*

Am Ende des Textes (Zeilen 45–51) diskutiert der Autor das Schwarz-Sein und den Rassismus. Die Frage ist sachlich zu beantworten: Man wird lediglich nach der Meinung des Autors gefragt und muss sie nicht selber kommentieren.

Musterantwort: *In his opinion, it is not possible to call black people racist, even if they themselves have certain prejudices, because they do not belong to the group of people who play a leading role in society. This implies that racism can only be expressed by people who have power over those they look down on. He also says that he cannot be racist as he has a lot of white friends. This, however, may be meant ironically, as white people often say that some of their best friends are black as proof that they are not racist.*

> **Checkliste** **4 Textanalyse**
> - Was ist der Hauptinhalt des Textes?
> - Was sagt mir die Überschrift über den Text?
> - Woher stammt der Text und was sagt er mir das über das Zielpublikum?
> - Habe ich auch alle Fuß- und Endnoten gelesen, um nach hilfreichen Zusatzinformationen und Vokabeln zu suchen?
> - Habe ich den Text gründlich gelesen und die Schlüsselwörter markiert?
> - Habe ich alle Fragen sorgfältig gelesen, bevor ich anfange, sie zu beantworten?
> - Nachdem ich die Fragen gelesen habe, habe ich den Text nochmals durchgelesen und nach Inhaltspunkten gesucht, die in den Fragen vorkommen?
> - Habe ich beim zweiten Lesen des Textes Wörter und Phrasen markiert, die für die Fragen relevant sein könnten?
> - Habe ich mir gemerkt, wie viele Punkte jede Frage wert ist, als Orientierung, wie viel ich ungefähr schreiben muss?
> - Habe ich die Fragen – so weit wie möglich – mit meinen eigenen Worten beantwortet, um zu zeigen, dass ich sowohl die Frage als auch den Text wirklich verstanden habe?
> - Habe ich aus dem Text zitiert, um meine Antwort klarer zu machen, ohne aber größere Textmengen ohne Erklärung einfach abzuschreiben?
> - Falls angegeben wurde, mit wie vielen Wörtern eine Frage beantwortet werden soll, habe ich mich ungefähr daran gehalten und mich bemüht, nicht zu wenig aber auch nicht zu viel zu schreiben?
> - Was für eine Art Text liegt vor (Romanauszug, Fabel, Märchen, Kurzgeschichte, Gedicht oder Theaterstück; beim Sachtext vielleicht ein Zeitungsartikel oder Artikel aus einer Fachzeitschrift)?
> - In was für einem Stil ist der Text geschrieben (förmlich, informell, lyrisch, umgangssprachlich usw.)?
> - Was ist die Erzählperspektive des Textes (Ich-Erzähler, personale Erzählperspektive, allwissender Erzähler, beschränkte Erzählperspektive)?
> - Was ist die Erzählweise (berichtend, szenisch, innerer Monolog, Bewusstseinsstrom)?
> - Welche stilistischen Mittel werden im Text benutzt (z. B. Alliteration, Metapher, Personifikation, Vergleich usw.)?

Textproduktion 5

Dieses Kapitel erklärt Ihnen einige Techniken, die man für die Erstellung eines eigenen Textes auf Englisch gut gebrauchen kann. Von einer Anleitung zum Schreiben einer Zusammenfassung über Tipps zum Sammeln und Gliedern von Ideen bis hin zu konkreten Beispielen finden Sie hier vieles, was Ihre eigene Kreativität anspornen kann.

5.1 Wie man eine Zusammenfassung schreibt

Generelle Tipps

Hier finden Sie einige nützliche Hinweise, wie man an die Aufgabe herangeht, eine Zusammenfassung zu schreiben.

Lesen Sie den Text sorgfältig durch. Vergewissern Sie sich dabei, dass Sie wirklich verstehen, worum es in dem Text geht.

Entscheiden Sie, was die Hauptaussagen des Autors sind. Auf diese müssen Sie sich dann konzentrieren.

Lesen Sie den Text noch einmal durch und versuchen Sie diesmal zu entscheiden, welche Teile der Information für die Kernbotschaft des Textes überflüssig sind. Sie können diese Teile durchstreichen oder in Klammern setzen.

Notieren Sie die Hauptaussagen des Textes auf einem gesonderten Blatt Papier.

Schreiben Sie eine Zusammenfassung dieser Hauptaussagen. Verwenden Sie dabei möglichst immer Ihre eigenen Worte. Es ist nicht Ziel einer Zusammenfassung, einfach Wörter und Phrasen aus dem Originaltext zu kompilieren (aneinanderzureihen), sondern zu zeigen, dass Sie verstanden haben, was der Autor sagen will.

Benutzen Sie verschiedene Satzverknüpfungen, um einen schönen fließenden Text zu erstellen und nicht nur eine Auflistung der einzelnen Punkte.

Unnütze Information erkennen

Sehen Sie sich den folgenden Text über London an: Die unterstrichenen Teile beinhalten Zusatzinformationen, die für die Hauptaussage nicht notwendig sind.

BEISPIEL: unnütze Informationen erkennen

It is impossible to be bored in London. <u>Samuel Johnson once said "When a man is tired of London, he is tired of life", and this statement is just as true today as it was nearly 300 hundred years ago, when Johnson made it. It goes without saying</u> that London is a completely different place in the 21st century than it was the 18th, but it still has something for everyone.

One thing that some people find it hard to get used to is the size of the city, and how crowded it is. Over 7 million people live there, <u>which is about 12% of the total population of Britain.</u> The population of London has a diverse ethnic mix, <u>with about 8% Asians, 7% black people from the Caribbean and Africa, and many others, too.</u> There are some parts of the city which are dominated by ethnic minorities, <u>such as Brixton in south London which has a large number of black residents.</u>

However, just because London is big, it doesn't mean it is difficult to get around. The underground system alone – always called the 'tube' by locals – is (<u>usually</u>) fast and efficient. <u>It should be pointed out, though,</u> that the system can be confusing at first to those who are unfamiliar with it. <u>I remember once being stopped by a Japanese tourist who was trying to get to Highgate on the Northern Line, but had not realised that the Northern Line branches off at Camden Town and that she should have taken a High Barnet train instead of one going to Edgware. It took me a good five minutes (and a lot of pointing at a large tube map on the wall) to explain her mistake to her.</u>

<u>As I was saying,</u> the tube system can be complicated: some of its larger stations, <u>for example King's Cross,</u> are extremely confusing, <u>like a labyrinth,</u> but, due to the huge amount of traffic <u>above ground,</u> it's still the fastest way to get around. <u>Having said this,</u> the mayor of London, <u>Boris Johnson,</u> is doing his best to improve the situation by the introduction of the controversial 'congestion charge'. This is a fee that motorists have to pay to drive into part of central London, <u>and a high one at that</u>: £5. <u>Although there have been a lot of protests from drivers about this charge,</u> it has been welcomed by environmental organisations, and does, <u>in fact</u>, seem to be effective in reducing the number of cars <u>in the city centre.</u>

What are the actual points that the writer has made?

1st paragraph:	London could never be boring as there is so much to do there.
2nd paragraph:	London has a large population, including many people from ethnic minorities.
3rd paragraph:	it is easy to get around London using the tube once you know how the system works.
4th paragraph:	there is too much traffic in London, but a new charge has been introduced to reduce it.

Wir können an diesem Beispiel sehen, welche verschiedenen Arten von Zusatzinformationen es geben kann:

- → **Zitate**
- → **Füllphrasen** wie *it goes without saying*
- → **Statistiken**
- → **Beispiele**, die ein Argument veranschaulichen
- → **Anekdoten,** z.B. die Geschichte mit den japanischen Touristen. Diese Anekdote macht den Gesamttext interessanter. Für die Zusammenfassung ist die Geschichte aber irrelevant.
- → **Wiederholungen**, z.B. Sätze, die mit Phrasen wie *as I was saying* anfangen. Weitere Beispiele für Wiederholungen in dem Text oben sind *Although there have been a lot of protests from drivers ...*, weil der Autor schon vorher erwähnte, dass die Gebühr umstritten (*controversial*) ist, sowie die letzte Erwähnung von *in the city centre*, weil wir schon wissen, dass der Autor über Fahrzeuge in der Londoner Innenstadt und nicht an einem anderen Ort spricht.
- → **Stilmittel**, z.B. Vergleiche *(like a labyrinth)*
- → **Namen von Personen** können auch unerheblich sein. So ist es im vorliegenden Text nicht nötig, den Namen des Londoner Bürgermeisters zu kennen, um die Kernaussage zu verstehen.

Sprache

Wenn Sie eine Zusammenfassung schreiben, gibt es eine Reihe von Satzverknüpfungen, die Sie nutzen sollten, um bloß parataktische Satzschlüsse zu vermeiden.

> **Merke** **Sinnvolle Satzverknüpfungen**
>
> | **Zusatzinformation** | **Ursache** | **logische Reihenfolge** |
> |---|---|---|
> | → moreover | → as | → first |
> | → furthermore | → since | → firstly |
> | → in addition to | → because | → first of all |
> | → likewise | → due to | → next |
> | → apart from | → to generate | → secondly, thirdly … |
> | → besides | → to provoke | → finally |
> | → as well as | → leads to | → lastly |
> | **Gegensätzliches** | **Ergebnis** | → in conclusion |
> | → although | → as a result | → to conclude |
> | → even though | → as a consequence | → in summary |
> | → despite | → consequently | → to sum up |
> | → in spite of | → the outcome was | |
> | → however | → to result in | |
> | → nevertheless | | |
> | → on the one hand | | |
> | → on the other hand | | |
> | → having said that | | |

Zusatzinformation geben

→ She has a very successful career as a professional tennis player. **Moreover/Furthermore**, she makes a great deal of money from advertising.

→ **In addition to** reducing your calorie intake, it is recommended that you take regular exercise if you want to lose weight.

→ The majority of households today have a personal computer. **Likewise**, more people have Internet access than ever before.

→ **Apart from/Besides** being the best at maths in his class, Jake is also a very talented musician.

→ The hotel, **as well as** being overpriced, was extremely dirty.

Gegensätzliche Ideen ausdrücken

- **Although/Even though** there were protests throughout the world, the war could not be stopped.
- The unemployment rate continued to rise, **despite/in spite of** the government's new policy.
- A lot of Britons are in favour of joining the European single currency. **However**, many others strongly oppose the idea.
- You can learn a lot from reading newspapers. **Nevertheless**, you shouldn't believe everything you read.
- **On the one hand**, professional sports people earn far too much money. **On the other hand**, in most cases their career is over by the age of 35.
- E-mail is a great way of keeping in touch with friends and family. **Having said that**, it is extremely annoying to receive several spam mails every day.

Die Ursache für etwas nennen

- Many small shops have been forced to close **as/since/because** more and more people now prefer to drive to big out-of-town shopping centres.
- Airlines have been experiencing a loss in sales in recent months **due to** fears of terrorist attacks.
- The rise in taxes **generated/provoked** nationwide protest.
- The new applications procedure has **led to** a great deal of confusion: no-one really understands it.

Ein Ergebnis festhalten

- The minister was involved in a financial scandal. **As a result/As a consequence/Consequently**, he was forced to resign.
- The **outcome** of the meeting with the trade union leaders was that the strike was called off.
- The petition **resulted** in an improvement in conditions for zoo animals.

Text in eine logische Reihenfolge bringen

→ **First/Firstly/First of all**, it is important to mention …
→ **Next**, I would like to point out that …
→ **Secondly/Thirdly**, there were several problems with …
→ **Finally/Lastly**, we have to take into consideration that …
→ **In conclusion/To conclude**, the whole project has been a great success.
→ **In summary/To sum up**, we cannot expect changes to happen overnight, but it seems that the long-term prospects are good.

Writing a summary: example

PRÜFUNGSBEISPIEL: **Does America still need the death penalty?**

The US doesn't need to torture people; we don't need to kill people in order to be safe and to punish them. I think life in prison without the possibility of parole is a harsher punishment. I think if I were a prisoner, I would prefer death. However, the death penalty issue is also a question of what's best for society, not whether a prisoner is comfortable with going to prison or whether a few people feel that a person deserves to be killed.

Here in Florida, where I live, one of the major newspapers did a study and showed that we would save a minimum of $51 million a year by abolishing the death penalty and going for life without parole instead. If that happened, I believe the money should be taken and put into prevention programs to stop more people from becoming victims.

Politicians often say the death penalty is a commodity for the victims. Every time there's an execution, the politicians say, "We're doing this for the victim's family members." Well, if that's true, what are they saying to all the victims' families where there isn't an execution? "Your loved one isn't valuable enough." I don't think that's a fair system.

Furthermore, when you look at the people who get executed and compare them to people who get life in prison without the possibility of parole, you really can't tell the difference in terms of their crimes. The people who are executed are not necessarily those who commit the worst crimes, but rather they're the ones who have the worst lawyers, or the ones who kill a white person, or the ones who are poor and can't afford a better lawyer. Sometimes it matters whether it's an election year. In many states, you have judges running for re-election and they have to appear to be tough on crime, or their challengers will say, "That judge didn't sentence that guy to death. I would have – and I will if I'm re-elected." Often this becomes a political issue rather than a question of the appropriate punishment.

I consider the Supreme Court's decision not to execute the mentally retarded is a good one. I think a similar decision will be made soon regarding juvenile offenders. Another issue that is likely to come up concerns wrongful conviction. We're letting several people off death row each year who have been wrongfully convicted and have spent years in prison.

Abraham Bonowitz, quoted in *Spotlight Magazine*, November 2002

Musteraufgabe:

Write a summary of the arguments put forward in the text above

(approx. 150 words)

Musterantwort:

The author of this text gives several reasons why he is against the death penalty.

Firstly, there would be a huge reduction in costs if the death penalty were abolished, which could be used for crime-prevention programs instead. Moreover, since not all criminals are executed, it does not make sense to say that executions are intended to help the victims' families.

Besides this, the system is not the same for everyone. People are not necessarily executed because of their actual crime, but, for example, because they cannot afford a good lawyer.

Politics can also play a role: judges must be seen to take a hard line if they want to be re-elected.

The author approves of the decision to stop executing mentally retarded people. Finally, he points out that mistakes are often made and, as a consequence, many people are sentenced to death for crimes they did not commit.

(149 words)

5.2 Wie man einen Aufsatz schreibt

In diesem Kapitel finden Sie nützliche Hinweise, wie man an die Aufgabe herangeht, einen Aufsatz zu schreiben.

Ideen sammeln

Vielen Leuten fällt es schwer, mit dem Schreiben zu beginnen. Das ist auch in der Literatur gelegentlich Thema: Der Schriftsteller mit dem leeren Blatt Papier vor sich. Diese Scheu vor dem Beginn ist natürlich besonders bei einer Prüfung von Nachteil. Im Folgenden finden sich einige Vorschläge, wie man viele Ideen zu einem Thema entwickeln kann, besonders wenn die Zeit knapp ist. Man muss hierbei anmerken, dass es nicht die eine richtige Methode gibt – es handelt sich um einen individuellen Prozess, und jeder muss die Methode wählen, die ihm am besten liegt.

> **Merke** **Ideen sammeln**
> → *mind maps*
> → *fast writing*
> → *wh*-Fragen
> → *pros and cons*
> → Erinnerungen

Mindmaps: Benutzen Sie diese, um so viele Ideen zu einem Thema zu entwickeln wie möglich. Diese Gedanken müssen noch nicht organisiert sein, alle Einfälle sind in diesem Stadium akzeptabel. Vergessen Sie beim Zusammentragen einer Mindmap nicht, über Ihre persönliche Einstellung zum Thema nachzudenken, sowie über die Punkte, die Sie selbst damit assoziieren. Versuchen Sie, schon an spezielle Beispiele zu denken, wie in diesem Fall: Was bedeutet Ihnen eine Großstadt, was gefällt oder missfällt Ihnen daran?

BEISPIEL: Mindmap zum Thema „Großstädte"

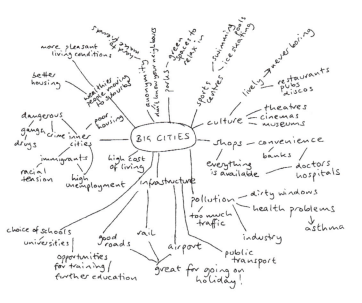

Fast writing: Ein ähnlicher Prozess wie das Erstellen einer Mindmap. Man schreibt einfach so schnell wie möglich alles auf, was einem zu dem speziellen Thema einfällt. Am einfachsten ist es, eine Liste mit den Einfällen anzulegen.

‚wh-"Fragen: Schreiben Sie sich die Fragen zum Thema auf, die mit *when, where, what, who, why, which, how* (nicht immer sind alle Fragewörter angemessen) anfangen, und versuchen Sie, diese zu beantworten. Dies gibt Ihnen reichhaltiges Material für den Aufsatz.

BEISPIEL: wh-Fragen stellen

Beispielaufgabe: *Explain what is meant by the "electronic church" in the USA and give your opinion of this phenomenon.*

- → Why is it called the "electronic church"?
- → What are its main features?
- → Where can it be found?
- → Who runs it?
- → What kind of people worship there?
- → How popular is it?
- → Why is this form of worship used?
- → What points of criticism exist about it?
- → What do I think about it? Why?

Vor- und Nachteile (*pros and cons*): Wenn Sie eine Erörterung schreiben, in der Sie die Vor- und Nachteile eines Themas diskutieren sollen, ist es bei der Ideensammlung sehr hilfreich, eine Liste mit zwei Spalten zu erstellen, in der man einfach alle Vor- und Nachteile zusammenträgt und einander gegenüberstellt.

BEISPIEL: Pro und contra

Frage: *"Should school uniforms be introduced in Germany?"*

pros
- → everyone is dressed the same = equality
- → differences in family income are less obvious
- → don't have to worry about what to wear
- → good to have different clothes to wear in free time
- → sense of school identity
- → can save money if 'free time' clothes are not worn out so quickly
- → helps to concentrate on reason you are at school: to learn, not to be fashionable
- → many young people wear the same kinds of clothes anyway: it's already a kind of uniform

cons
- → loss of individuality
- → it is not nice to be told what you must wear
- → feels like you are in the army or police force
- → some uniforms are unattractive
- → can be impractical to wear, e.g. skirts in winter
- → uniforms can be expensive to buy
- → what you wear makes no difference to the way you behave
- → it is bad enough if you have to wear a suit when you start work: young people should be able to enjoy their freedom while they can

Beispiele, um eine These zu veranschaulichen: Erinnern Sie sich an persönliche Erfahrungen; Ereignisse, die Bekannte von Ihnen miterlebten; Geschichten aus der Zeitung; was Sie über das Thema schon früher gelesen haben; wie die verschiedenen Medien (Zeitschriften, Fernsehen, Radio) mit dem Thema umgehen. Diese Einfälle werden Ihren Aufsatz lebendiger und damit interessanter machen, denn Sie können anschauliche Beispiele einfügen, anstatt sich nur generell über das Thema zu äußern.

Organisieren Sie Ihre Einfälle

Der zweite Schritt einer jeden Schreibaufgabe sollte die logische Gliederung der Einfälle sein, die man im ersten Schritt gesammelt hat. Eine Mindmap zu erstellen, ist nicht das gleiche wie eine Gliederung zu schreiben! Es ist wirklich wichtig, dass man sich die Zeit nimmt, seine Ideen so zu arrangieren, dass die Gesamtargumentation Sinn ergibt und der Leser dem Gedankengang folgen kann.

Auswählen und aussortieren: Lesen Sie sich noch einmal die Überschrift durch und sehen Sie sich anschließend sorgfältig Ihre Ideensammlung an. Denken Sie daran, dass es Ihre Aufgabe ist, eine begrenzte Anzahl Wörter zu diesem Thema zu schreiben. Es wird Ihnen daher nicht möglich sein, all Ihre Ideen einzubringen.

Welche Ihrer Einfälle sind für das Thema besonders relevant/am interessantesten/veranschaulichen am besten Ihre Argumentation? Unterstreichen Sie diese oder markieren Sie sie mit einem farbigen Stift. Streichen Sie alles durch, was Sie verwerfen. Alternativ können Sie Ihre besten Einfälle noch einmal auf einem separaten Blatt zusammentragen.

Planen Sie Ihre Abschnitte! Sie sind der Schlüssel für eine gelungene Aufsatzorganisation. Die generelle Gliederung eines Aufsatzes sollte folgende Punkte enthalten:

→ **Einleitung** (Was ist das Thema?/Was ist Ihre Meinung zu dem Thema?)
→ **Hauptteil** (Argumente dafür und dagegen/Veranschaulichung Ihrer Meinung durch Beispiele)
→ **Schluss** (Zusammenfassung).

Innerhalb dieser Einteilung sollten Ihre einzelnen Ideen jeweils in eigenen Absätzen stehen.

Sobald Sie sich entschieden haben, was die generelle argumentative Richtung der jeweiligen Abschnitte ist, überlegen Sie sich, welche Ihrer Ideen Erwähnung finden sollten und sortieren Sie diese in eine logische Abfolge. Ihre Argumentation im Aufsatz sollte folgendermaßen aussehen: ⟶ und nicht so: ⤳

Beispielhafte Aufsatzgliederungen

GLIEDERUNGSBEISPIEL 1: Pro-/Contra-Erörterung

Ihr Aufsatz hat das Thema: *No-one nowadays would live in a large city like London or New York by choice. Discuss.*

Sehen Sie sich jetzt die Mindmap über Großstädte auf → Seite 177 an und überlegen Sie sich, welche Ideen so relevant sind, dass man sie übernehmen sollte.

Hier eine mögliche Gliederung für dieses Thema:

1. intro:
don't think this is true → although there are disadvantages to living in a large city, there are also many plus points

2.1 disadvantages of city life:
high cost of living; anonymous → hard to make friends; pollution → unhealthy place to live

2.2 advantages of city life:
everything available → e.g. shops.
Example: different things you can buy; entertainment → never boring. Example: things to do in the evening
infrastructure → flexibility; mobility.
Example: young people not dependent on parents to drive them everywhere

3. conclusion:
can understand why some people don't like cities, but there are still plenty of reasons why people would choose to live there.

Es ist in diesem Stadium nicht wichtig, in ganzen Sätzen zu schreiben. Sie schreiben die argumentative Gliederung, nicht den Aufsatz selbst.

Organisation:

Nützlich ist folgendes Schema:
Wenn man gegen das Thema argumentiert (wie in diesem Fall): Einleitung → Pro-Argumente → Contra-Argumente → Zusammenfassung
Wenn man für das Thema argumentiert: → Einleitung → Contra-Argumente → Pro-Argumente → Zusammenfassung

Der Grund, diese Reihenfolge zu wählen, ist, dass Leser bei einer Erörterung meistens diejenigen Argumente am besten in Erinnerung behalten, die sie zuletzt gelesen haben. Das gilt besonders dann, wenn diese Argumente noch einmal in der Zusammenfassung erwähnt werden. Deshalb ist es geschickt, die Punkte, mit denen man nicht übereinstimmt, an den Anfang zu stellen. Damit zeigt man, dass man die andere Seite der Argumentation kennt, und kann anschließend diese Punkte durch seine eigenen starken Argumente entkräften, um den vertretenen Standpunkt zu stützen.

GLIEDERUNGSBEISPIEL 2: Beschreibende Aufsätze

In einigen Aufsätzen muss man ein Thema nicht diskutieren, sondern etwas beschreiben und anschließend seine persönliche Meinung zu diesem Thema äußern. Diese Themen haben oft etwas mit Landeskunde zu tun. Das bedeutet natürlich, dass man entsprechendes Hintergrundwissen über Großbritannien oder die Vereinigten Staaten benötigt, um die Frage beantworten zu können. Von → Seite 177 nehmen wir folgendes Beispiel:

Explain what is meant by the "electronic church" in the USA and give your opinion of this phenomenon.

Ideensammlung
Für diese Art Aufsatz ist zur Ideensammlung, wie wir gesehen haben, die Methode der „wh-Fragen" gut geeignet (→ Seite 178).

Gliederung

1. intro:
brief definition → 'electronic church' = use of media, e.g. TV and radio by fundamentalist churches to spread their message

2. explanation:
definition of fundamentalism;
location → normally southern states of US;
purpose → to spread the Christian message as defined by them;
popularity → millions watch the TV shows

3. points of criticism:
scandals involving TV evangelists, e.g. misuse of money donated by worshippers; criticism of fundamentalism in general → political power and implications of this

4. conclusion:
my opinion → in principal there's nothing wrong with spreading a religious message in this way, but it isn't so good if the influence becomes too strong.

> **Abi-Tipp: Strukturierte Aufsätze**
>
> → Schreiben Sie nicht sofort los, auch wenn die Zeit knapp ist. Planung ist nie Zeitverschwendung.
>
> → Beachten Sie die Schritte zur Ideensammlung und der Planung des Aufsatzes, die oben aufgeführt sind.
>
> → Schreiben Sie einen ersten Entwurf Ihres Aufsatzes.
>
> → Falls Ihnen während des Schreibens einfällt, dass Sie einen wichtigen Punkt vergessen haben, schreiben Sie ihn nicht einfach in den nächsten Satz, sondern schreiben Sie ihn z. B. an den Fuß der Seite und markieren mit einem Stern (*) die Stelle, wo dieser Satz eingefügt werden soll. Beim Verfassen der Schlussversion kann dieser Extrasatz an der richtigen Stelle eingefügt werden.
>
> → Wenn möglich (z. B. bei Hausaufsätzen) sollten Sie die Rohfassung Ihres Aufsatzes für einen oder zwei Tage zur Seite legen, um ihn dann mit neuer Aufmerksamkeit noch einmal zu lesen. Dabei ist es oft hilfreich, den Aufsatz laut vorzulesen. Gehen Sie sicher, dass das, was Sie zu Papier gebracht haben, auch sinnvoll ist und dass all Ihre Argumente in einer logischen Reihenfolge stehen.

GLIEDERUNGSBEISPIEL 3: Einfache Erörterung

In einigen Fällen wird es Ihre Aufgabe sein, nur eine Seite einer Frage zu erörtern und nicht sowohl Vor- als auch Nachteile darzustellen. Es folgt ein weiteres Beispiel zu dem sich eine Stoffsammlung auf → Seite 178 findet, hier aber als einfache Erörterung und nicht als Pro/Contra.

Aufgabenstellung: School uniforms are a good idea and should be introduced into German schools. Say whether you agree with this statement.

1. intro:

German schools don't have uniforms
→ most pupils wouldn't want them
→ I personally wouldn't mind
→ other countries have school uniforms – no lasting damage is done.

2. practical reasons:
costs → fewer clothes needed; less pressure on poorer families;

3. effect on pupils:

everyone is the same; focus on reason for being at school
→ *learning; not judging by appearance*

4. conclusion:
uniforms are helpful for creating an identity and a sense of equality
→ *pupils should only be judged on academic ability*

Auch hier gilt, dass die Argumente, die gegen Ende des Aufsatzes vorgebracht werden, wahrscheinlich besser im Gedächtnis des Lesers haften bleiben. Achten Sie daher bei der Planung des Aufsatzes darauf, dass diejenigen Argumente am Ende stehen, von denen Sie denken, dass es die schlagkräftigsten sind – die Argumente, die den Leser überzeugen werden, mit Ihrer Sicht übereinzustimmen.

Verwirrung vermeiden

Verworrenes Schreiben bedeutet nicht-organisiertes Schreiben. Ihr Aufsatz sollte nicht chaotisch von einem Einfall zum nächsten springen oder ein Argument wieder aufnehmen, das man schon einmal gebracht hat. Dies führt nur dazu, dass Ihr Aufsatz schlecht zu lesen ist und der Leser verwirrt wird.

Diese Art des nicht organisierten Schreibens ist das Ergebnis einer schlechten Planung – oder überhaupt keiner Planung! Sehen Sie sich das folgende Beispiel eines verworrenen Aufsatzes genau an.

EIN NEGATIV-BEISPIEL ...
Die Autorin versuchte folgende Frage zu beantworten: *In what ways has the world been shaped by the USA in the last 100 years?*

Wherever you go in the world you will see, to a greater or lesser extent, the influence of the United States. This starts with the fact that there are hardly any countries in the world today that do not have at least a couple of McDonald's. American culture is everywhere, from clothes and music to computer games, and while young people in particular do not mind this, others are worried about the loss of traditional cultures in a wave of 'Americanisation'.	**Kommentare:** Allgemein: es gibt keine Absätze, alle Ideen fließen ungeordnet zusammen.

This certainly helped to shape western Europe, making it a wealthy, capitalist society. <u>As I mentioned before</u>, some people do not like this, but Germany, for example, could never have recovered from the war so quickly without the help of the US.<u>(Some terrorist organisations, such as Al-Qaida, take their dislike one step further, and attempt to destroy the 'American way of life' with their campaigns of terror.)</u> <u>Incidentally</u>, America also radically improved the 'Old World' through its inventions. A large percentage of the appliances and gadgets that we take for granted today – fridges, lifts, electric lights – were invented or developed in the USA, and gradually spread to the rest of the world. Therefore America has contributed a great deal to making our lives easier. <u>Another point is that</u> the USA have taken upon themselves the role of the 'world's police', which has caused a great deal of protest and resentment in some countries. Many people in Iraq, for example, do not believe that the Americans understand the problems they face, because their set of values is so different, and think that the US has no right to tell others how to run their country. <u>Anyway</u>, there are a lot of McDonald's restaurants around the world. Their popularity has led to changes in the way people eat: far too many people nowadays eat fast food instead of cooking a meal from scratch and sitting down to enjoy it with their family. As Americans eat so much fast food, a significant percentage of them are seriously overweight, and this trend is spreading to the rest of the world, too.

Phrasen wie *as I mentioned before* zeigen, dass jetzt zu einem früheren Argument Zusatzinformationen kommen. Es ist besser, alle zusammengehörenden Argumente/Informationen auch zusammen aufzuführen.

Offensichtlich ist auch der in Klammern eingefügte Satz ein zusätzlicher Gedanke. Er ist zwar insgesamt für das Thema relevant, passt aber nicht wirklich an diese Stelle. Durch die Verwendung der Klammern zeigt uns die Autorin auch, dass ihr bewusst ist, dass dieser Punkt nicht wirklich zum vorherigen Satz passt.

Incidentally wird hier benutzt, um eine Zusatzinformation einzuführen, die nicht wirklich etwas mit dem Argument zu tun hat, das die Autorin gerade formieren will. Es ist offensichtlich, dass ihr diese Information gerade eingefallen ist und sie diese anbringen will, ob sie passt oder nicht.

Mit der Phrase *Another point is that ...* zeigt die Autorin, dass sie ein neues Argument beginnt. Warum macht sie in diesem Fall nicht auch einen Absatz?

Das Wort *anyway* zeigt, dass die Autorin zu einem früheren Argument zurückkehrt. Wenn sie aber wirklich noch mehr zu diesem Argument zu sagen hat, hätte sie dies an der früheren Stelle tun sollen und nicht jetzt.

... UND WIE ES BESSER GEHT:

Die Autorin hätte ihre Ideen folgendermaßen ordnen können:

1. introduction: the world has been shaped by the USA in several different ways, both positive and negative.
2. history: Europe after World War Two → help from US
3. inventions: useful items for the rest of the world
4. "Americanisation" of culture: clothing; changing eating habits → influence of McDonald's
5. US as "world police": interference in other countries → in some cases this has resulted in terrorist attacks
6. conclusion

Die Autorin muss sich auch über den Inhalt ihres Aufsatzes Gedanken machen. Sie hat eine große Anzahl Ideen in den Aufsatz eingebracht, aber nur wenige Beispiele, um ihre Argumente zu veranschaulichen. Gerade bei solch einem relativ kurzen Text wäre es besser, die Anzahl ihrer verschiedenen Punkte zu reduzieren und statt dessen lebhafte Beispiele einzufügen, um die Argumentation zu verdeutlichen.

Nicht vom Thema abweichen

Wenn man einen Aufsatz schreibt, besteht immer die Gefahr, dass man zu allgemein bleibt und einfach den gleichen Punkt auf verschiedene Art wiederholt, anstatt passende Beispiele für das Argument zu bringen. Autoren solcher Aufsätze erwecken immer den Eindruck, dass sie nichts zu sagen haben, sondern nur Zeilen füllen wollen.

Hier einige Tipps, wie man beim Thema bleibt:

Schreiben Sie eine klare Einleitung

Die Einleitung dient den Lesern als Orientierungshilfe. Sie wollen den Text einordnen können und wissen, worum es geht. Dementsprechend sollte die Einleitung möglichst knapp gehalten werden und noch keine Details enthalten.

Stellen Sie sich vor, Ihre Leser wüssten nichts über das Thema. Wie können Sie sichergehen, dass sie verstehen, wovon Sie sprechen?

BEISPIEL: Kommen Sie auf den Punkt!
In my opinion, the attitude of the British is very short-sighted, because Britain does most of its business with the rest of Europe. It is therefore vital for their future that they reconsider this question.

Der Autor dieser Einleitung lässt seine Leser im Unklaren darüber, worüber er eigentlich schreibt. Alles, was sie erfahren, ist, dass es etwas mit Großbritannien und Europa zu tun hat. Es bleibt aber im Dunkeln, was Großbritanniens Einstellung zu was ist, warum das schädlich ist und welche Frage die Briten neu beantworten sollten.

There has been a lot of heated discussion in the past few years about whether Britain should join the single European currency or not. Although some British think they should, most argue that the British economy is strong enough as it is and would be weakened if they had the Euro. In my opinion, this attitude is very short-sighted, because Britain does most of its business with the rest of Europe. The British government recently decided not to vote on joining the Euro for at least another year. It seems to me, however, that it is vital for the future of Britain that they reconsider this question.

Die Einleitung wurde überarbeitet. Jetzt wird absolut klar, worüber der Autor schreibt, da er seinen Lesern alle notwendigen Hintergrundinformationen gibt.

Schreiben Sie einen sauberen Schluss

Hören Sie nicht einfach zu schreiben auf, wenn Sie nichts mehr zu sagen haben oder wenn Sie die verlangte Wortzahl erreicht haben. Ein paar abschließende Sätze sind unbedingt notwendig, um einen Aufsatz abzurunden. Das Ende sollte kurz die Gesamtargumentation des Aufsatzes zusammenfassen und Ihre Meinung zu diesem Thema verdeutlichen. Das Ende sollte keine neue Gedanken oder Argumente enthalten.

Vermeiden Sie „Einkaufslisten"

Verdeutlichen Sie Ihr Argument lieber mit einem Beispiel als mit einer ausführlichen Liste.

BEISPIEL: Aufzählung ist langweilig!
Personally, I like living in a big city because there are lots of different shops, banks, restaurants, pubs, museums, art galleries, and sports centres.

Dies ist ein Beispiel für eine typische ‚Einkaufsliste' von Dingen, die es in einer Großstadt gibt. Offensichtlich ist dies nicht sonderlich interessant. Der

folgende Textausschnitt ist ein viel gelungeneres Beispiel für den inhaltlich gleichen Punkt:
Personally, one of the reasons I like living in a big city is that I'm a real shopaholic, and I love having a wide choice of places to shop. No matter what I want to buy: handmade candles, a mattress, or tropical fish, I know I'll find it somewhere.
In diesem Fall hat sich die Autorin auf nur einen speziellen Grund, warum sie gerne in einer Großstadt lebt, konzentriert und dafür eine detaillierte Erklärung gegeben.

Drücken Sie Ihre Meinung aus

Zeigen Sie Ihrem Leser, was Sie über das Thema denken, anstatt nur Allgemeinplätze zusammenzufassen. Stellen Sie sich vor, Sie müssten den Leser überzeugen, Ihrer Meinung zuzustimmen. Schreiben Sie, was sie von dem Thema halten und warum. Im Folgenden finden Sie Tipps, wie man auf Englisch seine Meinung ausdrücken kann.

Eine Meinung äußern – nützliche Begriffe

- → *In my opinion*, smoking should be banned from all public places.
- → *From my point of view*, parents must take more responsibility for the amount of television their children watch.
- → *In my view*, it is not the job of the United States to act as the world's police, whatever they themselves may believe.
- → *As far as I'm concerned*, computer games are no more harmful than any other free-time activities.
- → *I (personally) feel/believe* that more should be done to help refugees.
- → *As I see it,* the relationships between the countries of the European Union will grow stronger in the future, despite the disagreements that occur from time to time.
- → *I completely agree* that all children should have to learn at least one foreign language.
- → *I have to say that I am also in favour* of providing language courses for immigrants.
- → *I agree up to a point* with the statement that smoking should be banned from public places, but I think the ban should be limited to places like restaurants.
- → *I don't really agree* that the USA is still a dream destination for immigrants.

- Many people are *opposed to* the idea of introducing identity cards in Britain.
- She *completely disagrees* with the idea that religion should be taught in schools.
- It is a *controversial issue* whether abortion should be legal or not.
- Many people *hold the view* that there should be a speed limit for the German „Autobahn".

Beispielaufsätze

Sie sollten jetzt genügend Informationen haben, um gut lesbare Aufsätze zu verfassen. Um Sie noch ein wenig zu inspirieren, finden Sie im Folgenden einige Beispielaufsätze. Die Vorbereitung für diese Aufsätze finden Sie in den vorigen Abschnitten.

Musteraufgabe: *No-one nowadays would live in a large city like London or New York by choice. Discuss.*

Musterlösung: Der Autor hat beschlossen, dem Thema nicht zuzustimmen. Natürlich ist es auch möglich, die genau entgegengesetzte Meinung zu vertreten.

It is clear that not everyone likes big cities. They are dirty, overcrowded, and some areas can be dangerous, too. However, I do not think it is true to say that no-one would live there by choice. There are plenty of people – and I am one of them – for whom the advantages of big cities outweigh the disadvantages.

Obviously, one cannot deny that there is a downside to city life. For one thing, the cost of living tends to be higher than elsewhere, which makes things difficult for low-income families. After all, there is little point in living in a place where everything is available if you cannot afford to buy any of it.

Then there is the anonymity. Most people there tend to keep themselves to themselves, and anyone who is new to the city will often find it difficult to meet people and make friends.

In addition to this, there are people who argue that the quality of life in a city is not particularly good. My grandparents, who grew up in the heart of the countryside, are always talking about the fact that there are few green spaces, the air is polluted, and people are far more likely to suffer from illnesses such as asthma. The hectic pace of city life, they believe, is extremely unhealthy, and should be avoided at all costs.

In my view, however, big cities still have a great deal going for them. One of the biggest advantages of living in a large city, as I see it, is that the residents have everything they need close at hand, everything from airports to zoos. It does not matter whether you are looking for a rare kind of exotic Indian spice, a designer wedding dress or a beautiful plant to match your new garden furniture – in a city like London or New York you are sure to find it. In fact, large cities are perfect for anyone who loves variety. Just consider how much there is to do in the evenings. Personally, the first thing I do when visiting London is buy an events guide, so that I can decide whether to go and see that new play, try out an Egyptian restaurant or take part in a guided night-time walking tour of London's spookiest streets.

Furthermore, as someone who grew up in a small village in the middle of nowhere, I personally feel that one cannot underestimate the flexibility and mobility that result from the good infrastructure and public transport in cities. Before I was old enough to drive, when I went out at the weekends I either had to return in the early evening on the last bus, or rely on my parents to pick me up. The evening was always dictated by how I was to get home again. Friends of mine who grew up in a city, on the other hand, were able to go home when they chose to do so, because the public transport ran late and was reliable. They had the sort of independence that I didn't experience until I was well over eighteen.

In conclusion I have to say that, of course, it is a matter of personal preference. There will always be people who dislike big cities and avoid them at all costs, but there are also plenty of others who would choose to live there. As I have tried to show, city life is certainly not all bad.

Musteraufgabe: *Explain what is meant by the "electronic church" in the USA and give your opinion of this phenomenon.*

Musterlösung: *In the USA, the term "electronic church" refers to the way in which fundamentalist churches use the media, especially television* *and radio, to spread their evangelical message. Often also referred to as "TV evangelism", it is a method of preaching that has become increasingly widespread in the past few decades, as, of course, it is an easy way to reach a large audience.*

First of all, it is necessary to explain what is meant by "fundamentalism". This is the name given to the most conservative, right-wing, and politically influential branch of what can be broadly called the "evangelical" churches, which, among other things, insist on a traditional, and in some cases very literal, interpretation of the Bible. The largest number of followers of the fundamentalist movement can be found in the southern states of America, such as Alabama.

One obvious advantage of the "electronic church" is that it can be used to reach a wide audience – and it is successful in achieving this aim. Not only do large numbers of people attend prayer meetings to hear the well-known TV evangelists preach, but many millions more tune in when these meetings are broadcast. As a consequence, this has proved to be an extremely effective way of spreading both the word of God and the fundamentalist interpretation of this. This interpretation includes a strong emphasis on family values, and being against certain "evils" of society such as abortion, sex outside marriage and homosexuality, attitudes which have many supporters.

On the other hand, it should be pointed out that TV evangelism certainly has its critics. One reason for this is a number of scandals that have occurred in the past involving, for example, TV evangelists who have stolen money donated to their ministries and used it for their own purposes. In addition to this, there are people who are critical of the fundamentalism movement, for example its campaigns to prevent the teaching of evolution in schools as a scientific fact, and therefore dislike any methods which are used to spread this message further.

In my opinion, in general there is nothing wrong with using the media to spread a religious message: after all, if someone objects to this, they can switch off their television. However, I get the impression that the "electronic church" is being used not only for religious purposes but also, at a more subtle level, to spread a political message about certain values which this particular group wishes to promote. In my view, there is a lot of intolerance contained in this message, and I do not think it should be so easy to spread it through television, a medium which, one would hope, should be neutral in a free country.

Musteraufgabe: School uniforms are a good idea and should be introduced into German schools. Say whether you agree with this statement.

Musterlösung: *It would be difficult to find more than a few German pupils who would welcome the idea of having a school uniform. However, I have to admit that I would be part of this minority: having thought a lot about it, I actually rather like the idea of wearing a uniform. Despite protests about loss of individuality – something that doesn't seem to have happened in any of the countries that do have uniforms, by the way – I believe that there is a lot to be said for them.*

To begin with, I would like to consider one or two practical factors. Clothes nowadays are not cheap, especially if you want to keep up with the latest fashions. That's why having a school uniform saves money, because it means that there is less need for a large amount of different things to wear. It's helpful for families with lower incomes, too, as the children do not have to nag their parents so often for more and more new clothes in order not to feel left out at school.

I also believe that wearing a uniform has a positive effect on pupils in other ways. Since everyone is dressed the same, a sense of identity is created. Physical or financial differences between different pupils become less obvious, and so there is less focus on judging people by what they look like, and more on considering what they can do. After all, the reason why children attend school is to learn things, not to display their fashion sense to their peers. There is plenty of opportunity to do this outside of school, if that is what they want.

To sum up, wearing a uniform is certainly not harmful in any way. On the contrary, it creates a sense of equality within a school and means that pupils are judged on one thing alone: their ability to do well academically.

Musteraufgabe: *The unlimited possibilities of the Internet: a blessing or a curse?*

Musterlösung: *Although the Internet has not existed for very long, today we take it completely for granted and cannot really imagine what life would be like without it. It is used by young and old, rich and poor, and there is hardly a single corner of the globe where it is not available. Above all, it really is possible to find information on any topic that you care to mention – if you look hard enough. It therefore seems safe to say that there is no limit to the possibilities of the Internet. Whether this is a good or a bad thing is, of course, another question.*

Nowadays, looking something up or checking information on the Internet is completely normal. On the whole, this makes life a lot easier. For example, you no longer need to go to the library to do research for a school project. Instead, you can find all the information you need in one of the free online encyclopaedias or other useful websites, and download it in the comfort of your own home. In addition to this, it is now extremely common to book your holiday on the Internet. You can search for locations, read reviews of the various hotels in the region, book your flight and even check whether you need any vaccinations to visit the country in question. Then there are the social networking sites, allowing you to keep up to date with friends, share photos and films, and make new contacts: such sites are ideal for people whose friends and family live a long way away.

However, the easy availability of just about everything online also has its negative side. There are sites run by Neo-Nazis, terrorist networks and extremists of all kinds, many of which are used to spread messages of hatred to a wider audience. Moreover, it is very difficult to censor undesirable websites: in some cases they can be closed down by the Internet provider, but others will quickly take their place. Since real censorship of the Internet is almost impossible, we have to accept that the more unpleasant aspects will continue to exist.

An additional point to consider is that some people find the possibilities of the Internet so fascinating that they become addicted to it, surfing for several hours a day and cutting off other social contacts in order to do so. This problem often affects young people, who become addicted to chatting online and end up spending more time in front of the computer than talking to their friends face to face. Furthermore, there is a hidden danger in this: because the Internet allows its users to be anonymous, people often do not really know who they are chatting to, and could therefore be putting themselves in danger without even realising it, especially if, as sometimes happens, they agree to meet up with someone that they only know from a chat room.

The conclusions that we can draw from all this are fairly obvious. In many ways the Internet is a blessing. It makes life easier by giving us access to an incredible amount of information, and it seems safe to say that the majority of people that use it regularly would not want to be without it. There are, however, certain dangers that cannot be ignored, and that can only be controlled to a certain extent, e.g. by parents limiting the amount of time their children spend online. Nevertheless, it is impossible to remove all of these dangers, and this is one aspect of the Internet that many people see as a curse. In my opinion, though, the Internet has more good aspects than bad ones, and I am glad to be able to take advantage of them.

Kontrolle

Sobald Sie mit Ihrem Aufsatz fertig sind, ist es natürlich sinnvoll, Ihre Arbeit noch einmal zu überprüfen. Selbst unter Zeitdruck, wenn es sich z. B. um eine Prüfungssituation handelt, ist es empfehlenswert, sich hierfür am Ende wenigstens fünf Minuten zu reservieren.

Wenn es sich um einen Hausaufsatz handelt, hilft es sehr, wie schon oben erwähnt, ihn ein oder zwei Tage liegen zu lassen und ihn dann noch einmal durchzulesen. Man sieht ihn dann noch einmal distanzierter, und man wird oft Fehler entdecken oder Sätze, die wenig sinnvoll sind und die man das erste Mal überlesen hat.

Beim Korrekturlesen Ihres Aufsatzes können Sie die Checkliste nutzen, die auf Seite 194 abgedruckt ist. Haken Sie die einzelnen Fragen ruhig ab, damit Sie sichergehen können, dass Sie nichts vergessen haben.

Abi-Tipp: Timing ist alles!

Es ist nicht einfach, unter Zeitdruck, zum Beispiel während einer Prüfung, einen guten Aufsatz zu produzieren. Mit Ideen sammeln, planen, schreiben und überprüfen hat man als Prüfling mehr als genug zu tun.
Sie haben in diesem Kapitel schon viele Tipps bekommen, wie Sie einen Text vorbereiten und schreiben können. Es lohnt sich zudem, sich wie in der Prüfung eine bestimmte Zeit zu geben, um einen Testaufsatz zu schreiben. Mit etwas Übung erkennen Sie, wie viel Zeit Sie für welchen Arbeitsschritt einkalkulieren müssen, um einen guten Text innerhalb der zur Verfügung stehenden Zeit zu schreiben.

Checkliste 5 Textproduktion

- → Habe ich die Frage beantwortet?
- → Ist mein Aufsatz in Abschnitte gegliedert?
- → Habe ich eine Einleitung und einen Schluss (Zusammenfassung)?
- → Habe ich meine Gedanken in einer logischen Reihenfolge geordnet?
- → Habe ich meinen Gedankengang mit Beispielen veranschaulicht?
- → Habe ich eine angemessene Sprache verwendet (z. B. Satzverknüpfungen; sprachliche Wendungen, um meine Meinung/Zustimmung/Ablehnung auszudrücken)?
- → Habe ich mich an die Wortzahl gehalten, falls eine angegeben ist? (Bei zu wenig Wörtern sieht es aus, als ob mir nichts eingefallen sei; bei zu vielen sieht es aus, als ob ich nicht auf den Punkt kommen kann.)
- → Ist die Grammatik so weit wie möglich korrekt? Habe ich auf mögliche „Fallen" geachtet und versucht, sie zu vermeiden?
- → Ist meine Rechtschreibung korrekt? Wenn ich den Text als Hausaufgabe auf dem Computer geschrieben habe, habe ich die englische Rechtschreibprüfung benutzt?
- → Wenn der Aufsatz Hausaufgabe war, habe ich ihn laut gelesen, um zu hören, ob er „englisch" klingt und ob mir irgendwelche Fehler auffallen?

Übersetzung

In diesem Kapitel können Sie nachlesen, wie man eine Übersetzung am besten angeht. Es werden unterschiedliche Methoden gezeigt, je nachdem, ob die Übersetzung zu Hause oder in einer Prüfungssituation stattfindet. Außerdem wird gezeigt, wie man typische Übersetzungsfehler vermeiden kann. Das Kapitel endet mit Schritt für Schritt erklärten Übersetzungsbeispielen.

6.1 Wie man an eine Übersetzung herangeht

Generelle Tipps

Hier finden Sie einige generell nützliche Tipps, wie man an eine Übersetzung herangeht.

Lesen Sie den ganzen Text mindestens **einmal komplett** durch, um einen Eindruck davon zu bekommen, wovon er handelt.

Denken Sie über den Stil des Textes nach: Ist die Sprache förmlich, gehoben, neutral oder handelt es sich um Umgangssprache? Dies hilft Ihnen später zu entscheiden, welche Wörter/welche sprachliche Ebene Sie wählen sollten.

Gehen Sie noch einmal den Text durch und **unterstreichen Sie** dabei **alle Worte, bei deren Bedeutung Sie sich nicht sicher sind.**

Vergessen Sie dabei nicht, nachzusehen, ob **am Ende des Textes eventuell Übersetzungen** von einigen Wörtern angegeben sind.

Versuchen Sie die **Schlüsselwörter** eines Textes zu **identifizieren** (mehr dazu gleich). Wenn Sie nicht sicher sind, was diese bedeuten, versuchen Sie ihre Bedeutung aus dem Kontext heraus zu erkennen (→ Seite 51).

Schreiben Sie die übersetzte Version des Textes. Wenn Sie den Text übersetzt haben, lesen Sie Ihre Übersetzung noch einmal sorgfältig durch, um sicherzugehen, dass er verständlich ist. Wenn es Teile gibt, die sich seltsam anhören, gehen Sie noch einmal zum Originaltext – es ist gut möglich, dass Sie etwas falsch übersetzt haben.

Wenn die Übersetzung eine Hausarbeit ist

Benutzen Sie ein gutes Wörterbuch und prüfen Sie, ob Sie die richtige Übersetzung gewählt haben! Denken Sie daran, dass viele Wörter mehr als nur eine Bedeutung haben. Wenn Sie ein Wort nachschlagen, nehmen Sie nicht einfach das erste Wort, das vorgeschlagen wird. Stattdessen lesen Sie alle Vorschläge durch und überlegen Sie sich, welches am Besten passt. Tipps zum richtigen Gebrauch eines Wörterbuchs finden Sie im →Kapitel „Vocabulary", Seite 49.

Seien Sie bei idiomatischen Redewendungen vorsichtig – manche können Wort für Wort übersetzt werden, oft ist das aber nicht der Fall. Hier ein Beispiel: Die Redewendung *„to give something/someone the green light"* kann wörtlich ins Deutsche übersetzt werden: „etwas/jemandem grünes Licht geben". Andererseits würde man bei der englischen Redewendung *„six of one and half a dozen of the other"* auf Deutsch „Jacke wie Hose" sagen. Darauf würde man nicht unbedingt kommen. Dies bedeutet, dass Sie, um sicher zu gehen, Redewendungen immer nachschlagen sollten, obwohl dies natürlich auch zeitaufwendiger ist. Nur wenn Sie sich wirklich sicher sind, die betreffende Redewendung zu kennen, können Sie auf das Nachschlagen verzichten. Siehe →Kapitel „Vocabulary", ab Seite 46. Dort finden Sie einige häufigen Redewendungen.

Denken Sie daran, dass Ihnen sogenannte *False Friends* unterkommen können. Versuchen Sie, die häufigsten dieser „gemeinen" *False Friends* zu lernen (einige typische Beispiele finden Sie im →Kapitel „Grammar", ab Seite 82).

Lassen Sie immer eine Zeile frei, damit es später leichter ist, noch etwas zu verändern.

Nach dem Verfassen der **Rohübersetzung** lassen Sie diese am besten eine Weile liegen (z.B. über Nacht), und gehen Sie sie dann später noch einmal sorgfältig durch. Es kann einen großen Unterschied machen, wenn man den Text noch einmal mit etwas Distanz betrachtet.

Es kann hilfreich sein, den **Text laut vorzulesen**. Oft hört man dadurch Fehler heraus, die einem sonst nicht unbedingt auffallen würden. Achten Sie auch darauf, ob Ihre Version wortwörtlich in die andere Sprache zurückübersetzt werden könnte. Ist dies der Fall, haben Sie wahrscheinlich viel zu „wörtlich" übersetzt und Sie müssen Ihren Text nochmal genau unter die Lupe nehmen.

> **Abi-Tipp: Gesamtsinn wiedergeben**
>
> Denken Sie daran, dass es bei einer Übersetzung nicht darum geht, den Text Wort für Wort von der einen Sprache in die andere zu übertragen, sondern darum, in der zweiten Sprache einen Text zu schaffen, der die **gleiche Bedeutung** wie das Original hat. Deshalb besteht auch kein Grund zur Panik, wenn man nicht jedes einzelne Wort im Text versteht.
>
> Überlegen Sie stattdessen, was der Sinn des Gesamtsatzes ist, und versuchen Sie dann, diese Grundbedeutung in korrektem Deutsch wiederzugeben.

Wenn die Übersetzung während einer Prüfung gemacht wird

Fangen Sie nicht gleich zu schreiben an: Es ist wirklich wichtig, dass Sie den ganzen Text durchlesen, ehe Sie mit der Übersetzung beginnen. Dadurch werden Sie zum einen den Text als Ganzes verstehen und zum anderen erklärt sich die Bedeutung von unbekannten Wörtern oft, wenn man weiß, wovon der Gesamttext handelt.

Benutzen Sie die Techniken aus dem →Kapitel „Vocabulary", ab Seite 46, um die **Bedeutung von unbekannten Wörtern** zu erschließen.

Wenn Sie ein Wort verstehen, Ihnen aber die passende Übersetzung nicht einfällt, versuchen Sie für dieses Wort ein **Synonym** zu finden, oder den betreffenden **Satz zu paraphrasieren**. Ihr Hauptziel ist es, Ihren Lesern die **Botschaft** des Autors zu vermitteln.

Kalkulieren Sie am Ende der Prüfung immer etwas Zeit ein, um Ihre Übersetzung zu überprüfen. Man findet immer kleine Fehler, die man vorher übersehen hat.

> **Merke — Für eine gute Übersetzung**
>
> **Allgemein:**
> → den Text komplett durchlesen
> → den Stil des Textes feststellen
> → alle unklaren Wörter/Textstellen anstreichen
> → Nachsehen, ob am Ende des Textes Wörter bereits übersetzt sind.
> → Identifizieren der Schlüsselwörter
>
> **Bei der Prüfung:**
> → immer zuerst den Text komplett lesen!
> → immer eine Zeile für Korrekturen frei lassen
> → Techniken benutzen, um unbekannte Wörter zu erschließen
> → Synonyme und Paraphrasieren helfen weiter bei Vokabellücken
> → Zeit für die Überprüfung einkalkulieren!

Natürlich hat man in einer Prüfung nicht viel Zeit, um Abstand zur eigenen Übersetzung zu gewinnen, wie oben vorgeschlagen. **Es ist aber möglich, die Übersetzungsaufgabe am Anfang der Prüfung zu erledigen.** Sie können dann am Ende der Prüfung darauf zurückkommen und sie auf Fehler überprüfen. So haben Sie die Möglichkeit, Ihren Text zumindest mit einigermaßen „frischen Augen" nochmals durchzulesen.

6.2 Einige typische Übersetzungsprobleme

Dieser Abschnitt soll Ihnen helfen, einige der typischen Problemfelder beim Übersetzen vom Englischen ins Deutsche zu erkennen.

Satzstrukturen

Im Folgenden finden Sie einige Regeln für englische Satzstrukturen, die vom Deutschen abweichen können.

Adverbien in der Satzmitte

→ Adverbien wie *always, usually, normally, often, sometimes, occasionally, seldom, rarely, never, ever, also, probably, definitely, already* etc. stehen normalerweise vor dem Verb, wenn es im Satz nur ein einziges Verb gibt:
  - *We **often** go skiing in winter.*
  - *Jack **probably** missed the bus.*
→ Folgende Wörter stehen im Normalfall hinter dem Verb *to be*:
  - *Tony is **seldom** on time for class.*
  - *I was **already** at home when Tom arrived.*
→ Sollte das Verb aus mehr als einem Wort bestehen, also aus Hilfs- und Vollverb (z. B. *should go, didn't buy, has been eaten*), steht das Adverb hinter dem Hilfsverb:
  - *You should **definitely** go to that new disco.*
  - *I have **never** been to South America.*
→ Vorsicht: *definitely, probably, certainly, obviously* stehen vor der Negation.
  - *Julie **definitely** won't come to the party.*
  - *I **certainly** didn't believe a word he said.*

Verb und Objekt

→ Im Englischen stehen das Verb und sein Objekt normalerweise zusammen:
  - *You **will find the scissors** in the top drawer.*
  - *She **loves Paris** more than any other city.*

→ Übersetzungsbeispiel:
- *When you turn the corner you'll see **a bank on your right**.*
  → Wenn du um die Ecke biegst, siehst du *auf der rechten Seite eine Bank*. ODER: Wenn du um die Ecke biegst, siehst du *eine Bank auf der rechten Seite*.
- Diese zwei Beispiele demonstrieren, dass die Satzstellung des Deutschen flexibler ist als die des Englischen. Beide deutschen Sätze sind akzeptabel, auf Englisch hingegen ist es nicht möglich zu sagen: ... *you'll see on your right a bank.*

Ort und Zeit

→ Das Verb und der Ort stehen normalerweise zusammen:
- *He **goes to school** in the next town.*
- *They **sat in a café**, drinking coffee.*
→ Wenn das Verb ein Objekt hat, ist die Reihenfolge Verb–Objekt –Ort:
- *Sandra picked me up **at the airport**.*
- *Have you ever found any money **on the street**?*
→ Aussagen zur Zeit (*when, how often, how long*) stehen normalerweise nach dem Ort:
- *We go to Italy **every summer**.*
- *I asked Andy to get here **by 6 o'clock**.*
→ Aussagen zur Zeit können aber auch am Anfang eines Satzes stehen:
- ***This time last year** I was still living in Boston.*
- ***Next September** I'm starting a new job.*
→ Übersetzungsbeispiele:
- *I never go to bed before midnight.*
  → Ich gehe nie vor Mitternacht ins Bett.
- *He has worked in that building for 10 years.*
  → Er arbeitet seit 10 Jahren in diesem Gebäude.
  Hier erkennt man, dass im Deutschen die normale Satzstellung Zeit – Ort ist, also genau entgegengesetzt zur englischen Satzstellung.

Relativsätze

Ein Relativsatz ist ein Teilsatz, der zusätzliche Information enthält. Er sagt uns genauer, **was** oder **welcher Art** eine Person oder ein Ding ist. Sehen Sie sich die folgenden Beispiele unterschiedlicher Relativsätze und ihrer Übersetzung genau an.

→ *The boy **who is standing over there** is my cousin.*
  *The boy **standing over there** is my cousin.*
    → Der Junge, der dort drüben steht, ist mein Cousin.

Im Englischen ist es möglich, *who is* auszulassen; auf Deutsch wird in beiden Fällen *der* verwendet.

> **Kommasetzung** — Merke
>
> Beachten Sie, dass im Deutschen ein Komma verwendet wird, um den Relativsatz vom Hauptsatz zu trennen. In dem Beispiel hier werden im Englischen keine Kommas verwendet. Dies liegt daran, dass es sich hier um einen sogenannten ***defining relative clause*** handelt, also einen Relativsatz, der notwendig ist, um den ganzen Satz zu verstehen (wir wollen wissen, von welchem Jungen die Rede ist).

→ *The table, which was completely covered with papers, stood in the middle of the room.*
  → Der Tisch, **der komplett mit Papieren zugedeckt war**, stand mitten im Zimmer.
  → **Der komplett mit Papieren zugedeckte** Tisch stand mitten im Zimmer.

Betrachten Sie die zwei Übersetzungsmöglichkeiten: Die erste Übersetzung entspricht praktisch der englischen Version, inklusive der Komma-Verwendung. Kommas werden im Englischen bei sogenannten *non-defining relative clauses* verwendet: Das sind Relativsätze, die zusätzliche Information beinhalten (wir müssen nicht wissen, dass der Tisch mit Papier bedeckt war, um zu verstehen, von welchem Tisch hier die Rede ist). Die zweite deutsche Übersetzung ist hingegen ein Beispiel für eine Satzstruktur, die so im Englischen nicht möglich ist. Im Deutschen können wir die Information des Relativsatzes vor das Substantiv, das näher erklärt wird (Tisch), stellen. Im Englischen ist dies so nicht möglich.

Verben

Der Gebrauch der englischen Verbformen wurde im →Kapitel „English Grammar", ab Seite 55 erörtert. Problematisch ist das Übersetzen von Verbformen, die zwar im Englischen, nicht aber im Deutschen existieren. Im Folgenden werden einige typische Beispiele aufgegriffen.

Aspekt: *simple und continuous* (Verlaufsform)

→ I *am reading* a very interesting book at the moment.
   → Ich *lese gerade* ein sehr interessantes Buch.
→ I *read* at least one book a month.
   → Ich *lese* mindestens ein Buch pro Monat/im Monat.

Sowohl *I am reading* als auch *I read* werden im Deutschen mit *ich lese* übersetzt. Es ist jedoch möglich, durch den Gebrauch von *gerade* auszudrücken, dass die Handlung noch nicht abgeschlossen ist.

Tempus: *present perfect*

Man ist leicht versucht, das englische *present perfect* mit dem deutschen Perfekt zu übersetzen. Das Problem dabei ist, dass die beiden Formen unterschiedlich verwendet werden, obwohl in manchen Fällen eine analoge Übersetzung möglich ist. Das deutsche Perfekt ist ganz klar eine Vergangenheitsform des Verbs, während das englische *present perfect* sich oft auf etwas in der Gegenwart bezieht.

→ I **have already seen** the film. → *Ich habe den Film schon gesehen.* Hier ist die deutsche Übersetzung so möglich, weil sich auch der englische Satz klar auf etwas in der Vergangenheit bezieht.
→ I **have known** him for years. → Ich *kenne* ihn seit Jahren. Hier bezieht sich der englische Satz auf die Gegenwart, d.h. darauf, dass man die Person *jetzt* schon seit Jahren kennt. Im Deutschen wird dies durch das Präsens ausgedrückt.
→ We **have been waiting** for you for over an hour. → Wir *warten* seit über eine Stunde auf dich. Einerseits hat der Aspekt *continuous* des Englischen (been waiting) im Deutschen keine Entsprechung, andererseits zeigt die Benutzung des *present perfect continuous* im Englischen (*have been waiting*), dass sich der Satz auf die Gegenwart bezieht (wir haben bis eben gewartet). Daher ist es wiederum am besten, den Satz im Deutschen einfach mit dem Präsens zu übersetzen.

Konditionalsätze

Die folgenden Beispiele zeigen, welche Zeiten im Englischen in Konditionalsätzen gebraucht werden und was ihre jeweiligen Entsprechungen im Deutschen sind.

- *First conditional*
  - *If I **have** time this afternoon, I'**ll** go jogging.*
    - → Wenn/Falls ich heute Nachmittag Zeit *habe*, *gehe* ich joggen.
- *Second conditional*
  - *If I **met** Matthew Perry, I **would ask** for his autograph.*
    - → Wenn ich Matthew Perry *treffen würde/träfe, würde* ich ihn um ein Autogramm *bitten*.
- *Third conditional*
  - *If she **had used** sunblock, she **wouldn't have burnt** herself.*
    - → Wenn sie eine Sonnencreme *benutzt hätte, hätte* sie keinen Sonnenbrand *bekommen*.

Modalverben

Es gibt einige deutsche Modalverben, die im Englischen, je nach Kontext, unterschiedliche Übersetzungen benötigen. Hier sind ein paar Beispiele dafür:

dürfen

- *to be allowed to do something*
  - *My little brother isn't allowed to play on the street.*
    - → Mein kleiner Bruder darf nicht auf der Straße spielen.
- Als Negation (etwas nicht tun dürfen): *must not (or ought not to) do something*
  - *We mustn't (or ought not to) miss the bus.*
    - → Wir dürfen den Bus nicht verpassen.
- *may/might/can*
  - *Can/May I give you some advice?*
    - → Darf ich dir einen Ratschlag geben?
- *should/ought to*
  - *That shouldn't be a problem.*
    - → Das dürfte kein Problem sein.

sollen

- *should/ought to (= advice)*
  - *Maybe you should go to the doctor's if it hurts.*
    → Vielleicht solltest du zum Arzt gehen, wenn es weh tut.
- *should/ought to (= the right thing to do)*
  - *Parents ought to be stricter with their children.*
    → Eltern sollten mit ihren Kindern strenger umgehen.
- *should/ought to (= must)*
  - *You ought to be ashamed of yourself!*
    → Du solltest dich schämen!
- *supposed to*
  - *I'm supposed to finish reading this book by tomorrow, but I don't think I'll manage it.*
    → Ich soll dieses Buch bis morgen fertig lesen, aber ich glaube nicht, dass ich es schaffen werde.
- *supposed to be (= apparently)*
  - *It's supposed to be a very interesting film.*
    → Das soll ein sehr interessanter Film sein.
- Das Ausdrücken der Zukunft aus dem Blickwinkel der Vergangenheit (*was to* etc.)
  - *When they checked into the hotel, they had no way of knowing that they were to meet Brad Pitt there later on.*
    → Als sie im Hotel eincheckten, konnten sie nicht ahnen, dass sie dort später Brad Pitt treffen sollten.

müssen

- *must/have to (= it is necessary)*
  - *I must/have to phone Matthew this evening.*
    → Ich muss Matthew heute Abend anrufen.
- *needn't/don't have to*
  - *You needn't/don't have to come with me if you don't want to.*
    → Du musst nicht mitkommen, wenn du nicht willst.
- **Hinweis:** *Mustn't* ist nicht das Gleiche wie *muss nicht*: Es bedeutet, etwas ist verboten oder nicht erlaubt. Hier ein Vergleich:

- *I'm very ill. I mustn't go to school tomorrow.*
  → Ich bin sehr krank. Ich darf morgen nicht in die Schule gehen.
- *Tomorrow is Saturday. I don't have to go to school.*
  → Morgen ist Samstag. Ich muss nicht in die Schule gehen.

→ *supposed to be/said to be*
- *Bali is supposed to be very beautiful.*
  → Bali muss sehr schön sein.

können

→ *can (= ability)*
- *She can speak Italian.* → Sie kann Italienisch.

→ *could (= in the past)*
- *I couldn't understand a word he said.*
  → Ich konnte kein Wort, was er sagte, verstehen.

→ *to be able to*
- *I was able to recover the lost files.*
  → Ich konnte die verlorenen Dateien wiederherstellen.

→ **Hinweis:** *can* (im Präsens) and *could* (im Präteritum) sind die einzigen zwei Formen dieses Verbs, die existieren. Daher muss man sich bei der Übersetzung von *können* in ein anderes Tempus mit einer Form von *to be able* to behelfen.
- *I won't be able to pick you up at the station.*
  → Ich werde dich nicht am Bahnhof abholen können.

→ **Hinweis:** In der Vergangenheit wird *could* für eine generelle Fähigkeit benutzt, wenn man aber darüber spricht, was in einer bestimmten Situation geschah, wird *was/were able to* oder *managed to* anstelle von *could* verwendet. Hier ein Vergleich:
- *He could swim very well as a child.*
  → Er konnte als Kind sehr gut schwimmen.
- *We managed to/were able to swim to the rock.*
  → Wir konnten bis zum Fels schwimmen.

Andere Fallstricke

since und *for*

Beide Wörter können verwendet werden, um anzuzeigen, seit wann etwas passiert.
- → *since* wird benutzt, wenn wir den Startpunkt erwähnen:
  - *since 1998; since January; since 9 o'clock*
- → *for* wird benutzt, um über die Zeitdauer zu sprechen:
  - *for ten years; for three months; for five minutes.*
- → Auf Deutsch werden beide Wörter in diesem Kontext mit **seit** übersetzt. Übersetzungsbeispiele:
  - *I've had this bag **for** three years.*
    - → Ich habe diese Tasche **seit** drei Jahren.
  - *She's been working here **since** 2002.*
    - → Sie arbeitet hier **seit** 2002.

lassen

Das deutsche Wort **lassen** kann auf verschiedene Weise ins Englische übersetzt werden.
- → *let/allow*
  - *She just sat there and let me do all the work.*
    - → Sie saß einfach da und ließ mich die ganze Arbeit machen.
- → *leave*
  - *Please leave the light on.*
    - → Lass das Licht bitte an.
- → *to have/get something done*
  - *I'm having my hair cut at the weekend.*
    - → Am Wochenende lasse ich mir die Haare schneiden.
- → *to make someone do something/keep someone doing something*
  - *She makes her patients sit in the waiting room for a very long time/ She keeps her patients sitting in the waiting room for a very long time.*
    - → Sie lässt ihre Patienten immer sehr lange im Wartezimmer sitzen.

remember/remind

Im Englischen gibt es einen Bedeutungsunterschied zwischen diesen beiden Wörtern, der so im Deutschen nicht ausgedrückt wird.
- *To remember something* bedeutet, dass jemandem etwas einfällt, eine Erinnerung hochkommt;
- *to be reminded of something* oder *to remind someone* zeigt an, dass ein äußerer Einfluss das Erinnern auslöst.
- Übersetzungsbeispiele:
  - *I **remember** my first kiss.*
    → Ich *erinnere mich* an meinen ersten Kuss.
  - *The smell **reminds me** of my childhood.*
    → Der Geruch *erinnert mich* an meine Kindheit.
  - *Please **remind me** to feed the cat.*
    → Bitte *erinnere mich* daran, die Katze zu füttern.

recognise/realise/notice

Der Kontext, in dem diese drei Wörter verwendet werden, kann für Deutsche verwirrend sein:
- *To **recognise** something* – etwas wiedererkennen, weil man es schon mal gesehen/gehört/gerochen/geschmeckt hat.
- *To **realise** something* – bedeutet, dass man (meistens plötzlich) eine bestimmte Situation versteht.
- *To **notice** something* – etwas wahrnehmen/bemerken, weil man sich dessen bewusst wird, besonders, wenn man etwas sieht.
  - *I **recognised** him by his laugh.*
    → Ich **erkannte** ihn an seinem Lachen wieder.
  - *Emily **realised** that the story wasn't true.*
    → Emily **erkannte**, dass die Geschichte nicht stimmte.
  - *He didn't **notice** my new hairstyle.*
    → Er **bemerkte** meine neue Frisur nicht.
- **Hinweis:** In einigen Fällen bedeuten *realise* und *notice* mehr oder weniger dasselbe:
  - *We just realised/noticed in time that we had nearly run out of petrol.*
    → Wir bemerkten gerade noch rechtzeitig, dass wir fast kein Benzin mehr hatten.

6.3 Schlüsselwörter

Die Schlüsselwörter eines Textes sind die, die die **Grundbotschaft des Autors** ausdrücken. Dabei handelt es sich meist um
→ Substantive (die aussagen, **um was oder wen** es im Text geht), es können aber natürlich auch
→ Verben (**was geschah**),
→ Adjektive (**welche Art** von Person oder Ereignis) oder auch
→ Adverbien (**wie** etwas geschah) sein.

Hat man die Schlüsselwörter eines Textes identifiziert, kann man durch sie herausfinden, worum es in dem Text generell geht. Außerdem helfen sie einem anschließend dabei, unbekannte Wörter aus dem Kontext zu erschließen.

BEISPIEL:
Last week I bought a great new pair of blue trousers. However, I had only worn them once, at Jenny's party, when I noticed a huge hole in one of the legs. Worst of all, the shop refused to give me my money back because I had lost my receipt.

→ Die Adjektive *great, new, blue* und *huge* geben zusätzliche Information, sind aber nicht notwendig.
→ Artikel *(a, the)*, Strukturwörter (um Zeiten zu formen, wie *had* bei *had worn*), Präpositionen *(in)*, Pronomen *(my)* und Adverbien *(only)* werden nicht benötigt, um den Text zu verstehen.
→ Die Zeitreferenz *last week* macht in diesem Fall keinen Unterschied für das Verständnis der Geschichte als Ganzes.
→ *However* und *Worst of all* legen eine besondere Betonung auf die jeweiligen Sätze, würden den Sinn der Geschichte aber nicht verändern, ließe man sie weg.
→ Der Relativsatz at *Jenny's party* ist irrelevant für die Kernbedeutung.
→ Die wichtigen Wörter (Schlüsselwörter) dieses Textes sind daher: *bought, trousers, worn, once, noticed, hole, leg, shop, refuse, give money back, lost, receipt.*

Das bedeutet, dass man mithilfe von nur 14 (von ursprünglich 50) Wörtern die gesamte Geschichte rekonstruieren kann.

Selbst wenn man nicht bei allen Wörtern sicher ist, was deren genaue Bedeutung ist, kann man diese durch die Kernaussage des Textes und mit einem generellen Hintergrundwissen erschließen.

Wenn man zum Beispiel das Wort *receipt* nicht kennt, so kann man aus dem Kontext heraus schließen, dass es etwas ist, das man benötigt, um in einem Geschäft sein Geld zurückzubekommen, wenn man dort gekaufte Waren umtauscht. Man erfährt schließlich in der Geschichte, dass die Erzählerin ihr Geld nicht zurückbekam, weil sie den *receipt* verloren hatte. Man kann sich daher denken, dass es sich dabei um den Kassenzettel handeln muss.

> **Abi-Tipp: Nehmen Sie es nicht zu wörtlich**
>
> Wer hat nicht schon über eine ganz schlechte Übersetzung in die eigene Sprache herzlich gelacht? Im Internet gibt es ja genug Beispiele von wörtlichen Übersetzungen oder welche, in den einfach das falsche Wort eingesetzt wurde. Dies ist besonders oft der Fall bei Online-Übersetzungswerkzeugen, mit den man auch selber viel Spaß haben kann. Dass aber andere Leute sich über Ihre Übersetzungen so amüsieren, wollen Sie bestimmt nicht. Deshalb gilt: Immer daran denken, **die Bedeutung des Textes und nicht nur die einzelnen Wörter gilt es zu übersetzen**. Ist der Text als Ganzes überhaupt sinnvoll? Denken Sie daran: Das Ziel einer Übersetzung ist, die Bedeutung eines Textes klar darzustellen. Es kann also gut sein, dass Sie Ihren Text etwas umschreiben müssen, um dessen Bedeutung klar zu vermitteln. Eine zu wörtliche Übersetzung dagegen kann Verwirrung stiften.

6.4 Example texts

Im Folgenden finden Sie zwei Beispieltexte, anhand derer Sie das Vorgehen und die Überlegungen bei einer Übersetzung nachvollziehen können. Beim ersten Beispiel wird der Text in Einzelsätze zerlegt und dann mit Anmerkungen versehen. Im zweiten Beispiel stehen Originaltext und Übersetzung in voller Länge unmittelbar nebeneinander, die Anmerkungen zur Übersetzung folgen.

BEISPIEL 1: *"Rome, AD ... Rome, DC?"*
Satzweise Übersetzung eines Ausschnitts des Textes von Seite 158/159:

[...] The US has learned a second lesson from Rome: realising the centrality of technology. For the Romans, it was those famously straight roads, enabling the empire to move troops or supplies at awesome speeds. It was a perfect example of how one imperial strength tends to feed another: an innovation in engineer-
5 ing, originally designed for military use, went on to boost Rome commercially. Today those highways find their counterpart in the information superhighway: the internet also began as a military tool, and now stands at the heart of American commerce. In the process, it is making English the Latin of its day – a language spoken across the globe.
10 However, Rome's greatest conquests came not at the end of a spear, but through its power to seduce conquered peoples. As Tacitus observed in Britain, the natives seemed to like togas, baths and central heating – never realising that these were the symbols of their "enslavement". Today the US offers the people of the world a similar cultural package, a cluster of goodies that remain
15 reassuringly uniform wherever you are. Today we have Starbucks, Coca-Cola, McDonald's and Disney, all paid for in the contemporary equivalent of Roman coinage, the global hard currency of the 21st century: the dollar.
There are some large differences between the two empires, of course – starting with self-image. Romans revelled in their status as master of the known world,
20 but few Americans would be as ready to brag of their own imperialism. Indeed, most would deny it. But that may come down to the US's founding myth. For America was established as a rebellion against empire, in the name of freedom and self-government. Raised to see themselves as a rebel nation, they can't quite accept their current role as master. [...]
25 The US has learned a second lesson from Rome: realising the centrality of technology. For the Romans, it was those famously straight roads, enabling the empire to move troops or supplies at awesome speeds.

Übersetzungsvorschlag: Die Vereinigten Staaten haben eine zweite Lektion von den Römern gelernt: Sie erkannten die zentrale Bedeutung der Technologie. Rom hatte damals die berühmten schnurgeraden Straßen, auf denen sich die kaiserlichen Truppen und der Nachschub mit ungeheurer Geschwindigkeit transportieren ließen.

Anmerkungen:
→ Bei dem Ausdruck *"for the Romans"* eine wörtliche Übersetzung, wie: „Bei den Römern waren das ..." zu verwenden, wäre unschön, und es soll ja auch der Gegensatz damals–heute herauskommen, besser also, Sie wählen eine Umschreibung wie „Rom hatte damals".

→ *„empire"* hier adjektivisch übersetzt mit „kaiserlich", ein probates Mittel, einem zu nominalen Stil im deutschen Satz entgegenzuwirken

It was a perfect example of how one imperial strength tends to feed another:

Übersetzungsvorschlag: Dies war ein Musterbeispiel dafür, wie die starke Seite eines Reiches oft andere Bereiche günstig beeinflusst:

Anmerkungen:
→ *„imperial"* kann sich auf den Herrscher bzw. das ganze Reich beziehen; es ist nicht „imperialistic".
→ *„tend to"* wird hier adverbial mit „oft" aufgelöst.
→ der bildliche Ausdruck „nähren" für *„feed"* kann hier schlecht beibehalten werden.
→ „andere Bereiche" sind gemeint, eine wörtliche Übersetzung klingt hier nicht gut.

an innovation in engineering, originally designed for military use, went on to boost Rome commercially.

Übersetzungsvorschlag: Eine technische Neuentwicklung, die ursprünglich für militärische Zwecke geplant war, verschaffte der römischen Wirtschaft einen kräftigen Auftrieb.

Anmerkungen:

→ *„originally designed ..."* Partizipkonstruktion in deutschen Relativsatz aufgelöst

Today those highways find their counterpart in the information superhighway: the internet also began as a military tool, and now stands at the heart of American commerce.

Übersetzungsvorschlag: Heute finden diese Schnellstraßen ihr Gegenstück in der Datenautobahn: Auch das Internet hatte seine Anfänge im militärischen Gebrauch und bildet nun das Kernstück des amerikanischen Handels.

Anmerkungen:

→ „Datenautobahn": wichtig für solche Prüfungen ist ein Wortschatz, der auf dem aktuellen Stand ist – Nachrichten sehen, Zeitung lesen hilft da sehr.

→ „das Kernstück": ein Bild *(heart of)* wird durch ein anderes ersetzt.

In the process, it is making English the Latin of its day – a language spoken across the globe.

Übersetzungsvorschlag: Nebenbei entwickelt sich Englisch dadurch zu dem, was Latein einst war – eine Sprache, die auf der ganzen Welt gesprochen wird.

Anmerkungen:

→ „entwickelt sich" lenkt den Blick auf den allmählichen Prozess, ausgedrückt in der *continous form „making"* bzw. auch *„in the process"*, das sonst oft mit „dabei" übersetzt wird.

→ Da im Deutschen nun „Englisch" zum Subjekt des Satzes wird statt „*it*", nämlich das Internet, wird „dadurch" eingesetzt, um den Bezug auf den Verursacher klarzumachen.

However, Rome's greatest conquests came not at the end of a spear, but through its power to seduce conquered peoples.

Übersetzungsvorschlag: Doch Rom machte seine größten Eroberungen nicht durch Speerspitzen, sondern mit seiner Fähigkeit, die besiegten Völker für sich zu gewinnen.

Anmerkungen:

→ wörtl.: „an der Spitze eines Speeres" wird zugunsten „durch Speerspitzen" ersetzt, das Bild bleibt erhalten

As Tacitus observed in Britain, the natives seemed to like togas, baths and central heating – never realising that these were the symbols of their "enslavement". Today the US offers the people of the world a similar cultural package, a cluster of goodies that remain reassuringly uniform wherever you are.

Übersetzungsvorschlag: Wie Tacitus in Britannien bemerkte, mochten die Einheimischen offenbar die Togas, Bäder und Zentralheizungen – ohne sich klar zu machen, dass dies die Symbole ihrer „Versklavung" waren. Amerika bietet den Völkern der Welt heute ein ähnliches „Kultur"-Päckchen an, eine Ansammlung an Konsumgütern, die überall auf der Welt auf so beruhigende Art gleich bleiben.

Anmerkungen:

→ *„cultural package"* ist auch im Englischen ungewöhnlich, kann daher so übersetzt werden.

→ *„goodies"*, die guten Sachen bzw. Süßigkeiten, sind hier wohl nicht gemeint, sondern Konsumgüter jeglicher Art

Today we have Starbucks, Coca-Cola, McDonald's and Disney, all paid for in the contemporary equivalent of Roman coinage, the global hard currency of the 21st century: the dollar.

Übersetzungsvorschlag: Heutzutage sind das Starbucks, Coca-Cola, McDonald's und Disney, alle bezahlt mit dem zeitgenössischen Äquivalent zur römischen Münze, mit der weltweiten harten Währung des 21. Jahrhunderts – dem Dollar.

Anmerkungen:

→ Normalerweise sollen Fremdwörter, wenn es ein gebräuchliches Wort dafür gibt, ins Deutsche übersetzt werden; hier kann es stehen, weil „Äquivalent" einen ähnlichen Grad an Fremdheit hat wie *„equivalent"* im Englischen – und *„counterpart"* kam schließlich weiter oben schon einmal vor.

There are some large differences between the two empires, of course – starting with self-image. Romans revelled in their status as master of the known world, but few Americans would be as ready to brag of their own imperialism. Indeed, most would deny it.

Übersetzungsvorschlag: Natürlich gibt es einige große Unterschiede zwischen den beiden Imperien – und das fängt mit dem Selbstverständnis an. Die Römer sonnten sich in ihrer Rolle als Herrscher der damals bekannten Welt, während sich wohl nur wenige Amerikaner mit ihrem Imperialismus brüsten würden. Die meisten würden ihn rundweg abstreiten.

Anmerkungen:
→ Hier haben wir zwei Beispiele für sogenannte Füllwörter („wohl" und „rundweg"), die im Deutschen zur Verstärkung oder für den harmonischeren Klang eines Satzes gerne verwendet werden.

But that may come down to the US's founding myth. For America was established as a rebellion against empire, in the name of freedom and self-government.

Übersetzungsvorschlag: Aber dies mag am amerikanischen Gründungsmythos liegen: Amerika wurde schließlich in einem Akt der Rebellion gegen ein Weltreich gegründet, im Namen von Freiheit und Selbstbestimmung.

Anmerkungen:
→ „in einem Akt" einzufügen, ist notwendig, weil man nicht sagen kann, ein Staat wurde als Rebellion gegründet

Raised to see themselves as a rebel nation, they can't quite accept their current role as master.

Übersetzungsvorschlag: Aufgewachsen mit dem Selbstbild, eine rebellische Nation zu sein, können die Amerikaner ihre Rolle als derzeitiger Herrscher nur schwer akzeptieren.

Anmerkungen:
→ Im Englischen ist es möglich, *„America ... they see themselves"* zu schreiben; im Deutschen müsste dann entweder der Singular folgen – Amerika sieht sich selbst – oder „die Amerikaner" eingefügt werden.

BEISPIEL 2: Ellis Island, Point of Arrival.

On 1 January 1892, because of massive immigration from Europe, the United States opened its main immigration centre on Ellis Island, outside New York City. Between 1892 and 1943, about 20 million immigrants went through its gates, most of them before the First World War.

By 1880, poverty and overpopulation in Europe had made many people want to leave; and the arrival of railways and steamships had made it practical to do so. Millions of young men went to America to find work, and their families followed. To handle these large numbers, the US converted Ellis Island, 400 metres from the mainland, from a fortress[1] to an immigration office and hospital.

It was assumed that many of the arriving passengers would one day become citizens of the United States. First- and second-class passengers were allowed to enter the US without formalities, because it was thought that if they had the money to buy such a ticket, they would not be a burden on the country. The 90 per cent who travelled third class, however, were questioned and given a health examination. The process took hours. From Ellis Island they could see, on another island nearby, the Statue of Liberty. Ten days in a crowded ship's cabin made some people sick. Most immigrants arrived with only a few dollars in their pockets.

The First World War made overseas transport difficult, and immigration from Europe nearly stopped. Also, many Americans no longer trusted foreigners. This and a stronger feeling of nationalism led the government to begin restricting immigration through quotas in the 1920s. To this day, quotas still determine how many immigrants from various parts of the world may enter America.

In 1943, the immigration office was closed and moved to smaller quarters in New York City. Today the old building houses a museum.

[1] fortress: Festung

Adapted from: *Spotlight*, 01/2002, www.spotlight-verlag.de

Ankunftspunkt Ellis Island

Aufgrund enormer Einwanderung aus Europa eröffneten die Vereinigten Staaten am 1. Januar 1892 ihr Haupteinwanderungszentrum auf Ellis Island, außerhalb von New York City. Zwischen 1892 und 1943 gingen ungefähr 20 Millionen Immigranten durch seine Tore, die meisten davon vor dem Ersten Weltkrieg.

Bis 1880 wollten viele Leute Europa wegen Armut und Überbevölkerung verlassen, und die Erfindung von Eisenbahn und Dampfschiffen machte dies möglich. Millionen junger Männer fuhren nach Amerika, um Arbeit zu finden, und ihre Familien kamen nach. Um diese großen Mengen zu bewältigen, wandelten die Vereinigten Staaten Ellis Island, 400 Meter vom Festland gelegen, von einer Festung in ein Immigrationsamt und Krankenhaus um.

Man vermutete, dass viele der ankommenden Passagiere eines Tages Staatsbürger der Vereinigten Staaten werden würden. Passagiere der ersten und zweiten Klasse durften ohne Formalitäten in die USA einreisen, weil man dachte, dass jemand, der das Geld für so eine Fahrkarte hatte, dem Land nicht zur Last fallen würde. Dagegen wurden die 90 Prozent, die dritter Klasse gereist waren, verhört und gesundheitlich untersucht. Das Verfahren dauerte Stunden. Von Ellis Island aus konnten sie die Freiheitsstatue auf einer nahe gelegenen Insel sehen. Manche waren krank geworden während der zehn Tage, die sie in einer überfüllten Schiffskabine verbracht hatten. Die meisten Immigranten kamen mit nur ein paar Dollar in der Tasche an.

Der Erste Weltkrieg erschwerte die Übersee-Schifffahrt, und die Immigration aus Europa hörte fast auf. Dazu kam noch, dass viele Amerikaner den Ausländern misstrauten. Dies und ein zunehmendes Nationalgefühl führten dazu, dass die Regierung in den 1920er-Jahren anfing, Immigration durch Quoten zu beschränken. Bis heute wird durch diese Quoten immer noch geregelt, wie viele Einwanderer aus den verschiedenen Teilen der Welt nach Amerika einreisen dürfen.

1943 wurde das Einwanderungszentrum geschlossen und in ein kleineres Büro in New York City verlegt. Heute ist ein Museum in dem alten Gebäude untergebracht.

Translation notes:

Zeile 1: „*massive*" ist hier ein Beispiel für einen „*false friend*". Im Englischen bedeutet es „eine große Zahl" und kann mit „enorm" oder „riesig" übersetzt werden.

Beachten sie die Position der Zeitangabe (Datum) im ersten Satz. Wie schon erläutert, stehen Zeitangaben ganz am Anfang eines englischen Satzes. Im Deutschen wirkt die Satzordnung natürlicher, wenn man mit dem Relativsatz beginnt und die Zeitangabe direkt hinter das Verb stellt.

Zeile 5: „*poverty*". Es ist nicht wirklich einfach zu erraten, dass dieses Nomen von „*poor*" abstammt. Deshalb ist es wichtig, unterschiedliche, aber verwandte Wortformen aufzuschreiben, wenn man ihnen begegnet, um seinen Wortschatz zu erweitern.

Zeile 5: „*overpopulation*". Ein weiteres Beispiel für eine Vorsilbe, in diesem Fall „*over-*", die uns beim Finden der Wortbedeutung hilft. In diesem Fall erleichtert uns die Übersetzung, dass man beide Wortteile als „Überbevölkerung" direkt ins Deutsche übersetzen kann.

Zweiter Absatz, erster Satz. Beachten Sie, dass das Subjekt des englischen Satzes (*poverty and overpopulation*) im Deutschen zum Objekt (Armut und Überbevölkerung) wird. Die Bedeutung ist jedoch die gleiche: Im englischen Text verursachte die Armut die Auswanderung, im deutschen Text wanderten die Leute wegen der Armut aus.

Zeile 6: „*the arrival of railways and steamships ...*". Das Wort „*arrival*" kann hier nicht wörtlich mit „Ankunft" übersetzt werden. Was der Autor ausdrücken möchte, ist „als Eisenbahnen und Dampfschiffe aufkamen", d.h. als sie erfunden wurden. Deshalb ist die deutsche Übersetzung „Erfindung" hier angemessen.

Zeile 6: „*practical*". Dies kann im Deutschen mit „praktikabel" übersetzt werden, denn die Bedeutung von „*practical*" in diesem Fall ist, dass u.a. die Eisenbahnen Immigration erst ermöglichten. Daher ist auch „möglich" eine korrekte Übersetzung.

Zeile 7: „*Millions of young men went to America ...*". Im Englischen kann man das Wort „*to go*" sehr flexibel für alle Arten der Fortbewegung und des Reisens verwenden. So ist es möglich zu schreiben: "*I'm going to Chicago next week*", selbst wenn klar ist, dass die Person meint, "*I'm flying/driving to Chicago*" (was vom jeweiligen Abreiseort abhängt). Im Deutschen ist es daher besser „*went*" in diesem Kontext mit „fuhren" zu übersetzen.

Zeile 8: „*handle*". Ein weiterer *false friend*, den man nicht mit „handeln" übersetzen darf! Wir können aus dem Kontext erschließen, dass es darum geht, mit etwas fertig zu werden. Somit können wir auf die Übersetzung „bewältigen" kommen.

Zeile 9: „*mainland*". Das Wort mag unbekannt sein, aber es ist nicht besonders schwer, seine Bedeutung aus dem Kontext heraus zu erschließen. Wir wissen, dass Ellis Island eine Insel ist (bei dem Namen logisch) und dass es von diesem „*mainland*" getrennt ist. Das Wort selbst besteht aus zwei Elementen: „*main*" = das Hauptsächliche, das Wichtigste und „*land*" = Land. Daraus kann man ableiten, dass „mainland" sich auf ein größeres Stück Land beziehen muss, also das eigentliche Amerika und daher das „Festland".

Zeile 11: „*would ... become*". Obwohl es sich um keine *if*-Konstruktion handelt, ist dies ein Konditionalsatz, der mit „werden würden" übersetzt wird.

Zeile 13: „*to enter the US*". Es ist wichtig, dass man überlegt, welche Übersetzung von „*enter*" hier angemessen ist. Obwohl die Grundübersetzung „hineingehen" sein könnte, wäre ein genaueres Wort hier besser. Wenn wir im Kontext des Reisens daran denken, ein anderes Land zu betreten, kommen wir darauf, dass „einreisen" hier den Sachverhalt genauer wiedergibt.

Zeile 14: „*burden*". Das ähnliche deutsche Wort „Bürde" hilft uns beim Verständnis des englischen Originals und bringt uns auf das Synonym „Last", das in diesem Kontext auch passend ist.

Zeile 16: „*examination*". Es ist in diesem Fall wieder sehr wichtig, sich über den Kontext Gedanken zu machen, ehe man sich für eine Übersetzung entscheidet. Offensichtlich bezieht sich der Autor nicht auf eine Schulprüfung, sondern auf eine medizinische Überprüfung, daher ist die richtige Übersetzung „Untersuchung".

Zeile 17: „*the Statue of Liberty*". Da es sich hierbei um einen Eigennamen handelt, wäre es möglich, den englischen Ausdruck einfach zu übernehmen. Da es im Deutschen aber eine gebräuchliche Entsprechung („die Freiheitsstatue") gibt, ist eine Übersetzung in diesem Fall nicht nur richtig, sondern auch anzuraten.

Zeile 21: „*Also*". Ein Ausdruck der „auch" beinhaltet, könnte hier benutzt werden, um dieses Wort zu übersetzen (z.B. „Es war auch der Fall, dass ..."), aber „Dazu kam noch" am Anfang des Satzes zu benutzen, ist stilistisch besser.

Zeile 22: "*... led the government to begin ...*" Wenn man diesen Satz so übersetzt, dass er die englische Satzstellung widerspiegelt, klingt das Ergebnis im Deutschen seltsam (probieren Sie es einmal aus). Daher müssen wir den Satz im Deutschen etwas umstellen: „[es] führte dazu, dass ... die Regierung anfing ..."

Zeile 25: „*quarters*". Dies bedeutet einfach, dass es an einen anderen Platz verlegt wurde. Im Deutschen ist es möglich zu sagen, dass es in ein kleineres Büro verlegt wurde, was das Gleiche ausdrückt.

> **6 Übersetzung** — Checkliste
> → Immer den Text komplett durchlesen, ehe ich zu schreiben anfange!
> → Ich muss nicht Wort für Wort übersetzen, sondern soll die Bedeutung des englischen Textes ins Deutsche übertragen. Ich kann den Text also etwas umschreiben und muss nicht jedes einzelne Wort kennen.
> → Bevor ich mit dem Übersetzen anfange, suche ich nach Schlüsselwörtern im Text, die mir beim Verständnis helfen.
> → Meine Übersetzung soll dem Stil des Originaltextes entsprechen.
> → Nicht wörtlich übersetzen – dies funktioniert meistens nicht! Nicht über „false friends" und andere typische „Übersetzungsfallen" stolpern!
> → Die Übersetzung immer nochmals durchlesen, im optimalen Fall mit etwas Zeitabstand – aber auch in der Prüfungssituation muss ich mir diese Zeit nehmen! Tipp: Erledigen Sie die Übersetzungsaufgabe zu Beginn der Prüfung, dann haben Sie am Ende schon etwas Abstand gewonnen.

Stichwortverzeichnis

A

Adverbien   199
Afghanistan   116
Africa   111
Akrotiri   113
A-levels   106
Alliteration   135
allwissender Erzähler   141
Amendment   114
American Dream   117
American English   125
American Revolutionary War   109
Anapher   135
Anekdote   135
Anguilla   113
anti-terrorist campaign   116
Antithese   135
Argentina   113
Argumentation   187
Artikel   92
Ascension Island   113
Aufsatz   176–194
auktoriale Erzählperspektive   141
Australia   110
Australia Act   110
Axis of evil   116

B

Bahamas   108
BBC   107
BBC World Service   126
berichtende Erzählweise   142
Bermuda   108
beschränkte Erzählperspektive   141
Bewusstseinsstrom   143
bildliche Sprache   137
Bill of Rights   114
Blankvers   146

Boston   108
Boston Tea Party   109
British Antarctic Territory   113
British dominion   110
British Empire   108, 109
British English   125
British Indian Ocean Territory   113
British Parliament   109
British Raj   111
British Virgin Islands   113
BTECs   105
Bush, George   101

C

Cambridge   124
Cameron, David   102, 103
Canada   109
Capital punishment   116
Cayman Islands   113
Charakterisierung   143–144
Checks and balances   114
Christian fundamentalism   121
Church of England   103–104
Civil Rights Movement   118
Commonwealth   108, 111, 112
Commonwealth realm   110
Comprehensive schools   104
Congress   114
Constitution   114
Continental Congress   109
Continuous forms   55–58
Countable nouns   93–94
Crime   116
Cultural Christianity   103
Cyprus   113

D

Declaration of Independence 109, 123
Devolution 98
Dhekelia 113
Dole 102
Dollar diplomacy 115
Drama 146–147
Drug-related crimes 117

E

East India Company 108, 110, 127
Education 104–106, 121–122
Egypt 111
Electronic church 121
Elementary school 121
Empire 124
Empress of India 111
Erzähler 140–141
Erzählperspektive 141
Erzählweise 142–143
Euphemismus 136
European Community 101
Eurosceptics 102

F

Fabel 144
Fairy tale 145
Falkland Islands 113
False Friends 82–86
Federalism 114
Figuren 143
First Fleet 110
Flat characters 143
förmlicher Stil 132–134
Formulierungshilfen 171–172, 187
Fundamentalism 121
Future continuous 59
Future forms 59
Future perfect 60, 62

G

GCSEs 105
Gedicht 145
Georgia 109
Gerund 73
Gibraltar 108, 113
Gliederung 179–187
Going-to-future 60, 62
Government of India Act 111
Grammar schools 104
Gulf War 101

H

Harvard 122
Health Insurance Marketplace 119
Higher education 106–107, 122–123
High school 121
Homeschooling 122
Homosexuality 104
House of Commons 97
House of Lords 97
Hudson Bay 108
Hyperbel 137

I

Ich-Erzähler 141
Idiome 37–44
Imperial Conference 111
Independent schools 105
India 108, 110
informeller Stil 132–134
innerer Monolog 143–144
Interior monologue 143–144
IRA 100
Iran 116
Iraq 116
Ireland 111
Iron Curtain 101
Ironie 137
Irregular verbs 70–72
ITV 107
Ivy League 122

J
Jamaica 108
Jamestown 108

K
King James Bible 123
Klimax 135
Klischee 135
Konnotation 136
Kurzgeschichte 145

L
Landeskunde 97–110
Latin 123
Legende 145–146
lingua franca 125
literarische Texte 140–146

M
Major, John 102
Märchen 145
Marshall Plan 115
Media 107
Medicaid 119
Medicare 119
Melting pot 117
Metapher 137
Mindmaps 176–177
Modalverben 203–205
Monarchy 98
Montserrat 113

N
Narrator 140–141
National Health Service 102
National Rifle Association 115, 127
native speaker 126
New England 108
Newfoundland 108, 109
New Hampshire 109
New South Wales 110
New York 108
New Zealand 110
Nomen 93–94
North America 108
North American colonies 108
North Korea 116
Novel 144

O
Obama, Barack 119
Obamacare 119
Objekt 199–200
Observer narrator 141
Omniscient narrator 141
Onomatopöie 137
Ort und Zeit 200
Oxford 124
Oxymoron 137

P
Pacific Rim 112
Paradoxon 137
Participles 75–76
Partizipialkonstruktionen 75–76
Partizipien 75–76
Passive 68–69
Past continuous 58
Past participle 76
Past perfect 65, 67
Past perfect continuous 65, 66
Past tense 58–59
Pennsylvania 108
Pentagon 116
personale Erzählperspektive 141
Personifikation 137
Phrasal verbs 78–81
Pilgrims 108
Pitcairn Islands 113
Plot 140
Plymouth colony 108
Poetry 140, 145
Point of view 141
Political lobbies 115
Politics
- Großbritannien 97–98
- USA 114–115

Post-colonial literature 124

Präfixe 52
Present continuous 56
Present participle 75
Present perfect 62, 64, 67
Present perfect continuous 63, 64
Present simple 55
Present tense 55–57
President 114
Primary school 104
Princeton 122
Private schools 104
Prosa 140
Protagonist 140
Protestant work ethic 120
Public education 121
Public schools 105
Puritans 108, 120

Q
Quality papers 107

R
Redewendungen 37–44
Reflexivpronomen 91
Reim 146
Relativsätze 201–202
Religion 120–121
religious instruction 122
rhetorische Mittel 135–139
Rhodesia 111
Rhythmus 146
Rogue states 116
Roman 144
Roosevelt Corollary 115
Round(ed) characters 144
Rückblende 136

S
Sachtext 158–168
Saint Helena 113
Sarkasmus 138
Satire 138
Satzverknüpfungen 172

Schauplatz 140
Schlüsselwörter 208–209
Scholastic Aptitude Test 122
Secondary school 104
Second World War, 101
Separation of powers 114
Setting 140
Short story 145
Showing 142
Simile 138
Simple forms 55–58
Simple past 57, 62, 67
Slang 133
Social welfare 118
South Africa 111
Southern Christian Leadership Conference 118
Southern Rhodesia 111
South Georgia 113
South Sandwich Islands 113
Sprachstile 132–134
Statute of Westminster 110, 112
stilistische Mittel 135–139
Suez Canal 111
Suffixe 52
Summary 169–175
Supreme Court 114
Symbol 138
Syria 116
szenische Erzählweise 142

T
Tabloids 107
Telling 142
Tenses 55–66
Texas 116
Textanalyse 128–168
The Second Empire 109
Thirteen Colonies 109, 123
Treaty of Paris 109
Tristan da Cunha 113
Tropen 136
Troubles, the 100
Truman Doctrine 115

Turks and Caicos Islands   113
TV evangelism   121

U

Übersetzung   195–217
Übersetzungsprobleme,
 typische   199–207
Übertreibung   136
Uncountable nouns   93–94
Understatement   139
unregelmäßige Verben   70
Untertreibung   139

V

Vergleich   138
Virginia Company of London   108
Vokabeln
- Cities   18–20
- Describing people's character   34–35
- Environment   10–12
- Media   13–14
- Medicine   23–24
- Politics   6–9
- Religion   24–26
- Society today   15–17
- Sport   29–31
- The arts   26–28
- Travel and tourism   32–33
- Work   20–22

Vokabeln lernen   46–48

W

War of Independence   109
Washington, D.C   118
West Indies   108
White Anglo-Saxon Protestants   120
Wiederholung   138
Will-future   59, 62
World language   123
World Trade Center   116
Wörterbücher   49–51
Wortspiel   138

Y

Yale   122

Z

Zimbabwe   111
Zusammenfassung   169–175